D1521985

IRISH TRACTS
1728—1733

Frontispiece

JONATHAN SWIFT, *1667-1745*

IRISH TRACTS
1728—1733

Edited by
Herbert Davis

BASIL BLACKWELL · OXFORD
1964

11,209

First published 1955
Reprinted 1964

PRINTED IN GREAT BRITAIN
BY THE COMPTON PRINTING WORKS (LONDON) LTD., LONDON,
FOR BASIL BLACKWELL & MOTT LTD
AND BOUND BY
THE KEMP HALL BINDERY, OXFORD

ACKNOWLEDGEMENTS

I AM indebted to Professors James Clifford and Irvin Ehrenpreis for drawing my attention to the autograph drafts of
Hints for Intelligencer Papers and for Maxims Examined
among the manuscript Fragments which they are editing; and
to the John Rylands Library for permission to make use of
them here. Mr. John Hayward first lent me a photostat of the
manuscript of Swift's comments *On the Bill for the Clergy's
Residing on their Livings*, which is in the possession of Mr.
William LeFanu, who very kindly allowed me to use it here.
It has the peculiar interest of showing both corrections and
additions in Swift's hand, and further changes which are
clearly the work of a later editor. And in this volume I have
particularly availed myself of permission to make use of a
number of manuscripts now in the Forster Collection at the
Victoria and Albert Museum Library. I have also been allowed
to reproduce title-pages of volumes from Trinity College
and the National Library in Dublin, from the Bodleian, from
the University Library, Cambridge, and from the libraries at
Harvard and at Yale.

H. D.

The CONTENTS

ILLUSTRATIONS

Fascimiles of Title pages, etc.

The INTRODUCTION

DURING the summer of 1727 Swift visited his friends in England for the last time. When he set out from Dublin in April his power and influence in Ireland was at its greatest height and his reputation elsewhere had been finally established by the success of *Gulliver's Travels* during the previous winter. He was welcomed by Pope and Bolingbroke and all his old friends, and he met Voltaire who provided him with letters of introduction to his friends in France. He planned to leave for Paris, but when on June 15 the news came of the death of George I on his way to Hanover, Swift was persuaded, in view of the expected changes in the political scene, to remain in London and await the turn of events. At the beginning of July he wrote to Sheridan that he was ill again with his old fits of giddiness and deafness, and that he designed to stay in the country, not liking any of the schemes in which his friends would have engaged him, and wished only to settle some business before leaving England for the last time.[1] Though he recovered enough to think of staying on during the winter and wrote for a further licence of absence, his illness returned and he grew so much worse that in September he suddenly decided to leave for Dublin. He had been much disturbed by alarming reports of the illness of Stella, and was in fear of 'the most fatal news' that could ever come to him. His mood while waiting for the boat at Holyhead can be seen in the jottings of the Journal which he kept from September 22–29, and the verses dated Holyhead Sept. 25, 1727.[2]

These verses and the Journal are almost the only writings of Swift which we possess, apart from letters, during the year

[1] *Corr.*, iii, 402 and 415.
[2] See Vol. V of this edition and *Poems*, Oxford, 1936, p. 420.

1727. He had given Pope some assistance in the preparation of their joint publication, *Miscellanies*, for the third volume of which he had asked Sheridan in July to copy out some of the poems to Stella.[1] And in London he had begun a 'Letter to the Writer of the Occasional Paper,' which he had showed to Bolingbroke, but which was never finished and printed only later.[2]

In Dublin he prepared to settle down at the Deanery to what he calls 'the life of a monk', and to take no further part in politics:

> As to politics; in England it is hard to keep out of them, and here it is a shame to be in them, unless by way of laughter and ridicule, for both which my taste is gone.[3]

He was ill again at the beginning of the year 1728, and was unable to leave the house at the time of the death of Stella, on January 28; in his misery he began at once to put down for his own satisfaction 'something of her life and character.'[4] Even at this worst moment he tried, as he recommended to Gay, to 'preserve some spice of the alderman, and prepare against age and dullness, and sickness, and coldness or death of friends'.[5] But he had not enough of this spirit to keep him out of trouble, and in the spring of 1728, he once more became active in Irish politics and took upon him again the rôle of Hibernian patriot, which led him to produce a number of important tracts on the state of Ireland during the following five years.

The first of these was a small pamphlet, *A Short View of the State of Ireland* printed by Sarah Harding in the same format as the first *Drapier Letter*. It was published on March 19; and at the end of the *Answer to A Memorial*, which was dated March 25, 1728, Swift states that he had sent out *A Short View* 'some days ago.'[6] It was issued anonymously, but the attack on the late Lord Chief Justice Whitshed would alone have been sufficient to indicate to most readers in Dublin

---

[1] *Corr.*, iii, 403.   [2] See Vol. XIV of this edition.   [3] *Corr.*, iii, 429.
[4] See Vol. V of this edition.   [5] *Corr.*, iv, 21.
[6] *Mist's Weekly Journal*, March 30, 1728. See also below, p. 122.

that it could have come from no other hand than the Dean of
St. Patrick's. It was written with the intention of exposing
the miserable state of the country, and making it very clear
that this was due not to any natural causes but to the restraints
upon trade and shipping and the general enslavement of the
country in the interests of England. It was addressed to the
gentry and the members of the Irish Parliament and to all
who were concerned with the state of affairs in Ireland. It
was above all an outcry against those who to please the court
were capable of talking about the flourishing condition of all
things in their neighbourhood. The mood from which it
proceeded is fully revealed in the lines on *Ireland*,[1] which
Swift had entered into the Holyhead note-book, during those
wretched days when he was waiting for the boat and raging
impatiently for a passage to that

> land of slaves
> Where all are fools, and all are knaves
> Where every knave and fool is bought
> Yet kindly sells himself for nought . . .
> While English sharpers take the pay,
> And then stand by to see fair play.

He goes on to describe the blandishments of the Lord
Lieutenant and the way in which he wins over the Irish gentlemen to the support of the government's policy in trade and
agriculture which was leading to the ruin of the country.

> He whisperd publick things at last,
> Askt me how our elections past.
> Some augmentation Sir you know
> Would make at least a handsom show
> New Kings a compliment expect
> I shall not offer to direct
> There are some prating folks in town,
> But Sir we must support the Crown.

In *A Short View* he tries to explain to these same Irish gentlemen the real sources of the miserable state of Ireland—the
encouragement of grazing instead of agriculture, the restrictions on the export of native commodities and manufacture,

[1] *Poems*, pp. 421–23.

half of the rent and profits of the whole Kingdom annually exported and spent in England, and all kinds of luxuries allowed to be imported. In all the papers that Swift wrote in the following five years, he continued to repeat his bitter tale of the complete enslavement of Ireland and the increasing wretchedness and poverty of her people and to expose to shame those natives and inhabitants who could be so stupid or so debased as in the face of all the evidence to maintain that the Kingdom was flourishing and well-governed.

A few days after the publication of *A Short View*, a small tract of eight pages appeared anonymously, addressed To The R——d Dr. J——n S——t, *The Memorial of the poor Inhabitants, Tradesmen, and Labourers of the Kingdom of Ireland*. It contained a proposal to provide against the scarcity of bread corn for the following winter by raising a fund of ten thousand pounds to import corn from the plantations abroad and some neighbouring countries where it is cheap and plentiful. Swift is asked to consider the proposal and if he approves of it to recommend it to the Lord Lieutenant and the Parliament.

To this Swift replied in *An Answer* etc., dated March 25, printed also by S. Harding, and ascribed on the title-page to the Author of the *Short View of the State of Ireland*. He first shows that dearness and scarcity of corn is due to the poor methods of Irish farmers which ruined their agricultural land, and led their landlords to turn all into grass. He then exposes the absurdity of thinking that there is enough money in Ireland to pay for the proposed importation of corn, and instead suggests that funds should be contributed to support the poor in potatoes and butter-milk until the new corn comes in. He is willing, however, to assume that the paper is written with good will and therefore must be the work of someone who is a stranger to Ireland. He was in fact aware who had written it, because he had been informed by the man who had been entrusted by the author to deliver the little book. This we know from the letter written by the author, John Browne, to Swift on April 4, 1728, in which he asks Swift 'to conceal what chance has revealed to you, and . . . judge of me not from the report of my enemies, but from what I appear in the little tracts which have waited on you.' Swift had violently attacked Browne in his *Drapier's Letters*, because he had appeared as a witness for Wood before the Privy Council in London, and had seemed to him then a traitor to the cause of Ireland; but he was brought to change his attitude after he had read Browne's pamphlets on Irish trade, and he kept the secret of the authorship, and finally even took the trouble to remove the passage in which Browne had been condemned from later editions of the *Drapier's Letters*.[1]

Swift devotes the last pages of *An Answer* to deal with the objections that had been raised against his attack upon the late Lord Chief Justice Whitshed in *A Short View*. He insists that 'people distinguished for their Villainy have as good a Title for a Blast from the proper Trumpet [of Fame], as those who are most renowned for their Virtues.'[2] And then he sounds an even louder and longer blast than before against Whitshed and his like; for 'although their memories will rot, there may be some Benefit for their Survivors to smell it while it is rotting.'

In these papers Swift appears again as champion of the liberties of Ireland, though he refuses to accept Pope's kind opinion of him as a patriot; 'what I do is owing to perfect rage and resentment, and the mortifying sight of slavery, folly, and baseness about me, among which I am forced to live.'[3] But however much he may have been prompted to write by resentment, there was little exaggeration in his account of the miserable state of Ireland. Those in authority were also concerned, as shown in a remark of Marmaduke Coghill, Judge of the Prerogative Court, writing to Edward Southwell at the end of the year, on December 14, 1728:

> In my last I gave you an account of the circumstances of this Kingdom, which grows worse every day, by the Lds Justices great caution in not prohibiting the exportation of corn . . . I

[1] *Corr.*, iv, 24–28; and *Drapier's Letters*, Clar. Press, 1935, pp. 37, 226–8.
[2] See below, p. 23.   [3] *Corr.*, iv, 34.

wish the mobb may not rise and do mischief . . . I have herewith
sent a paper which we think to be Swifts, in which you will see
the genius and spirit of the man with his usual indiscretion.[1]

But neither Swift's indiscretions nor the threatening situation
disturbed the equanimity and satisfaction of the Irish Parliament, which closed a long session in May 1728 with fervent
addresses of loyalty to the new monarch, who had done so
much 'to encourage the Trade, and increase the Wealth of
the Kingdom'; and with speeches of thanks to the Lord
Lieutenant from the Commons, in recognition of his 'entire
knowledge of the Condition and true Interest of the Kingdom'
and his 'tender Concern for its Prosperity and Happiness.'[2]

As soon as the session was over Swift started a small
weekly paper, called the *Intelligencer*; the first number appeared
on May 11, 1728. It did not last long because the work fell
entirely on Swift and Sheridan. Writing to Pope about it
some years later, he says:

> If we could have got some ingenious young man to have been
> the manager, who should have published all that might be sent
> to him, it might have continued longer, for there were hints
> enough. But the printer here could not afford such a young
> man one farthing for his trouble, the sale being so small, and the
> price one halfpenny; and so it dropped.[3]

He then gives particulars of the papers he contributed himself,
and though the nineteen numbers had been reprinted in
London in 1729, Pope included four of them in the last
volume of their *Miscellanies*, 1732. The fifth and seventh
were printed together under a new title—'An Essay on the
Fates of Clergymen'; the ninth as 'An Essay on Modern
Education.' These three and Number III, Swift's admirable
defence of Gay's *Beggar's Opera*, were printed with Swift's final
corrections in Volume I of his collected works, and in that
form are reproduced in this volume. Number XIX, which
he had described to Pope as 'only a parcel of facts relating
purely to the miseries of Ireland, and wholly useless and un-

---

[1] B.M. Add. MSS. 21, 122.
[2] *Journals of the House of Commons of Ireland*, III, 566–67.
[3] *Corr*, iv, 307; and see Appendix B.

entertaining,' was nevertheless reprinted by him with his other
Irish papers in Volume IV of the collected works. Number I
is also included in its original form since Swift states definitely
that he wrote it. He may have thought that it was not worth
reprinting, as it is such a slight performance merely suggesting
what the aim of the *Intelligencer* was to be. It was 'to inform,
or divert or correct, or vex the Town' and was to provide
another opportunity of drawing attention to the condition of
Ireland. Number VI is an excellent paper by Sheridan,
describing vividly the wretchedness of the people to be met
on any of the roads in the country, and the poverty of their
tumbled-down dwellings; Number XV is a reprint, with an
introduction by Sheridan, of Swift's pamphlet, *A short View
of the State of Ireland*; and Number XIX is an account of conditions in County Down in the form of a letter from a country
gentleman, a landlord there with two hundred tenants.

Perhaps it would be as well to explain here why this volume
does not contain another pamphlet, which perhaps chiefly
by reason of its title has been attributed to Swift, namely
*The Present Miserable State of Ireland: In a Letter from a Gentleman
in Dublin, to his Friend S. R. W. in London*, several times reprinted without a date, and finally with the imprint Dublin,
1735. It had appeared[1] in *The Weekly Journal or Saturday's Post*,
for Saturday, September 30, 1721, with this introductory note:

> We shall consider the present State of *Ireland*, with regard to
> its Trade, Learning, Religion and Policy.
> As to the first; we find ourselves happily provided upon this
> Head, with a Letter from an eminent *Dublin* Trader in the
> Woollen Affair, a Person of Integrity, good Sense, and thorough
> Experience, to an Irish Gentleman of Distinction settled in
> *London*.

The letter is dated Dublin, March 15, 1720–21, and signed
S.T., and at the end there is this further comment:

> We are in good Hopes, the Fears the Author of this Letter
> was disturbed with, are greatly quieted by the Magnanimous
> Resolutions of the *Irish* Parliament, and are apprehensive he

[1] See note, *Poems*, p. 844, and R. H. Wagner, Bibliography, p. 5.

must be deceived in his Opinion of the Scarcity of Money in his Country, or surely such a thing as a Publick Bank would never be projected.

Swift was by no means alone during this whole period from 1720 onwards, in drawing attention to the miserable state of Ireland. On matters of trade and coinage and agriculture and absentee landlords there was a steady flow of often well-written and well-argued papers, from some of which he was not unwilling to borrow information. Sometimes he himself refers to them and to the authors of them; and we can be fairly sure that nothing printed in Dublin at this time was written by him if it was not sooner or later included in the Dublin edition of his collected works.

But six papers which we know he wrote in 1729 were apparently put aside; at least they are not known to have been printed in his lifetime. *The Letter on Maculla's Project about Halfpence* was first printed by Faulkner in 1758, but a fragment of it has been preserved in autograph, sufficient to establish its authenticity. The rest were all printed by Deane Swift for the first time in 1765 from Swift's manuscripts, two of which are now in the Forster Collection, namely the *Letter to the Archbishop of Dublin concerning the Weavers*, dated April, 1729, and the *Answer to Several Letters from Unknown Persons*. These are printed from the manuscript, and a comparison with Deane Swift's text shows that he may be relied upon as a fairly accurate editor for the text of the others of which the manuscripts are not now available.

The real problem is to explain why they were not printed. It is evident that they were written for the public. For Swift says towards the end of *A Letter to the Archbishop of Dublin:*

> What I have said may serve as an answer to the desire made me by the Corporation of Weavers, that I would offer my notions to the publick.[1]

And again in *An Answer to Several Letters from Unknown Persons*, he begins by referring to the letter he had received from them the previous summer, to which he had ordered an answer to

---

[1] See below, p. 71.

be printed, namely the *Intelligencer*, Number XIX, dated December 1728, and proposes to deal with their second letter in the same fashion:

> I do imagine you intended that the world should not only know your Sentiments, but my Answer, which I shall impartially give. . . . I have ordered your Letter to be printed, as it ought to be, along with my answer; because, I conceive, it will be more acceptable and informing to the Kingdom.[1]

Though he complains in the same letter, that without 'subscribing our names, we cannot prevail upon a printer to be at the charge of sending it into the world, unless we will be at all or half the expence' it is difficult to believe that in 1729 Swift could not have found a printer, if he really wanted something published. It is more likely that he changed his mind, and decided to do nothing, in that mood of despondency to which he often gives expression in these unpublished pieces:

> I am tired with letters from many unreasonable well-meaning people, who are daily pressing me to deliver my thoughts in this deplorable juncture; which, upon many others, I have so often done in vain. What will it import, that half a score people, in a coffee-house, may happen to read this paper . . .?[2]

Or again, in his *Answer to Several Letters from Unknown Hands*, though he approves of some of their suggestions and proceeds to set down several particulars which Parliament might well take into consideration, he does not think they would be well received 'if handed into the public by me.' And when he mentions his plan 'to abolish the Irish language . . . in order to civilize the most barbarous among them' and wishes that some public thoughts could be employed upon it, he confesses that he is himself too desponding to produce it.[3]

Although only the *Letter to the Archbishop* is dated April 1729, it is evident that most of these pieces were written in the early part of that year, perhaps before Swift left Dublin in June for a long summer stay with the Achesons at Market Hill, which lasted until the beginning of October. *A Letter*

---

[1] See below, p. 75.   [2] See below, p. 80.   [3] See below, p. 89.

B

concerning Maculla's Project must also have been written in the spring while he was still in Dublin, because he mentions that Maculla had called and left a copy of his book at the Deanery when he was too indisposed to see him, and that he had afterwards returned this visit and had some conversation with him at his own house. The fragment of manuscript which remains is not dated and is addressed only 'S^r' but Faulkner assumed that the letter was written to Dr. Delany. Like the rest of these manuscripts it is written in the right-hand column of each page only, leaving the left for additions and corrections, which in these four pages are quite considerable. Maculla's proposals are treated with respect, only some of his charges are criticized; and an alternative plan is suggested to ensure greater economy and security. This recommends that a company should be formed of ten public-spirited gentlemen, who would undertake to finance and manage the coinage of a limited amount of copper of the best quality for a profit of only one per cent more than the legal interest rate for the capital they would advance. But the working out of the financial details was done in such a casual fashion, that the first charges for preparing the necessary equipment and the rent of the house to work in were added as an after-thought. But the difficulties in getting such a plan into operation were clearly foreseen:

> It is not so hard to find an honest Man, as to make this honest Man active, vigilant and skilful, which I doubt will require a Spur of Profit greater than my Scheme will afford him, unless he will be contented with the Honour of serving his Country and the Reward of a good Conscience.[1]

It is probable that this letter was put aside when Swift went off early in June for his long summer visit at Market Hill. His giddiness and deafness had left him, and he was able to take to riding again. But though he was living in the country, and writing verses for the amusement or annoyance of his friends, he was not able to throw off his anxiety and his

---

[1] See below, p. 102.

resentment at the miseries of Ireland. His feelings are fully expressed in a letter to Pope, written on August 11, 1729:

> As to this country, there have been three terrible years' dearth of corn, and every place strewed with beggars; but dearths are common in better climates, and our evils here lie much deeper. Imagine a nation the two thirds of whose revenues are spent out of it, and who are not permitted to trade with the other third, and where the pride of women will not suffer them to wear their own manufactures, even where they excel what come from abroad. This is the true state of Ireland in a very few words. These evils operate more every day, and the kingdom is absolutely undone, as I have been telling often in print these ten years past. What I have said requires forgiveness but I had a mind for once to let you know the state of our affairs, and my reason for being more moved than perhaps becomes a clergyman, and a piece of a philosopher, and perhaps the increase of years and disorders may hope for some allowance to complaints, especially when I may call myself a stranger in a strange land.[1]

This statement reveals Swift's state of mind when he set about writing the greatest of all the Irish pamphlets, in which he shows his most daring use of irony. It is unlikely that he had then actually begun the *Modest Proposal*, for at the end of August, in two letters written on the 30th, he says that he intends to be soon back in town. But he changed his mind and stayed on through the whole of September and did not reach Dublin until October 8, when he 'was received with great joy by many of our principal citizens, who also on the same occasion caused the bells to ring in our cathedrals, and had bonfires and other illuminations.'[2]

They did not then know what Swift had been writing in those last weeks in the country, but before the end of October *A modest Proposal* appeared in its first Dublin edition, with the same imprint and in the same small format as *A short View* and the *Drapier's Letters*. The following advertisement of it appeared in the *Dublin Intelligence* for November 8:

> The late apparent spirit of patriotism, or love to our country, so abounding of late, has produced a new scheme, said in public

[1] *Corr.*, iv, 89–90.   [2] *Dublin Intelligence*, Oct. 11, quoted *Corr.* iv., 103.

to be written by D—— S——, wherein the author ... in-
genuously advises that one fourth part of the infants under two
years old, be forthwith fattened, brought to market and sold
for food, reasoning that they will be dainty bits for landlords,
who as they have already devoured most of the parents, seem
to have the best right to eat up the children.
   N.B. This excellent treatise may be had at the printer's hereof.

It was immediately reprinted in London, and in the following
year three other editions were separately printed in London,
while it was also included in several collections both in London
and Dublin.

It was a plan, 'calculated only for Ireland, and for no other
that was, is, or I think ever can be upon earth;' and it was
therefore addressed directly to an Irish audience; but it was
novel and startling enough to draw readers from elsewhere,
and was indeed intended to arouse attention in England even
among those who were not intimately acquainted with all
the problems or aware of all the miseries of the state of Ireland.
And for Swift himself it served, instead of letters to the Archbishop about the Weavers, or to Delany about the coinage of
copper, or to unknown persons about the scarcity of corn,
as a general answer. He had been wearied out for many
years with offering vain, idle, visionary thoughts, and at
length utterly despairing of success fortunately fell upon this
proposal; 'which as it is wholly new, so it hath something *solid*
and *real*, of no Expence and little Trouble, full in our own
Power, and whereby we can incur no Danger in *disobliging*
ENGLAND.'[1]

Its irony is so effective because it follows exactly the shape
and form of all these various proposals of one kind and another
with very specific details worked out, and with careful calculations of all the possible advantages and disadvantages of the
scheme. It is a fair, cheap and easy method, not like some of
the schemes which had been submitted to Swift, needing the
raising of large sums of money, or the finding of gentlemen
public-spirited enough to provide capital without the hope of
an exorbitant return. It deals with the most pressing problem,

[1] See below, p. 117.

what to do with the children of beggars and poor people, and offers a solution for lessening the population better than other suggestions such as allowing the young men to be recruited for service in foreign armies, or sending them out to the plantations in America. As for the old, the diseased and the maimed, they are already dying off as quickly as can reasonably be expected. The author professes himself still quite ready to listen to any alternate proposals, but believes that there is no other way for Ireland which is so sure to provide what is necessary—the public good of the country, 'by advancing Trade, providing for Infants, relieving the Poor, and giving some Pleasure to the Rich.'

This is really Swift's last word on the state of Ireland. It left nothing further to be said, and little further to be done, except to prepare his will and to leave his money for the founding of a hospital for the insane. But only a few weeks later he was stirred to action again by the news of a Bill being debated in the Irish Parliament, which had been called into session just before his return to the city. On November 29, 1729, the *Old Dublin Intelligence*, printed by R. Dickson, had reported the proceedings of the House of Commons, in contempt of the order of the House, and it became generally known that a Bill had been introduced for an additional duty on wine, and a tax of 4 shillings in the pound on the salaries of Absentees, and that this was to be applied to pay the interest at 6 per cent and discharge a capital sum of 200,000 pounds from the National Debt. Swift immediately set to work on *A Proposal that all the ladies should appear constantly in Irish Manufactures*, in which he was largely concerned to use all his influence to oppose the additional duty on French wines. He sets down six powerful reasons against such a tax and then proceeds to recommend three methods which might do something to improve conditions, namely to lessen the importation of unnecessary commodities, to tax heavily the incomes of absentees, and to allow Ireland a free trade. And finally in order to stop the waste due to the cost of luxuries to gratify the pride and vanity of women, he proposes that there should be a vote in both Houses of Parliament that every senator, noble or plebeian, should guarantee to the utmost of his power that his family, his friends and tenants should use nothing but the growth and manufacture of the kingdom.

This paper also was not published, but here I think the reason is clear. While Swift was writing it, the Bill had been read three times and passed in the House of Commons on December 20. It was immediately sent up to the House of Lords, passed and given Royal Assent by the Lord Lieutenant on December 22. Moreover, in his Address to the Lord Lieutenant on the same day, the Speaker of the House of Commons drew attention to the speed with which this business had been finished in very difficult circumstances:

> At their first Meeting, they found the Nation in very difficult Circumstances: The Calamities of the Times, which no human Wisdom could prevent or remedy, had occasioned a great Deficiency in the Revenue, and thereby a considerable Arrear to the Establishment; and these Calamities, which had been the principal Cause of the great Increase of the National Debt, made it more difficult to find proper and effective Means to discharge it.
>
> But great as these Difficulties were, his Majesty's faithful Commons with Cheerfulness and Unanimity, resolved to use their utmost Endeavours to surmount them: . . . they have given larger Supplies than ever granted in any previous Session: and they present the Bills thus early to your Excellency to receive the Royal Assent, though they have not yet been able to finish the many useful and necessary Laws depending before them for the Good of their Country.[1]

Swift had certainly planned to print his objections in time to influence opinion in the House against the Bill, for he says:

> As to the additional duty on wine, I think any person may deliver his opinion upon it, until it shall have passed into a law; and, until then, I declare mine to be positively against it.

Once it had passed it was too late for him to protest, and he put away what he had written. He may well have gone on

---

[1] *Journals of the House of Lords of Ireland*, III, 111–13.

with another task which seems to have occurred to him during
the writing of the *Proposal*, for he had said

> I could undertake to name six or seven of the most uncon-
> trolled maxims in government, which are utterly false in this
> Kingdom.[1]

Among the scraps of Swift autograph manuscripts found by
Professor James Clifford among the Piozzi papers, which are
now in the John Rylands Library[2], are two leaves headed
MAXIMS EXAMIN'D followed by six short maxims and
below, and on another torn leaf a first draft of some 'heads'
which include sentences to be found in the text of *Maxims
controlled in Ireland*. Though left incomplete and never printed
by Swift himself, this original draft is proof of the authenticity
of what was later printed by Deane Swift. It was evidently
begun in order to elucidate and exemplify a point he was constantly repeating, namely that it was futile to propose methods
for improving the trade of Ireland, by drawing upon the
experience or referring to the practice of other nations. He
takes certain accepted principles in economics or politics and
then demonstrates why they are not applicable in Ireland.
There, for instance, it would be false to argue that the high
price of the necessities of life and the low interest rates on
money indicate that money is plentiful; and as for the great
maxim that people are the riches of a nation this could only
be true in such a beggarly country if the miserable natives could
be sold for slaves to foreigners.

He breaks off at a point where he is about to deal with the
much discussed matter of the Absentees, and the manuscript
was presumably put aside unfinished.

As we look at this group of papers which Swift did not
bother to finish or to publish, we should do well to remember

[1] See below, p. 124. It has been suggested to me by Mr. Oliver Ferguson
that these *Maxims* were probably written in 1728. This may be correct; at least,
the original hints were among fragments of *Intelligencer* papers, certainly of
that year. But this reference seems to indicate that Swift may have developed
them in 1729 after (or possibly just before) writing his *Modest Proposal*. Cf. also
last lines of p. 66 below, written April 1729.

[2] See Appendix B.

what he wrote in a letter to Pope, about a year later, January 15,
1730–31:

> I write pamphlets and follies merely for amusement, and
> when they are finished, or I grow weary in the middle, I cast
> them into the fire, partly out of dislike, and chiefly because I
> know they will signify nothing.[1]

We now know that he did not cast them all into the fire,
but he may well have wished to avoid rousing Pope's curiosity
about manuscripts, which, being concerned with particular
Irish matters, were not suitable for publication in England.

There are two other short pieces, written early in 1730,
which were most certainly addressed to the public at the time,
although I have not been able to find any printed copy and
have had to take the text from later editions. They are both
concerned with the occasion on which the Dean of St.
Patrick's was honoured by being presented with the Freedom
of the City of Dublin. This had been proposed on Friday,
January 16, 1729–30:

> At the Tholsel there was a general Assembly of the Right
> Honourable the Lord-Mayor and Common-Council of this City,
> who generously and unanimously agreed to present that truly
> worthy Patriot, the Revd. Dr. Swift, Dean of St. Patrick's, with
> the Freedom of this City, in a Gold Box, made for the Purpose,
> on which is engrav'd the City Arms.[2]

Swift was just at this time writing one of his most violent
political verse satires, called *A Libel on D—— D—— And a
Certain Great Lord*,[3] which appeared in Dublin on February 2,
1729–30. His theme is the rottenness of political patronage:

> True *Politicians* only Pay
> For solid Work, but not for Play:
> Nor ever chuse to Work with Tools
> Forg'd up in *Colleges* and *Schools*.

---

[1] *Corr.*, iv, 194.   [2] *Dublin Journal*, Jan. 20, 1729–30.
[3] 'The best thing I writ, as I think.' See *Poems*, p. 475 and p. 483.

He even attacks the Vice-Roy, though he loves the man, Lord Carteret:

> He comes to *drain* a *Beggar's Purse:*
> He comes to tye our Chains on faster,
> And shew us, England is our Master:
> Caressing Knaves and Dunces wooing,
> To make them work their own undoing.

And a very dangerous meaning could be assumed to lie beneath the generalization of the concluding lines:

> For, no imaginable things
> Can differ more than God and Kings
> And, *Statesmen* by ten thousand odds
> Are Angels, just as Kings are Gods.

Perhaps it was not quite so surprising as Swift would have us believe that Lord Allen on February 13, 'at the Privy Council, the Lord Mayor being sent for, accused me for the author, and reproached the city for their resolution of giving me my freedom in a gold box, calling me a Jacobite, libeller, etc., and has now brought the same affair into the House of Lords, that the printer, etc., may be prosecuted.'[1] The authorities, however, took no action against the printer, but Swift, at the height of his power, did not delay in taking action publicly against his accuser. The *Advertisement by Dr. Swift, in his defence against Joshua Lord Allen* was dated February 18, 1729–30.

But he was not content to leave the matter there. He had a further opportunity to deal with the accusation of Lord Allen, when the Lord Mayor and some of the Aldermen came to present the Dean with his Freedom. I have been unable to find a record of the actual date when the presentation was made;[2] but Lord Allen evidently succeeded in causing some delay, and producing some embarrassment which Swift did nothing to lessen. It is disappointing that we have no account of what took place, except that which was carefully written down by Swift himself, giving 'The Substance of what was

---

[1] *Corr.*, iv, 126–27.

[2] Dr. Hayes, Librarian of the National Library in Dublin, very kindly had the minutes of the City Council and the newspapers searched for me, but found nothing.

said by the Dean of St. Patrick's to the Lord Mayor and some of the Aldermen, when his Lordship came to present the said Dean with his Freedom in a Gold Box.' This paper has not, I think, been given the attention it deserves. It is in the form of an account by one who had gathered all the particulars from some who had been there as far as they could recollect them, but every sentence bears the mark of the Dean's own vivid recollection of the ceremony, and shows the satisfaction he derived from being able to use this official occasion to vindicate himself against the charges of Lord Allen, and gently to chide the city authorities for their delays and hesitancies in honouring him. The Dean adopts exactly the same tone as Gulliver at the court of Lilliput.

> When his Lordship had said a few words, and presented the instrument, the Dean gently put it back, and desired first to be heard. He said, He was much obliged to his Lordship and the city for the honour they were going to do him, and which, as he was informed, they had long intended him: That it was true, this honour was mingled with a little mortification, by the delay which attended it; but which, however, he did not impute to his Lordship or the city: And that the mortification was the less, because he would willingly hope the delay was founded on a mistake; for which opinion he would tell his reason.[1]

And so he proceeds to the accusations of Lord Allen, and argues gravely that there must have been a mistake in assuming that they were levelled at himself, because at that very time Lord Allen was caressing him and courting his friendship. Then he vindicates himself against all charges of Jacobitism and gives some account of all that he had done for Ireland over a period of twenty years, acknowledging himself to be the author of the *Drapier's Letters*, and recalling what he had suffered by a most iniquitous judge. Finally,

> The Dean concluded with acknowledging to have expressed his wishes, that an inscription might have been graven on the box, shewing some reason why the city thought fit to do him that honour, which was much out of the common forms to a person

[1] See below, p. 145.

in a private station; those distinctions being usually made only to chief governors, or persons in very high employments.

He was clearly anxious to let it be known that he could only accept the honour offered to him, if it was understood that it was something different from the ordinary formality, such as was bestowed upon Hoadly, the newly appointed Archbishop of Dublin, who received the freedom of the city in a gold box on April 11, 1730.[1]

In the meantime he had been preparing a further exposure of the treachery and villainy of Lord Allen, and on the very day 'the Parliament was up, and as soon as the Lord Lieutenant came from the House' a paper was cried about in the streets, entitled *A Vindication of his Excellency, the Lord Carteret*, which was calculated to amuse and compliment the Lord Lieutenant, and at the same time provide an excuse for attacking Lord Allen and his supporters with impunity. Allen is introduced as that 'miserable Creature *Traulus*,' who has been imprudent enough to rouse 'the Resentment of an incensed political Surgeon, who is not much in Renown for his Mercy upon great Provocation.' He is warned that this surgeon, without waiting for his death is ready to flay and dissect him alive—and all for threepence. This was duly carried out in a verse dialogue, *Traulus*,[2] which shortly appeared in two separate parts, and amply fulfilled Swift's promise to lay open all the disordered cells of his brain to the view of mankind. In the *Vindication* he also singled out for special mention Pistorides, namely Sir Richard Tighe, the leader of the Whig patriots,' and 'Squire Hartly Hutcheson,' who had arrested two newsboys for crying the 'Libel on Dr. Delany.' But these matters were only the subject of a digression; the paper was in the main an ironical apology for the unfortunate tastes of Lord Carteret, which led him to prefer the company of men of learning as a result of his old-fashioned academic education. This had given cause for the suspicion that he has shown favour to Tories, such as Swift's friends

[1] Reported under that date in the *Dublin Intelligence*.
[2] *Poems*, pp. 794–801.

Dr. Thomas Sheridan and Dr. Delany and Sir Arthur Acheson. To answer this accusation, a very careful account is drawn up of the value of all preferments and benefits, conferred by the Lord Lieutenant on these persons. The result is a balance sheet, computed per annum, showing a satisfactory balance in favour of the Whigs of some £27,405. But it must be remembered that when Lord Carteret was appointed Lord Lieutenant for a second time, the power of disposing Deaneries was omitted from his commission; and this is said to have been done because he had given away three out of four deaneries to high Tories. Furthermore, in spite of his liking for Delany and his promise of preferment, he had refused him what he wanted and told him plainly that he could not give it to him, because he was suspected to be somewhat of a Tory.[1] And Swift, while admitting that Delany had become 'so domestick at the Castle of Dublin' is able to show that his present preferments are still less than he had given up when he was Senior Fellow of Trinity College, and further maintains that he cannot be justly accused of any Tory doctrines, since he had not in his writings, his actions or his discourse 'discovered one single principle of either Whig or Tory.' In examining the case of Dr. Sheridan, Swift does not hesitate to refer to that unfortunate sermon which he preached at Cork, on his way to take over the Church living to which he had just been presented.

> It *happened* to be the first of *August*; and the first of *August happened* that year to light upon a *Sunday*: And it *happened* that the Doctor's text was in these Words; *Sufficient unto the day is the Evil thereof*: And lastly, it *happened* that some one Person of the Congregation, whose loyalty made him watchful upon every Appearance of Danger to his Majesty's Person and Government, when Service was over, gave the Alarm.[2]

It was Sir Richard Tighe who gave the alarm, and managed to get Sheridan's name struck off the list of Chaplains as though he was a dangerous Tory. Swift had always disliked Tighe, and had carefully avoided him when they were in London together in 1711. After his action against Sheridan Swift

[1] *Corr.*, iv, 1, *note*.   [2] See below, p. 163.

pursued him mercilessly in some of the most scurrilous verses he ever wrote, the longest of which—'A Dialogue between Mad Mullinix and Timothy' was published as Number VIII of the *Intelligencer*.

In the course of his report on the patronage exerted by the Lord Lieutenant, which might have given rise to suspicions of his partiality, Swift is able with urbanity to compliment Lord Carteret on the excellence of his government, and at the same time vindicate himself against the charge of being a dangerous Jacobite, by letting it thus be known to what an extent he and his friends had been distinguished by the friendship and the regard of his Majesty's chief representative. The impression we get of Swift's relations with Carteret from this pamphlet and from his verses is strengthened by the more personal and intimate remarks that we come across in their letters. For instance, Swift wrote to Gay on November 19:

> I believe my Lord Carteret, since he is no longer Lieutenant, may not wish me ill, and I have told him often that I only hated him as Lieutenant. I confess he had a genteeler manner of binding the chains of this kingdom, than most of his predecessors, and I confess, at the same time, that he had, six times, a regard to my recommendation, by preferring so many of my friends in the Church, and the last two acts of his power were to add to the dignities of Dr. Delany and Mr. Stopford.[1]

If there is any doubt as to Carteret's attitude towards Swift in this whole affair, it can be settled on the evidence of his own remark in a letter to Swift, later, when he could speak quite freely, on March 6, 1734–35:

> When you see me forgetful of [liberty] . . . may you treat me like Traulus and Pistorides.

And in the same letter he adds:

> my compliments to Dr. Delany, for whom I have a most hearty esteem, though I know he thinks me not serious enough upon certain arduous points of antiquity.[2]

Swift was not on such close terms with the next Lord Lieutenant, the Duke of Dorset, and when his appointment

---

[1] *Corr.*, iv, 179.   [2] *Corr.*, v, 142.

had first been rumoured, he had remarked to Pope how unfortunate it was for him that Lady Allen, whose husband he
had treated so roughly, 'has been an old favourite of the Duke
of Dorset, and consequently will use all means to put me on a
worse foot than my station requires me to be with a chief
governor.'[1] But Dorset did not arrive in Ireland until September 1731, and during the previous year, while Parliament
remained prorogued, Swift was less involved in public affairs.

There was, however, one matter which caused some trouble
for a few months during the winter of 1730, namely the appearance in Dublin of some French officers who had been allowed
to raise recruits in Ireland for service in the armies of France.
Even Archbishop Boulter, who had been asked to afford
protection to Colonel Hennecy, the French officer in charge
of recruiting, was unhappy about the business, and mentions
that the Lords Justices 'apprehend there will be greater difficulties in this affair than at first offered.'[2] He is much relieved
to be able to report on December 31, that the Colonel had
behaved with great prudence during his stay, and had kept
his officers from appearing in public; and especially to hear
that they had received orders to quit the kingdom:

> I am glad this affair is at last happily concluded, after having
> been the occasion of so great a noise here, and of a much greater
> in England.

The first newspaper accounts reached Dublin in October,
and on November 7, the *Craftsman* had taken up the matter,
and protested vigorously against the rashness of such a proceeding. The writer had, as it were, challenged Swift to enter
the fray by referring to his *Modest Proposal*.

> Such a Method of providing for Persons, whose Principles
> render them unserviceable in *our Army*, is indeed a little more
> charitable than a *late Project* for preventing *Irish Children* from
> being starved, by fatting them up, and selling them to the
> *Butcher*.[3]

[1] Letter to Pope, May 2, 1730; see *Corr.*, iv, 151.
[2] Letter to the Duke of Newcastle, October 14, 1730; see *Letters of Hugh
Boulter, etc.* (Dublin, 1770), ii, 25–35.
[3] See below, Appendix C. In Swift's reply, as printed later by Faulkner
and in all editions where this *Craftsman* has been reprinted it is referred to as

It gave Swift a perfect opening, and he replies in the character of a loyal Whig, defending this policy of the government
against the objections of the Tory *Craftsman*:

> I detest reading your Papers, because I am not of your
> Principles, and because I cannot endure to be convicted. . . . You
> are pleased to reflect on a Project I proposed . . . and you venture
> to assert that your own Scheme is more charitable. . . . But now,
> when there is a most lucky Opportunity offered to begin a Trade,
> whereby this Nation will save many Thousand Pounds a Year,
> and *England* be a prodigious Gainer, you are pleased, without a
> Call, officiously and maliciously to interpose with very frivolous
> Arguments.[1]

What could be better than to let sixty thousand recruits be
exported to serve in the armies of France and Spain, when in
due course they would be destroyed, and so many Popish
friends of the Pretender would be lost. He then proceeds to
recommend a number of other policies which would have the
desired effect of contributing further profits and benefits of
trade to England and reduce Ireland to a state of Arcadian
simplicity, where the people would 'live with Comfort on
Potatoes and Bonnyclabber, neither of which are vendible
Commodities abroad.' This paper was first included in Swift's
collected Works, as a supplement to Vol. IX, published in
Dublin in 1758, where it is described as a Letter written
to the author of the *Craftsman* 'full of wit and the finest turns
of irony.' Faulkner states specifically in his preface to the
Reader, that he has printed it 'from the original Manuscript,
that was sent to England, and handed about there.' There
can be no doubt as to its genuineness.

No other occasional pieces in prose seem to have survived
from the year 1731, which can be accepted as Swift's work,
although several pamphlets printed during the year have been
attributed to him. *An Infallible Scheme to pay the publick Debt*

No. 232, of December 12. This is, of course, an impossible date, as by then the
matter was almost over. This number and date derive from the collected
edition, published in July 1731, in which the order of the papers has been
changed and the dates and numbers altered without warning. The original
paper is No. 227, dated Nov. 7. See my note in *The Book Collector*, Vol. 2, no. 4.
[1] See below, p. 173.

of this Nation in Six Months appeared anonymously, with no
imprint, in Dublin and was reprinted in London, with the
name D——n S——t on the title-page; it was also included
in 'Schemes from Ireland' and in *'Miscellanies. The Third
Volume*,' 1732. This is a very good example of the way in
which things were picked up in London, and sold with the
help of his name. Even his friends believed it to be his, and
Faulkner, his printer, was apparently willing to make a wager
on it, for Swift wrote to him on March 29, 1732:

> Without the least regard to your wager, I do assure you,
> upon my word and reputation, that I am not the author of one
> single line or syllable of that pamphlet, called an Infallible
> Scheme to pay the Debts of the Nation; and, as it is very unjust,
> so it is equally an imprudent and fallible proceeding, to pronounce
> determinately on our taste and knowledge of style or manner
> of writing, where very good judges are often deceived, and in
> this case, few men have suffered so much as myself, who have
> borne the reproach of many hundred printed papers, which I
> never saw.[1]

and later, he repeats the same to Pope, and adds that it was
written by 'a young clergyman whom I countenance: he told
me it was built upon a passage in Gulliver, where a projector
hath something upon the same thought.'[2] This was, of course,
the Rev. Matthew Pilkington.

Another anonymous pamphlet without an imprint appeared
in Dublin, in 1731 *A Proposal Humbly offered to the P——t,
For the more effectual preventing the further Growth of Popery*, and
was reprinted in London with some of Swift's verses to make
a sixpenny pamphlet. This *Proposal* was in part a reprint of a
Tatler for September 4, 1710, and has nothing in it to suggest
the hand of Swift. Indeed, although it imitates his ironical
manner, it is plainly the work of a Whig, who has no love for
the Established Church; and the original Dublin edition, on
the evidence of the printer's ornaments, was certainly printed
by S. Powell, who later published some of the more important
Whig tracts in favour of the repeal of the Test Act.

Swift was indeed fully occupied at this time in writing

---

[1] *Corr.*, iv, 286–87.   [2] Ibid., p. 309.

verse. Apart from lines addressed to Gay and to Pulteney, and those three Hogarthian pieces—*A Beautiful Young Nymph going to Bed, Strephon and Chloe,* and *Cassinus*—we know that he was working on his long poem, the *Verses on the Death of Dr. Swift,* which shows his final mastery of familiar occasional writing and is at the same time a humorous conversational piece, a study of the Dean and his friends as well as an apologia for his life and work. Writing to Gay on December 1, 1731, he speaks of it as almost finished; and he says that he has been at work upon it for several months, and that it takes him a week to add two lines and blot out four and alter eight. There is evidence, moreover, to show that he went on working at it and annotating it during the winter.[1] Besides as he had mentioned in an earlier letter to Gay, he had also been occupied during the summer in the country with two other great works in prose, *Polite Conversation* and *Directions to Servants*.[2] He has moreover begun to feel that the time for writing is almost past:

> My invention and judgement are perpetually at fisticuffs, till they have quite disabled each other; and the merest trifles I ever wrote are serious philosophical lucubrations in comparison to what I now busy myself about, as, to speak in the author's phrase, the world may one day see.[3]

One of the trifles which is dated 1732, though first published both in Dublin and in London the following year, consists of *The humble Petition of the Footmen in and about the City of Dublin,* addressed to the Honourable House of Commons. It adopts the usual form and prays for protection against certain counterfeits, who have appeared for some months in the streets of Dublin trying to pass themselves off as *real Footmen.* Seditious motives are suspected and the government is urged to issue warrants for the investigation of such disorderly persons who are bringing a scandal upon the true fraternity of footmen. Apart from the jokes at the expense of the footmen it is amusing as an expression of Swift's

---

[1] *Poems,* p. 553.   [2] See Vol. XIII of this edition.   [3] *Corr.,* iv, 261.

C

dislike of the *Toupees*, a name denoting a certain kind of peri-wig then in fashion as well as the people who wore them.

Another of the trifles he was busied about was printed in the spring of 1732 under the title *An Examination of Certain Abuses, Corruptions, and Enormities in the City of Dublin*. Its subject was *City Cries Instrumental and Vocal*, which was the alternative title of the London edition. It contained a series of amusing glimpses of the city streets, the habits and the phrases of the hawkers, the proverbs and slang in local use. He had always been sensitive to such things, and noted them down when he was in London to make use of them in his verses on 'A Description of the Morning' or to amuse Stella, with his complaints of being disturbed:

> Here is a restless dog crying Cabbages and Savoys plagues me every morning about this time, he is now at it, I wish his largest Cabbage was sticking in his Throat.[1]

And he had been amusing himself recently again writing 'Verses made for Women who cry Apples' etc.[2]

The pamphlet begins innocently enough in the same tone with a complaint that no stranger to Dublin could possibly understand the meaning of the jargon of the hawkers, who shout *Muggs, Juggs and Porringers up in the Garret and down in the Cellar*, when they have a farthing's worth of milk to sell; and with a protest against the shamelessness of those who solemnly cry, *Herrings alive, alive here*, or *Salmon alive, alive*, when the former have been a day and a night on dry land and the latter have been cut up into a dozen pieces. But cries such as 'Sweet-hearts' and 'Dirt to carry out' may be positively dangerous, because of their political insinuations, and street diversions like the 'Cossing of a Dog' reveal the violence of party faction. The signs that are set over those houses that invite the passers-by to punch are nothing better than Popish and Jacobite gew-gaws; and the very drinking of punch, involving the squeezing of an orange, is obviously intended as a curse on the glorious memory of King William III.

After the pamphlet had been printed in Dublin Swift gave

---

[1] *Journal to Stella*, December 13, 1712.   [2] *Poems*, pp. 951–53.

Pilkington a copy to arrange for its printing in London. This copy contained an additional paragraph, which seems to be intended to ridicule even more extravagantly the absurdity of some of the suspicions entertained by the Court against all Tories and Jacobites. For it is suggested that those ciphers G.R.II on the signs of the King's Head, cannot mean King George the Second, but George the second King—a clear proof of treason even in the capital city. We may here, perhaps, detect another indication of Swift's bitterness against Queen Caroline, which appears in the *Verses on the Death of Dr. Swift* and in his letters to the Countess of Suffolk in 1731, in which he replies to the preposterous charge that he could have been capable of writing the 'Counterfeit Letter to the Queen.'[1]

However, in the second of these letters to the Countess, dated October 26, he promised to refrain from causing his Majesty's government any further embarrassment by writing about the condition of Ireland:

> If any state scribble here should happen to reach London, I entreat your Ladyship would continue to do me the justice of believing my innocence, because I lately assured the Duke of Dorset that I would never have a hand in any such thing, and I gave him my reason before his Secretary, that looking upon this kingdom's condition as absolutely desperate, I would not prescribe a dose to the dead.

That must have been soon after the Lord Lieutenant's arrival in Dublin on September 11. Nevertheless, within a few months he had plunged into an attack upon the Bishops in the Irish House of Lords who were supporting two bills which Swift believed would have serious consequences for the inferior clergy. On December 2, 1731, the 'Lord Bishop of Ossory introduced Heads of a Bill more effectually to enable the Clergy having cure of souls, to reside upon their several and respective Benefices, and to build upon their respective Glebe-Lands.'[2] On the 9th the Archbishop of Dublin reported on Amendments to the Bill, and on the following day it was read a third time. Some of the clergy thereupon presented a petition to the Lord Lieutenant and Council that they might

[1] *Corr.*, iv, 246, 266.   [2] *Journals of the House of Lords of Ireland*, III, 167.

be heard against the Bill, but this was rejected. Then they went to the Dean of St. Patrick's for his advice and help.

Some time in January 1731–32, Swift began to write a paper 'On the bill for the Clergy's residence on their livings.' The manuscript[1] of this first draft, which breaks off in the middle of the eighth page consists of two quarto half sheets, entirely in Swift's hand, which can be definitely dated after December 28, 1731, because the second of these half-sheets has on the bottom of page 8 two lines of a letter of that date, which had evidently been put aside. It is an interesting document in that it reveals Swift's first thoughts on the subject, which were not concerned with the merits of the proposal, but with the fact that it was brought forward by the Bishops, who characteristically showed no feeling for the inferior clergy, while being very careful to guard their own financial interests. He begins by a few comments on the bench of Bishops to make sure that his readers will share to the full his dislike and distrust of them and their proposal. He commends those who have given up tolerable preferments in England for their condescension in leaving their native country to promote Christianity in Ireland; and as an afterthought, adds between the lines this comment:

> and therefore, in my opinion, both their Lordships and the many Dependers they bring over, may justly claim the merit of Missionaries sent to convert a Nation from Heresy and Heathenism.

Then he points out the differences between the circumstances of the English clergy and those of Ireland. This section slightly rearranged, is used in the paper which, redrafted, with a new title, *Considerations upon two Bills, &c.*, and dated February 24, 1731–32, he definitely addressed to the House of Commons, at the moment when the Bill had been returned to them. The counter-proposal to reduce the value of the rich Deanery of Down, and create some more rectories in that diocese, is also introduced into the revised pamphlet of

---

[1] The manuscript belongs to Mr. William Lefanu, who has most kindly allowed me to use it here.

February 24. During that month, the clergy had sought to be heard in the House of Lords. On the 17th they presented a petition

> setting forth that they would be greatly prejudiced if a Bill, intituled An Act more effectually to enable the Clergy, having care of Souls, to reside upon their several and respective Benefices, and to build upon their respective Glebe-Lands, should pass, etc.

This was referred to a committee and the petitioners were appointed to be heard by their Counsel.[1] On the 21st, after hearing counsel, the Bill passed at a third reading, by twenty-six votes against seventeen, and was sent back to the Commons. The second Bill for dividing larger livings passed without opposition on February 24. Two days later there appeared in the *Dublin Journal* of February 26 an abstract of some of the points of Swift's argument:

> The following Queries are an Extract from a Pamphlet, in the Press, writ by the Rev. Dr. S. D.S.P.D., which being somewhat long, and the Time passing, it was though fit to publish these Queries, that contain some of the Arguments, made use of in the said Pamphlet, etc.

> Some Queries humbly offered
> Whether the House of Commons may not think the Bishops have power enough already?
> Whether a Gentleman would not rather have a creditable Parson than a Beggar to converse with?
> Whether this Scheme of multiplying beggarly Clergymen may not by their Numbers have great Influence upon Elections, being intirely under the Dependance of their Bishops?
> Whether a Clause against Parsons having Votes should not be inserted?
> Whether Gentlemen and Farmers would not be easier in their Tythes with a rich Minister, than a poor one; for a hungry horse bites sore, etc.?

> If the Bills depend so long, as to print the Pamphlet entire, or shall be thrown out, the said pamphlet shall be publish'd

next Monday for the Satisfaction of those who may desire to read the Arguments against them.

Swift had evidently realized that the matter would be brought up in the House of Commons before the full pamphlet could be printed, and so arranged for the 'Queries' to appear in the *Dublin Journal* on the very day, February 26, when the counsel for the petitioners were heard at the bar of the House of Commons, where both bills were rejected.[1]

But on the same day in the House of Lords a complaint was made against Faulkner, the printer of the *Dublin Journal* for inserting 'Some Queries highly reflecting upon the honour of the House.' He was ordered to attend the following Monday. When he did not appear an order for his arrest was made. But there the matter stood until more than eighteen months later, when on October 1, 1733, it was again ordered that he should be taken into custody. After another fortnight he presented a petition for his release, and was brought before the bar of the House, reprimanded and discharged.[2]

As the bills had both been defeated, and as action had already been taken against the printer, the pamphlet was apparently not published in Dublin. But the *Dublin Journal* of 21–25 March, 1732, printed a report that 'the clergy and young gentlemen in the universities were wonderfully pleased with a pamphlet,'[3] just published in London under the title *Considerations upon Two Bills sent down from the R—— H—— the H—— of L—— To the H——ble H—— of C—— Relating to the Clergy of I****d.* Though his arguments were no longer needed, Swift was evidently willing to have them known, as a witness to the folly of the Bishops and his triumph over them.

He had suggested some possible amendments to the bill, which might serve to make their Lordships hesitate before raising the matter again; the first of these being a proposal that the Bishoprics in Ireland might be divided into 'two, three or four parts, as occasion shall require.' And he had

---

[1] *Journals of the House of Commons of Ireland*, IV, pt. i, 54.
[2] *Journals of the House of Lords of Ireland*, III, 230; 233–34.
[3] See Landa, L. A., *Swift and the Church of Ireland*, Clar. Press, 1954, p. 115*n*.

pointed out that the late Archbishop of Dublin had a very different way of encouraging the clergy of his diocese to residence, a good example which the rest of the Bishops had not followed. Nevertheless, the pamphlet was written with commendable restraint, and rarely shows the full force of Swift's dislike. That found expression in his verses *On the Irish Bishops*,[1] which appeared in the *Gentleman's Magazine* for June 1732, in which he triumphs over their defeat:

> Our B——s puft up with Wealth and with Pride
> To Hell on the Backs of the Clergy wou'd ride;
> They mounted, and labour'd with Whip and with Spur,
> In vain—for the Devil a Parson wou'd stir.
> So the *Commons* unhors'd them, and this was their Doom
> On their Crosiers to ride, like a Witch on a Broom.

And then he compliments the three Bishops who voted against the bill;

> Lord Bolton's good Grace, Lord Carr and Lord Howard
> In spite of the Devil would still be untoward.
> They came of good Kindred, and cou'd not endure,
> Their former Companions should beg at their Door.

and ends with his blessing on the House of Commons:

> So God bless the Church, and three of our Mitres;
> And God bless the *Commons* for *Biting* the *Biters*.

He also printed in Dublin a *Proposal for an act of Parliament to pay off the Debt of the Nation* by selling the Bishops' lands. For this purpose the Irish House of Commons had recently imposed fresh Duties and Taxes, but Swift proposed to do it 'without taxing the subject' and promised that 'no person will be the poorer or contribute one farthing to the charge.' He felt sure that no law could be more popular, and that therefore the Bishops would heartily support the proposal, out of gratitude to his Majesty and as a way of removing all causes of envy and all charges of oppression, and of bringing them somewhat nearer to 'the practice of the apostles, whose Successors they are deemed to be.'

[1] *Poems*, p. 801.

This sort of writing would cause the Lord Lieutenant no trouble, and could even be taken by the Bishops as a good joke. But in another matter of great concern to the Church, in which half the Bishops were with him, Swift was engaged in opposing a scheme which the Duke of Dorset had undertaken to press as much as possible on behalf of the government, namely to bring forward legislation in Ireland for the repeal of the Test Act. The situation is well described in a letter from Archbishop Boulter to the Duke of Newcastle, when the trouble was over:

> When my Lord Lieutenant first came thither this time, he let the Dissenters and others know, that he had instructions, if it could be done, to get the test repealed; and he has since spoke to all any ways dependant on the government, as well as to others whom he could hope to influence, to dispose them to concur with the design, and so have others done that have the honour to be in his Majesty's service.
>
> But it was unanimously agreed, that it was not proper to bring that affair in to either house of parliament till the supply was secured. However, as the design could not be kept secret, and as the Dissenters sent up agents from the north to solicit the affair among the members of parliament, it soon occasioned a great ferment both in the two houses and out of them, and brought a greater number of members to town than is usual. There came likewise many of the clergy from the several parts of the kingdom to oppose the design; and a pamphlet war was carried on for and against repealing the test, in which those who wrote for it shewed the greatest temper.[1]

In such a controversy it was not likely that Swift would keep silent; and there was no doubt on which side he would be found. It was the same question on which he had first broken with the Whigs, when he wrote a *Letter concerning the Sacramental Test*,[2] dated December 4, 1708, to oppose the attempt being then made by the Earl of Wharton to take off the Test. He entered the campaign in its first winter, for his paper entitled 'The Advantages propos'd by Repealing the Sacra-

---

[1] *Letters*, II, 86.   [2] See Vol. II of this edition, p. 109.

mental Test impartially considered,' was advertised in the *Dublin Journal* for February 5–8, 1731–32, and published first by Faulkner in Dublin and later reprinted in London. His arguments were evidently prepared to influence opinion in the Parliament of Ireland, where it was then expected that a Bill would be put forward for the repeal of the Test. Therefore he avoids any appeal to party loyalties, and puts aside all consideration of the different claims of the Church and the Protestant sects, and simply maintains the need for the establishment of one national religion, and the importance of admitting to civil or religious offices only those who conform to the legal worship. He argues simply that so long as there is an established church, whatever it may be, it would be inconsistent to do away with the law which requires those who hold office under the Crown to give proofs of their conformity. He admits that the repeal of the Test would probably not affect church patronage, and shrewdly observes that the bishops in their wisdom and piety may well consent to the repeal of the Test. At the same time he warns the Dissenters of Ireland that even if the Act is repealed and they are qualified for all secular employments, they will have to go to great lengths to overcome the disqualification of having been born in Ireland, before any employments are likely to be bestowed upon them.

There appeared also in 1732 a very different kind of tract addressed to churchmen—*Queries Wrote by Dr. J. Swift, in the Year* 1732. It was printed on a half sheet with a large head title to catch the eye, and the rubric 'Very proper to be read at this Time by every Member of the Established Church.' Here there is no attempt to hide his bias against Dissenters, Low Churchmen and Deists, and to emphasize the greater danger to the Established Church from this side than from the Papists. In these *Queries* Swift was less concerned with the situation in Ireland, than with the need he felt to rouse the whole church to oppose the attempts which the Dissenters were making from every quarter to stir opposition to the Test

Acts. In a letter to Ford, December 9, 1732, Swift shows how carefully he was watching their activities in London:

> We are full of your intentions to repeal the Test; The spirituall Leaders will encourage that project to a man. We conclude the same thing will be attempted here next winter, and have the same advocates, but we hope, without success.[1]

Ford replied that there was no real danger of the Test being repealed; and the matter is not further mentioned between them until Swift's letter of 20 November, 1733; which shows what his feelings were in the matter at that moment and also throws some light on his own part in the controversy:

> It is reckoned that the Test will be repealed. It is said that £30,000 have been returned from England; and £20,000 raised here from Servants, Laborers, Farmers, Squires, Whigs &c to promote the good Work. Half the Bishops will be on their side. Pamphlets pro and con fly about. One is called *The Presbyterian Plea of Merit examined*: perhaps if you saw it, you might guess the writer. Dr. Tisdel writes a weekly Paper called the *Correspondent*, generally very poor and spiritless. But we all conclude the Affair desperate. For the money is sufficient among us—to abolish Christianity it self. All the People in Power are determined for the repeal, and some of your acquaintance, formerly Toryes, are now on the same side. I have been in no condition to stir in it.[2]

This enables us to settle the date of *The Presbyterian Plea of Merit etc.*, which was evidently written in 1733 (not in 1731 as Monck Mason suggested) and first published by Faulkner to be ready for the opening of Parliament on October 4. It also proves that Swift had nothing to do with the *Correspondent*, of which Nos. III and IV were attributed to him by John Nichols in 1779.

Judging from the tone of Swift's letter, it seems safer to conclude that the only other papers which he wrote in 1733 were *Reasons for repealing the Sacramental Test &c. in favour of the Catholics*, and a small fragment, *Some few Thoughts concerning the Repeal of the Test*. The latter is a cynical comment reminding

---

[1] *Letters to Ford*, p. 144 and *note*.   [2] Ibid., pp. 160–61.

the Dissenters how few employments ever fall to the share of those English who have been born in Ireland, and what a snuffling there will be for these few scraps thrown among so many. This thought had first been put into Swift's head by a shrewd Quaker who had remarked that even the Quakers would doubtless find a way of claiming their share, once the Test had been removed.

The chief argument in favour of the repeal of the Test Act in Ireland was that it would strengthen the Protestant interest in a country where Papists were still so strong. The case had been put with great cogency and with some urbanity by John Abernethy in his *The Nature and Consequences of the Sacramental Test considered. With Reasons humbly offered for the Repeal of it*, printed in Dublin in 1731. He is able to show what support and encouragement had been given to the Dissenters in both houses of Parliament, and even by the Bishops themselves; and to point out that the importance of the part played by them at the time of the Revolution, their loyalty and support of William had been recognized in official resolutions of Parliament both in England and Ireland.

Now at the beginning of the new session of Parliament, which opened on October 4, 1733, there were signs that the Dissenters were to get their reward. In his address to the Parliament, the Lord Lieutenant had referred to the marriage arranged between the Princess Royal and the Prince of Orange as a strengthening of the Protestant interest; and had claimed that the King 'esteems it his chief Glory to protect us in the full Enjoyment of all our Civil and religious Rights.' He therefore appealed for 'a firm Union among all Protestants, who have one common Interest, and the same common Enemy.'[1] Further reasons for Swift's anxiety may be found in a paragraph, which may possibly have been inserted at his suggestion, in Faulkner's *Dublin Journal*, October 6:

> We are credibly informed, there are great Numbers of the most considerable Dissenting Teachers and Elders come to Town, from most Parts of this Kingdom, to sollicit the Repeal

[1] *Journals of the House of Commons of Ireland*, IV, pt. i, p. 70.

of the Sacramental Test; and that they are applying to all Persons who are presum'd to have Interest in the Members of either House to obtain a Repeal of that Law. It is not doubted but such of the established Clergy in the Country, who have best Interest, and are most capable to oppose their Designs, will immediately come to Town, and join with their Brethren of the City, at this critical Juncture: nor is it to be doubted but their respective ——— will not only indulge, but encourage their coming to Town.

For this indicates not only the amount of pressure which would be brought to bear on the Irish Parliament to introduce a bill for the repeal of the Test, but also the possible unwillingness of some of the bishops to oppose it.

Swift must have felt when he began to write again at this time that it was too late, and his case was lost. All the resources of power and influence would be exerted, and considerable funds made available to support the Dissenters; for the repeal of the Test would obviously increase the power of the Whig party, and establish more firmly all those whose influence he most distrusted in the affairs of church and state. He was moreover himself in rather an odd position, opposing as usual the designs of the Whig ministry in Ireland, who were supported by the most Whiggish among the bishops; but at the very moment when he was flouting the authority of the Crown and these Bishops, his chief case against the Dissenters was that in their whole history they had shown themselves to be rebels and schismatics, disturbing the unity of the kingdom, and as soon as they had gained power, overthrowing both the monarchy and episcopacy.

Perhaps that is the real reason why *The Presbyterians Plea of Merit . . . impartially examined* is so ineffective, except as a mere party pamphlet to arouse bigotry and rancour. But it has a special interest none the less, in showing that Swift could not confine himself to such a narrow rôle, without giving himself away. In his account of the past history of the Presbyterians over the course of a hundred and fifty years before the Revolution, and especially of their behaviour in 1688, he shows that 'he is resolv'd never to own that the Presbyterians did one good thing; for when he can't deny the

Fact, he arraigns the Intention.' This was a not unfair comment by the author of a well-written reply, entitled *A Vindication of the Protestant Dissenters from the Aspersions cast upon them in a late pamphlet, intitled, The Presbyterians Plea of Merit, etc.* where Swift's inconsistency is detected in the two passages in which he has given himself away.[1] First, when he admits that he may have been influenced by his reading of the ancient histories of Greece and Rome:

> This Writer himself tells us, that he is far from condemning all Commonwealths, and which is very odd, gives broad hints that he himself is turned Republican . . . so good a Churchman, and one that was educated in the highest Reverence for Monarchy (as he himself intimates) has by long *Experience*, and by observing and *detesting* the Corruptions of Mankind, and not improbably by his Discontents at the present Government, been brought to have such favourable Thoughts of a Republick.

And, secondly, when he is unable to hide his dislike of those churchmen who are not as Tory as he is, though his argument requires that he maintain a clear line of division with the loyal established church on the one side and the sects, as rebellious fanatics, on the other:

> This Writer does not confine his Invectives to the Dissenters alone; he cannot abstain from abusing the *whole Set of zealous Whigs*, as he calls them, whom he represents as hating the Tories more than the Papists themselves, and excluding them, even from the *smallest offices*, though *professing the same Loyalty to the same Protestant King and his Heirs*.

Swift was more successful with the other pamphlet that he printed before the end of the year, entitled *Reasons for repealing the Sacramental Test &c. in favour of the Catholics*, a theme, however ironically handled, which was well calculated in Ireland to raise doubts about the advisability of tampering with the Test. Perhaps when he came to write this, he had learned that there was less cause for anxiety than he had feared. But even if he is not less concerned, the fact that he is here adopting the rôle of one who would appeal to the Parliament

[1] *A Vindication etc.*, London, 1733, pp. 5, 17.

of Ireland on behalf of the Catholics frees him from his own dilemma, and from all appearance of rancour or bias, so that he is able with easy mastery to elaborate his case 'drawn partly from Arguments as they are Catholics, and partly from Arguments common to them with their Brethren the Dissenters.'

He is able to insinuate, as Monck Mason says, that their 'pretensions, founded upon their former services, and attachment to the government, had greater weight than those of the Presbyterians.' 'The arguments pretended to be urged by the Roman Catholics, consist partly of true statements and partly of ironical allusions, which are combined together into such a trellis work, as to render it almost unassailable.'[1]

Swift dates this tract in November, and it is probable that the matter was settled before he had time to publish it. To bring things to a head a vote was passed in the House of Commons, on Tuesday, December 11, 'That no Bill, or Heads of a Bill, be received after Friday next, for the Repeal of any Clause in any Act to prevent the further Growth of Popery.'[2] And in his letter of December 18 to the Duke of Newcastle, Archbishop Boulter reported that

> it was concluded at a meeting at the Castle on Wednesday morning and another on Thursday morning, where some of the agents for the Dissenters were present, to be most for the credit of the government and the peace of the kingdom, not to push for a thing which plainly appeared impracticable.[3]

He further gave it as his opinion that even if it had passed in the Commons it would have miscarried among the Lords; and he reminds the Duke that the Archbishop of Dublin had told the ministry in London that he thought such a repeal could not pass, and says that since the opening of the session he had shared that opinion. He does not suggest that the opposition in either House was increased by the public controversy, and it would be foolish to claim that Swift's pamphlets were responsible for stopping the attempt to repeal the Test.

---

[1] *History of St. Patrick's, Dublin*, p. 389.
[2] *Journals of the House of Commons of Ireland*, IV, pt. i, p. 99.
[3] *Letters*, II, 87.

Those he printed in Dublin between 1731 and 1733 were reprinted in London, and furnished High-Churchmen with some of their strongest arguments. Two of them were again reprinted in a volume with an authoritative pronouncement by the Bishop of London: *The Dispute adjusted About the Proper Time of applying for a Repeal of the Corporation and Test Acts: by shewing that No Time is proper.* By the Right Reverend Father in God, Edm. Lord Bishop of London. To which are added, *The Advantages propos'd by repealing the Sacramental Test*: As also, *Some Queries relating thereto.* By the Reverend Dr. J. S. D.S.P.D.

In such a controversy Swift may seem to some of his readers to-day to be more than ordinarily caught by party prejudice, involved in a narrow dispute which at the proper time settled itself, and in some respects to be unlike himself, as he is revealed in the full sweep of his satire in his verses *On Poetry: A Rapsody*, written at this same time and published on December 31, 1733. How should one who has so little respect for kings and bishops be so positive against the Dissenters because they were once involved in killing a king and overthrowing the bishops?

Swift might have replied in words that he had written long before that he was not unaware 'what a bundle of Inconsistencies and Contradictions would appear' if a man would register all his opinions 'upon Love, Politicks, Religion, Learning, and the like'; but it was not his business to express those inconsistencies any more than the doubts that come unbidden into the mind. For in all controversy 'positiveness' is a necessary quality, 'because whoever would obtrude his Thoughts and Reasons upon a Multitude, will convince others the more, as he appears convinced himself.' Nevertheless, he would perhaps have admitted also that his experience of such controversies had led him to confirm another observation he had noted down when he was a young man:

> We have just Religion enough to make us *hate*, but not enough to make us *love* one another.[1]

[1] See *Thoughts on Various Subjects*, Vol. I, p. 241 of this edition.

A Short View of the State of Ireland

of Ireland

A

Short VIEW

OF THE

STATE

OF

IRELAND.

D U B L I N:
Printed by *S. HARDING*, next Door to
the *Crown* in *Copper-Alley*, 1727-8.

A
Short VIEW
OF THE
STATE of *IRELAND*.

Written in the Year 1727.

I AM assured, that it hath, for some Time, been practised as a Method of making Men's Court, when they are asked about the Rate of Lands, the Abilities of Tenants, the State of Trade and Manufacture in this Kingdom, and how their Rents are paid; to answer, that in their Neighbourhood, all Things are in a flourishing Condition, the Rent and Purchase of Land every Day encreasing. And if a Gentleman happen to be a little more sincere in his Representations; besides being looked on as not well affected, he is sure to have a Dozen Contradictors at his Elbow. I think it is no Manner of Secret why these Questions are so *cordially* asked, or so *obligingly* answered.

BUT since, with regard to the Affairs of this Kingdom, I have been using all Endeavours to subdue my Indignation; to which, indeed, I am not provoked by any personal Interest, being not the Owner of one Spot of Ground in the whole *Island*; I shall only enumerate by Rules generally known, and never contradicted, what are the true Causes of any Countries flourishing and growing rich; and then examine what Effects arise from those Causes in the Kingdom of *Ireland*.

THE first Cause of a Kingdom's thriving, is the Fruitfulness of the Soil, to produce the Necessaries and Conveniences of Life; not only sufficient for the Inhabitants, but for Exportation into other Countries.

THE Second, is the Industry of the People, in working up all their native Commodities, to the last Degree of Manufacture.

THE Third, is the Conveniency of safe Ports and Havens, to carry out their own Goods, as much manufactured, and bring in those of others, as little manufactured, as the Nature of mutual Commerce will allow.

THE Fourth is, that the Natives should, as much as possible, export and import their Goods in Vessels of their own Timber, made in their own Country.

THE Fifth, is the Priviledge of a free Trade in all foreign Countries, which will permit them; except to those who are in War with their own Prince or State.

THE Sixth, is, by being governed only by Laws made with their own Consent; for otherwise they are not a free People. And therefore, all Appeals for Justice, or Applications for Favour or Preferment, to another Country, are so many grievous Impoverishments.

THE Seventh is, by Improvement of Land, Encouragement of Agriculture, and thereby encreasing the Number of their People; without which, any Country, however blessed by Nature, must continue poor.

THE Eighth, is the Residence of the Prince, or chief Administrator of the Civil Power.

THE Ninth, is the Concourse of Foreigners for Education, Curiosity, or Pleasure; or as to a general Mart of Trade.

THE Tenth, is by disposing all Offices of Honour, Profit, or Trust, only to the Natives, or at least with very few Exceptions; where Strangers have long inhabited the Country, and are supposed to understand, and regard the Interest of it as their own.

THE Eleventh, is when the Rents of Lands, and Profits of Employments, are spent in the Country which produced them, and not in another; the former of which will certainly happen, where the Love of our native Country prevails.

THE Twelfth, is by the publick Revenues being all spent and employed at home; except on the Occasions of a foreign War.

THE Thirteenth is, where the People are not obliged, unless they find it for their own Interest or Conveniency, to receive any Monies, except of their own Coinage by a publick Mint, after the Manner of all civilized Nations.

THE Fourteenth, is a Disposition of the People of a Country to wear their own Manufactures, and import as few Incitements to Luxury, either in Cloaths, Furniture, Food, or Drink, as they possibly can live conveniently without.

THERE are many other Causes of a Nation's thriving, which I cannot at present recollect; but without Advantage from at least some of these, after turning my Thoughts a long Time, I am not able to discover from whence our Wealth proceeds, and therefore would gladly be better informed. In the mean Time, I will here examine what Share falls to *Ireland* of these Causes, or of the Effects and Consequences.

IT is not my Intention to complain, but barely to relate Facts; and the Matter is not of small Importance. For it is allowed, that a Man who lives in a solitary House, far from Help, is not wise in endeavouring to acquire, in the Neighbour-hood, the Reputation of being rich; because those who come for Gold, will go off with Pewter and Brass, rather than return empty: And in the common Practice of the World, those who possess most Wealth, make the least Parade; which they leave to others, who have nothing else to bear them out, in shewing their Faces on the *Exchange*.

As to the first Cause of a Nation's Riches, being the Fertility of the Soil, as well as Temperature of Climate, we have no Reason to complain; for, although the Quantity of unprofitable Land in this Kingdom, reckoning Bogg, and Rock, and barren Mountain, be double in Proportion to what it is in *England*; yet the native Productions which both Kingdoms deal in, are very near on Equality in Point of Goodness; and might, with the same Encouragement, be as well manufactured. I except Mines and Minerals; in some of which, however, we are only defective in Point of Skill and Industry.

IN the Second, which is the Industry of the People; our Misfortune is not altogether owing to our own Fault, but to a Million of Discouragements.

THE Conveniency of Ports and Havens, which Nature hath bestowed so liberally on this Kingdom, is of no more Use to us, than a beautiful Prospect to a Man shut up in a Dungeon.

As to Shipping of its own, *Ireland* is so utterly unprovided, that of all the excellent Timber cut down within these Fifty or Sixty Years, it can hardly be said, that the Nation hath received the Benefit of one valuable House to dwell in, or one Ship to trade with.

IRELAND is the only Kingdom I ever heard or read of, either in ancient or modern Story, which was denied the Liberty of exporting their native Commodities and Manufactures, wherever they pleased; except to Countries at War with their own Prince or State: Yet this Privilege, by the Superiority of meer Power, is refused us, in the most momentous Parts of Commerce; besides an Act of Navigation, to which we never consented, pinned down upon us, and rigorously executed; and a Thousand other unexampled Circumstances, as grievous, as they are invidious to mention. To go on to the rest.

IT is too well known, that we are forced to obey some Laws we never consented to; which is a Condition I must not call by its true uncontroverted Name, for fear of Lord Chief Justice *Whitshed's* Ghost, with his * *Libertas & natale Solum*, written as a Motto on his Coach, as it stood at the Door of the Court, while he was perjuring himself to betray both. Thus, we are in the Condition of Patients, who have Physick sent them by Doctors at a Distance, Strangers to their Constitution, and the Nature of their Disease: And thus, we are forced to pay five Hundred *per Cent.* to decide our Properties; in all which, we have likewise the Honour to be distinguished from the whole Race of Mankind.

As to Improvement of Land; those few who attempt that, or Planting, through Covetousness, or Want of Skill, generally leave Things worse than they were; neither succeeding in Trees nor Hedges; and by running into the Fancy of Grazing, after the Manner of the *Scythians*, are every Day depopulating the Country.

* Liberty and my native country.

WE are so far from having a King to reside among us, that even the Viceroy is generally absent four Fifths of his Time in the Government.

NO strangers from other Countries, make this a Part of their Travels; where they can expect to see nothing, but Scenes of Misery and Desolation.

THOSE who have the Misfortune to be born here, have the least Title to any considerable Employment; to which they are seldom preferred, but upon a political Consideration.

ONE third Part of the Rents of *Ireland*, is spent in *England*; which, with the Profit of Employments, Pensions, Appeals, Journeys of Pleasure or Health, Education at the *Inns* of Court, and both Universities, Remittances at Pleasure, the Pay of all Superior Officers in the Army, and other Incidents, will amount to a full half of the Income of the whole Kingdom, all clear Profit to *England*.

WE are denied the Liberty of Coining Gold, Silver, or even Copper. In the Isle of *Man*, they coin their own *Silver*; every petty Prince, Vassal to the *Emperor*, can coin what Money he pleaseth. And in this, as in most of the Articles already mentioned, we are an Exception to all other States or Monarchies that were ever known in the World.

AS to the last, or Fourteenth Article, we take special Care to act diametrically contrary to it in the whole Course of our Lives. Both Sexes, but especially the Women, despise and abhor to wear any of their own Manufactures, even those which are better made than in other Countries; particularly a Sort of Silk Plad, through which the Workmen are forced to run a Sort of Gold Thread that it may pass for *Indian*. Even Ale and Potatoes are imported from *England*, as well as Corn: And our foreign Trade is little more than Importation of *French* Wine; for which I am told we pay ready Money.

NOW, if all this be true, upon which I could easily enlarge; I would be glad to know by what secret Method, it is, that we grow a rich and flourishing People, without *Liberty*, *Trade*, *Manufactures*, *Inhabitants*, *Money*, or the *Privilege of Coining*; without *Industry*, *Labour*, or *Improvement of Lands*, and with more than half the Rent and Profits of the whole *Kingdom*, annually exported; for which we receive not a single Farthing: And to make up all this, nothing worth mentioning, except the Linnen of the *North*, a Trade casual, corrupted, and at Mercy; and some Butter from *Cork*. If we do flourish, it must be against every Law of Nature and Reason; like the Thorn at *Glassenbury*, that blossoms in the Midst of Winter.

LET the worthy *Commissioners* who come from *England*, ride round the Kingdom, and observe the Face of Nature, or the Faces of the Natives; the Improvement of the Land; the thriving numerous Plantations; the noble Woods; the Abundance and Vicinity of Country-Seats; the commodious Farmers Houses and Barns; the Towns and Villages, where every Body is busy, and thriving with all Kind of Manufactures; the Shops full of Goods, wrought to Perfection, and filled with Customers; the comfortable Diet and Dress, and Dwellings of the People; the vast Numbers of Ships in our Harbours and Docks, and Ship-wrights in our Seaport-Towns; the Roads crouded with Carriers, laden with rich Manufactures; the perpetual Concourse to and fro of pompous Equipages.

WITH what Envy, and Admiration, would those Gentlemen return from so delightful a Progress? What glorious Reports would they make, when they went back to *England*?

BUT my Heart is too heavy to continue this Irony longer; for it is manifest, that whatever Stranger took such a Journey, would be apt to think himself travelling in *Lapland*, or *Ysland*, rather than in a Country so favoured by Nature as ours, both in Fruitfulness of Soil, and Temperature of Climate. The miserable Dress, and Dyet, and Dwelling of the People. The general Desolation in most Parts of the Kingdom. The old Seats of the Nobility and Gentry all in Ruins, and no new ones in their Stead. The Families of Farmers, who pay great Rents, living in Filth and Nastiness upon Butter-milk and Potatoes, without a Shoe or Stocking to their Feet; or a House so convenient as an *English* Hog-sty, to receive them. These, indeed, may be comfortable Sights to an *English* Spectator; who comes for a short Time, only *to learn the Language*, and returns back to his own Country, whither he finds all our Wealth transmitted.

Nostrâ miserià magnus es.

THERE is not one Argument used to prove the Riches of *Ireland*, which is not a logical Demonstration of its Poverty. The Rise of our Rents is squeezed out of the very Blood, and Vitals, and Cloaths, and Dwellings of the Tenants; who live worse than *English* Beggars. The Lowness of Interest, in all other Countries a Sign of Wealth, is in us a Proof of Misery; there being no Trade to employ any Borrower. Hence, alone, comes the Dearness of Land, since the Savers have no other Way to lay out their Money. Hence the Dearness of Necessaries for Life; because the Tenants cannot afford to pay such extravagant Rates for Land, (which they must take, or go a-begging) without raising the Price of Cattle, and of Corn, although themselves should live upon Chaff. Hence our encrease of Buildings in this City; because Workmen have nothing to do, but employ one another; and one Half of them are infallibly undone. Hence the daily Encrease of *Bankers*; who may be a necessary Evil in a trading Country, but so ruinous in ours; who, for their private Advantage, have sent away all our Silver, and one Third of our Gold; so that within three Years past, the running Cash of the Nation, which was about five Hundred Thousand Pounds, is now less than two; and must daily diminish, unless we have Liberty to coin, as well as that important Kingdom the Isle of *Man*; and the meanest Prince in the *German* Empire, as I before observed.

I HAVE sometimes thought, that this Paradox of the Kingdom growing rich, is chiefly owing to those worthy Gentlemen the BANKERS; who, except some Custom-house Officers, Birds of Passage, oppressive thrifty 'Squires, and a few others who shall be nameless, are the only thriving People among us: And I have often wished, that a Law were enacted to hang up half a Dozen *Bankers* every Year; and thereby interpose at least some short Delay, to the further Ruin of *Ireland*.

YE are idle, ye are idle, answered *Pharoah* to the *Israelites*, when they complained to *his Majesty*, that they were forced to make Bricks without Straw.

ENGLAND enjoys every one of those Advantages for enriching a Nation, which I have above enumerated; and, into the Bargain, a good Million returned to them every Year, without Labour or Hazard, or one Farthing Value received on our Side. But how long we shall be able to continue the Payment, I am not under the least Concern. One Thing I know, that *when the Hen is starved to Death, there will be no more Golden Eggs.*

I THINK it a little unhospitable, and others may call it a subtil Piece of Malice; that, because there may be a Dozen Families in this Town, able to entertain their *English* Friends in a generous Manner at their Tables; their Guests, upon their Return to *England*, shall report, that we wallow in Riches and Luxury.

YET, I confess, I have known an Hospital, where all the Household-Officers grew rich; while the Poor, for whose Sake it was built, were almost starving for want of Food and Raiment.

To conclude. If *Ireland* be a rich and flourishing Kingdom; its Wealth and Prosperity must be owing to certain Causes, that are yet concealed from the whole Race of Mankind; and the Effects are equally invisible. We need not wonder at Strangers, when they deliver such Paradoxes; but a Native and Inhabitant of this Kingdom, who gives the same Verdict, must be either ignorant to Stupidity; or a Man-pleaser, at the Expence of all Honour, Conscience, and Truth.

An Answer to a Paper called A Memorial

A N
A N S W E R
TO A
P A P E R,
CALLED
A Memorial

Of the Poor *Inhabitants*, *Tradesmen* and
Labourers of the KINGDOM of

I R E L A N D.

By the AUTHOR of the SHORT VIEW of the
State of *I R E L A N D*.

D U B L I N:
Printed by S. HARDING, next Door to the
Crown in *Copper-Alley*, 1728.

AN

ANSWER

TO A

PAPER,

CALLED

A Memorial *of the poor* Inhabitants, Tradesmen, *and*
Labourers *of the Kingdom of* Ireland.

Written in the Year 1728.

I Received a *Paper* from you, wherever you are, printed
without any Name of Author or Printer; and sent, I suppose,
to me among others, without any particular Distinction.
It contains a Complaint of the Dearness of Corn; and some
Schemes of making it cheaper, which I cannot approve of.

BUT pray permit me, before I go further, to give you a
short History of the Steps, by which we arrived at this hopeful
Situation.

IT was indeed the shameful Practice of too many *Irish*
Farmers, to wear out their Ground with Plowing; while,
either through Poverty, Laziness, or Ignorance, they neither
took Care to manure it as they ought; nor gave Time to any
Part of the Land to recover itself: And when their Leases were
near expiring, being assured that their Landlords would not
renew, they Ploughed even the Meadows, and made such a
Havock, that many Landlords were considerable Sufferers
by it.

THIS gave Birth to that abominable Race of Graziers, who,

E   17

upon Expiration of the Farmers Leases, are ready to engross great Quantities of Land; and the Gentlemen having been before, often ill paid, and their Land worn out of Heart, were too easily tempted, when a rich Grazier made him an Offer to take all his Land, and give him Security for Payment. Thus, a vast Tract of Land, where Twenty or Thirty Farmers lived together, with their Cottagers, and Labourers in their several Cabins, became all desolate, and easily managed by one or two Herdsmen, and their Boys; whereby the Master-Grazier, with little Trouble, seized to himself the Livelyhood of a Hundred People.

It must be confessed, that the Farmers were justly punished for their *Knavery*, *Brutality*, and *Folly*. But neither are the *'Squires* and *Landlords* to be excused; for to them is owing the depopulating of the *Country*, the vast Number of *Beggars* and the Ruin of those few sorry Improvements we had.

That *Farmers* should be limited in Ploughing, is very reasonable, and practiced in *England*; and might have easily been done here, by penal Clauses in their Leases: But to deprive them, in a manner, altogether from Tilling their Lands, was a most stupid Want of Thinking.

Had the *Farmers* been confined to plough a certain Quantity of Land, with a Penalty of Ten Pounds an Acre, for whatever they exceeded; and farther limited for the Three or Four last Years of their Leases; all this Evil had been prevented; the Nation would have saved *a Million of Money*; and been more populous by above *Two Hundred Thousand Souls*.

For a People denied the Benefit of *Trade*, to manage their Lands in such a Manner, as to produce nothing but what they are forbidden to trade with; or, only such Things as they can neither export, nor manufacture, to Advantage; is an Absurdity, that a *wild Indian* would be ashamed of; especially when we add, that we are content to purchase this hopeful Commerce, by sending to foreign Markets for our Daily Bread.

The *Grazier's* Employment is to feed great Flocks of *Sheep*, or *Black Cattle*, or both. With Regard to *Sheep*; as Folly is usually accompanied with Perverseness, so it is here. There is something so monstrous to deal in a Commodity, (further than for our own Use) which we are not allowed to export manufactured, nor even un-manufactured, but to *one certain Country*, and only to some *few* Ports in that Country; there is, I say, something so sottish, that it wants a Name, in our Language, to express it by: And, the Good of it is, that the more *Sheep* we have, the fewer human Creatures are left to wear the *Wool*, or eat the *Flesh*. *Ajax* was mad when he mistook a Flock of *Sheep* for his Enemies: But we shall never be sober, until we have the same Way of Thinking.

THE other Part of the *Grazier's* Business is, what we call *Black-Cattle*; producing *Hides*, *Tallow*, and *Beef* for Exportation. All which are good and useful Commodities, if rightly managed. But it seems, the greatest Part of the *Hides* are sent out raw, for want of *Bark* to *Tan* them; and that Want will daily grow stronger: For, I doubt, the new Project of *Tanning* without it, is at an End. Our *Beef*, I am afraid, still continues scandalous in foreign Markets, for the old Reasons. But, our *Tallow*, for any Thing I know, may be good. However, to bestow the whole Kingdom on *Beef* and *Mutton*, and thereby drive out half the People who should eat their Share, and force the rest to send sometimes as far as *Egypt*, for Bread to eat with it; is a most peculiar and distinguished Piece of publick Oeconomy; of which I have no Comprehension.

I KNOW very well, that our Ancestors, the *Scythians*, and their Posterity our Kinsmen the *Tartars*, lived upon the Blood and Milk, and raw Flesh of their Cattle; without one Grain of *Corn*; but I confess my self so degenerate, that I am not easy without *Bread* to my Victuals.

WHAT amazed me for a Week or two, was to see, in this prodigious Plenty of *Cattle*, and Dearth of *human Creatures*, and Want of *Bread*, as well as *Money to buy it*; that all Kind of *Flesh-meat* should be monstrously *dear*, beyond what was ever known in this Kingdom. I thought it a Defect in the Laws; that there was not some Regulation in the Price of *Flesh*, as well as *Bread*: But I imagine my self to have guessed out the Reason. In short, I am apt to think, that the whole Kingdom is over-stocked with *Cattle*, both *Black and White:* And, as it is observed that the poor *Irish* have a Vanity, to be rather Owners of two lean Cows, than one Fat, although with double the Charge of Grazing, and but half the Quantity of Milk; so I conceive it much more difficult, at present, to find a fat *Bullock*, or *Weather*, than it would be, if half of both were fairly knocked on the Head: For, I am assured, that the District in the several Markets, called *Carrion-Row*, is as reasonable as the Poor can desire; only the Circumstance of *Money to purchase it*; and of *Trade*, or *Labour*, to *purchase that Money*; are, indeed, wholly wanting.

Now, Sir, to return more particularly to you, and your Memorial.

A hundred thousand Barrels of *Wheat*, you say, should be imported hither; and Ten thousand Pounds, *Præmium*, to the Importers. Have you looked into the Purse of the Nation? I am no Commissioner of the *Treasury*; but am well assured, that the whole running *Cash* would not supply you with a Sum to purchase so much *Corn*; which, only at Twenty Shillings a Barrel, will be a Hundred thousand Pounds; and Ten thousand more for the *Præmiums*. But you will traffick for your *Corn* with other Goods: And where are those Goods? If you had them, they are all engaged to pay the Rents of *Absentees*, and other Occasions in *London*; besides a huge Ballance of Trade this Year against us. Will Foreigners take our Bankers Paper? I suppose, they will value it at little more than so much a Quire. Where are these *rich Farmers* and *Ingrossers of Corn*, in so bad a Year, and so little Sowing?

You are in Pain of two Shillings *Præmium*, and forget the Twenty Shillings for the Price; find me out the latter, and I will engage for the former.

Your Scheme for a *Tax* for raising such a Sum, is all visionary; and owing to a great want of Knowledge in the *miserable State* of this Nation. *Tea, Coffee, Sugar, Spices, Wine*, and *foreign Cloaths*, are the Particulars you mention, upon which this Tax should be raised. I will allow the two first, because they are unwholsome; and the last, because I should be glad if they were all burned; but I beg you will leave us our Wine, to make us a while forget our Misery; or give your Tenants leave to plough for *Barley*. But I will tell you a *Secret*, which I learned many Years ago from the Commissioners of the *Customs* in *London:* They said, when any *Commodity* appeared to be taxed above a *moderate Rate*, the Consequence was to lessen that Branch of the Revenue by one Half; and one of those Gentlemen pleasantly told me, that the Mistake of Parliaments, on such Occasions, was owing to an Error of computing Two and Two to make Four; whereas, in the Business of laying *heavy Impositions*, Two and Two never made more than One; which happens by lessening the Import, and the strong Temptation of running such Goods as paid high Duties. At least in this Kingdom, although the Women are as vain and extravagant as their Lovers, or their Husbands can deserve; and the Men are fond enough of Wine; yet the Number of both, who can afford such Expences, is so small, that the major Part must refuse gratifying themselves; and the Duties will rather be lessened than increased. But, allowing no Force in this Argument; yet so prœternatural a Sum, as one Hundred and ten Thousand Pounds, raised all on a sudden, (for there is no dallying with Hunger) is just in Proportion with raising a Million and a half in *England*; which, as Things now stand, would probably bring that opulent Kingdom under some Difficulties.

You are concerned, how strange and surprising it would be in foreign Parts, to hear that the Poor were starving in a RICH Country, &c. Are you in earnest? Is *Ireland* the *rich Country* you mean? Or are you insulting our *Poverty*? Were you ever out of *Ireland*? Or were you ever in it till of late? You may probably have a good Employment, and are saving all you can, to purchase a good Estate in *England*. But by talking so familiarly of one Hundred and ten Thousand Pounds, by a Tax upon a few *Commodities*; it is plain, you are either naturally or affectedly ignorant of our present Condition; or else you would know and allow, that such a Sum is not to be raised here, without a *general Excise*; since, in Proportion to our Wealth, we pay already in *Taxes* more than *England* ever did, in the Heighth of the War. And when you have brought over your Corn, who will be the Buyers? Most certainly, not the

Poor, who will not be *able* to purchase the Twentieth Part of it.

SIR, upon the whole, your Paper is a very crude Piece, liable to more Objections than there are Lines; but, I think, your Meaning is good, and so far you are pardonable.

IF you will propose a general Contribution, in supporting the Poor in *Potatoes* and *Butter-milk*, till the new Corn comes in, perhaps you may succeed better; because the Thing, at least, is possible: And, I think, if our Brethren in *England* would contribute, upon this Emergency, out of the Million they gain from us every Year, they would do a Piece of *Justice* as well as *Charity*. In the mean Time, go and preach to your own Tenants, to fall to the Plough as fast as they can; and prevail with your neighbouring 'Squires to do the same with theirs; or else die with the Guilt of having driven away half the Inhabitants, and starving the rest. For as to your Scheme of raising *one Hundred and ten Thousand Pounds*, it is as vain as that of *Rabelais*; which was to squeeze out Wind from the Posteriors of a dead Ass.

BUT, why all this Concern for the Poor? We want them not, as the Country is now managed; they may follow Thousands of their Leaders, and seek their Bread abroad. Where the Plough has no Work, one Family can do the Business of Fifty, and you may send away the other Forty-nine. An admirable Piece of Husbandry, never known or practised by the wisest Nations; who erroneously thought People to be the Riches of a Country.

IF so wretched a State of Things would allow it, methinks I could have a malicious Pleasure, after all the Warning I have in vain given the Publick, at my own Peril, for several Years past; to see the Consequences and Events answering in every Particular. I pretend to no Sagacity: What I writ was little more than what I had discoursed to several Persons, who were generally of my Opinion: And it was obvious to every common Understanding, that such Effects must needs follow from such Causes. A fair Issue of Things, begun upon Party Rage, while some sacrificed the Publick to Fury, and others to Ambition! While a Spirit of Faction and Oppression reigned in every Part of the Country; where Gentlemen, instead of consulting the Ease of their Tenants, or cultivating their Lands, were worrying one another, upon Points of *Whig* and *Tory*, of *High Church* and *Low Church*; which no more concerned them, than the long and famous Controversy of *Strops for Razors:* While *Agriculture* was wholly discouraged, and consequently half the Farmers, and Labourers, and poorer Tradesmen, forced to Beggary or Banishment. *Wisdom crieth in the Streets; because I have called and ye refused; I have stretched out my Hand, and no Man regarded. But ye have set at nought all my Counsel, and would none of my Reproof. I also will laugh at your Calamity, and mock when your Fear cometh.*

I HAVE now done with your Memorial, and freely excuse your Mistakes, since you appear to write as a Stranger, and as of a Country which is left at Liberty to enjoy the Benefits of Nature; and to make the best of those Advantages which God hath given it in Soil, Climate, and Situation.

BUT having lately sent out a Paper, entitled, *A Short View of the State of* Ireland; and hearing of an Objection, that some People think I have treated the Memory of the late Lord Chief Justice *Whitshed*, with an Appearance of Severity; since I may not probably have another Opportunity of explaining my self in that Particular, I chuse to do it here. Laying it therefore down for a Postulatum; which, I suppose, will be universally granted; That no *little Creature*, of so *mean* a Birth and Genius, had ever the *Honour* to be a *greater Enemy* to his Country, and to all Kinds of Virtue, than HE, I answer thus: whether there be two different Goddesses called *Fame*, as some Authors contend, or only one Goddess, sounding two different Trumpets; it is certain, that People distinguished for their *Villainy*, have as good a Title for a Blast from the *proper Trumpet*, as those who are most renowned for their *Virtues*, have from the other; and have equal Reason to complain, if it be refused them. And accordingly, the Names of the most *celebrated Profligates*, have been faithfully transmitted down to Posterity. And although the Person here understood, acted his Part in an obscure Corner of the World; yet his

Talents might have shone with Lustre enough in the noblest Scene.

As to my naming a Person Dead, the plain honest Reason is the best. He was armed with Power, Guilt, and Will to do Mischief, even where he was not provoked; as appeared by his prosecuting two *Printers*, one to Death, and both to Ruin, who had neither offended God, nor the King, nor Him, nor the Publick.

WHAT an Encouragement to Vice is this? If an ill Man be alive, and in Power, we dare not attack him; and if he be weary of the World, or of his own Villainies, he has nothing to do but die, and then his Reputation is safe. For, these excellent Casuists know just *Latin* enough, to have heard a most foolish Precept, that *de mortuis nil nisi bonum*; so that if *Socrates*, and *Anytus* his Accuser, had happened to die together, the Charity of Survivers must either have obliged them to hold their Peace, or to fix the same Character on both. The only Crime of charging the Dead, is when the least Doubt remains, whether the Accusation be true; but when Men are openly abandoned, and lost to all Shame, they have no Reason to think it hard, if their Memory be reproached. Whoever reports, or otherwise publisheth any Thing, which it is possible may be false, that Man is a Slanderer, *Hic niger est, hunc tu Romane caveto*. Even the least Misrepresentation, or Aggravation of Facts, deserves the same Censure in some Degree: But in this Case I am quite deceived, if my Error hath not been on the Side of Extenuation.

I HAVE now present before me the Idea of some Persons, (I know not in what Part of the World) who spend every Moment of their Lives, and every Turn of their Thoughts while they are awake, (and probably of their Dreams while they sleep) in the most detestable Actions and Designs; who delight in *Mischief*, *Scandal*, and *Obloquy*, with the *Hatred* and *Contempt* of all Mankind against them; but chiefly of those among their own Party, and their own Family; such, whose *odious Qualities* rival each other for Perfection: *Avarice*, *Brutality*, *Faction*, *Pride*, *Malice*, *Treachery*, *Noise*, *Impudence*, *Dulness*, *Ignorance*,

Vanity, and *Revenge*, contending every Moment for Superiority in their Breasts. Such Creatures are not to be reformed; neither is it Prudence, or Safety to attempt a Reformation. Yet, although their Memories will *rot*, there may be some Benefit for their Survivers, to smell it while it is *rotting*.

I am, SIR,

Your humble Servant,

A. B.

Dublin, March
    25th, 1728.

Intelligencer Papers

THE

Intelligencer;

NUMB. I.

For
May 11th,
continued

Saturday
1728. to be
Weekly.

DUBLIN:
Printed by S. HARDING, next Door
to the *Crown* in *Copper-Alley,* 1728.

THE
INTELLIGENCER

Number I

IT may be said, without offence to other *Cities*, of much greater consequence in the World, that our Town of *Dublin* doth not want it's due proportion of *Folly*, and *Vice*, both Native and Imported; And as to those Imported, we have the advantage to receive them last, and consequently after our happy manner to improve, and refine upon them.

But, because there are many Effects of *Folly* and *Vice* among us, whereof some are *general*, others confined to smaller Numbers, and others again, perhaps to a few *individuals*; there is a Society lately established, who at great expence, have Erected an *Office of Intelligence*, from which they are to receive Weekly Information of all *Important Events* and *Singularities*, which this famous *Metropolis* can furnish. Strict Injunctions are given to have the truest Information: In order to which, certain qualified Persons are employed to attend upon Duty in their several Posts; some at the *Play-house*, others in *Churches*, some at *Balls*, *Assemblies*, *Coffee-houses* and *meetings* for *Quadrille*; some at the several *Courts of Justice*, both *Spiritual* and *Temporal*, some at the *College*, some upon my *Lord Mayor* and *Aldermen* in their publick Affairs; lastly, some to converse with *favourite Chambermaids* and to frequent those *Ale-houses*, and *Brandy-Shops*, where the *Footmen* of great Families meet in a Morning: only the Barracks and *Parliament-house* are excepted, because we have yet found no *enfans perdus* bold enough to venture their Persons at either. Out of these and some other *Store-houses*, we hope to gather Materials enough to *Inform*, or *Divert*, or *Correct*, or *Vex* the Town.

But as *Facts*, *Passages* and *Adventures* of all kinds, are like to have the greatest share in our *Paper*, whereof we cannot always Answer for the Truth; due Care shall be taken to have them applyed to feigned Names, whereby all just Offence will be removed; for if none be guilty, none will have Cause to Blush or be angry; if otherwise, then the guilty Person is safe for the future upon his *present* Amendment, and safe for the *present*, from all but his *own Conscience*.

THERE is another Resolution taken among us, which I fear will give a greater and more general discontent, and is of so singular a Nature, that I have hardly confidence enough to mention it, although it be absolutely Necessary by way of Apology, for *so bold and unpopular an Attempt*. But so it is, that we have taken a desperate Counsel to produce into the World every distinguished Action, either of *Justice*, *Prudence*, *Generosity*, *Charity*, *Friendship*, or *publick Spirit*, which comes well attested to us. And although we shall neither here be so daring as to Assign Names, yet we shall hardly forbear to give some hints, that perhaps to the great displeasure of such deserving Persons may endanger a Discovery. For we think that even *Virtue it self*, should submit to such a *Mortification*, as by its *visibility* and *example*, will render it more useful to the World. But however, the *Readers* of these *Papers*, need not be in pain of being overcharged, with so dull and ungrateful a Subject. And yet who knows, but such an occasion may be offered to us, once in a Year or two, after we shall have settled a Correspondence round the *Kingdom*.

BUT after all our boasts of *Materials*, sent us by our several *Emissaries*, we may probably soon fall short, if the Town will not be pleased to lend us further Assistance towards entertaining it self. The *World* best knows it's own *Faults* and *Virtues*, and whatever is sent shall be faithfully returned back, only a little Embellished according to the Custom of AUTHORS. We do therefore *Demand* and *Expect* continual *Advertisements* in great Numbers, to be sent to the *PRINTER* of this *Paper*, who hath employed a *Judicious Secretary* to collect such as may be most useful for the *Publick*.

AND although we do not intend to expose our own Persons by mentioning Names, yet we are so far from requiring the same Caution in our *Correspondents*, that on the contrary, we expressly *Charge* and *Command* them, in all the Facts they send us, to set down the Names, Titles, and Places of Abode, at length; together with a very particular Description of the *Persons*, *Dresses*, and *Dispositions* of the several *Lords*, *Ladies*, *Squires*, *Madams*, *Lawyers*, *Gamesters*, *Toupees*, *Sots*, *Wits*, *Rakes* and *Informers*, whom they shall have occasion to mention; otherwise it will not be possible for us to adjust our Style to the different Qualities, and Capacities of the Persons concerned, and Treat them with the *Respect* or *Familiarity*, that may be due to their *Stations* and *Characters*, which we are Determined to observe with the utmost strictness, that none may have cause to Complain.

FINIS

THE
INTELLIGENCER

NUMBER III

——— Ipse per omnes
Ibit personas, & turbam reddet in unam.

Written in *Ireland* in the Year 1728

THE *Players* having now almost done with the Comedy called the *Beggar's Opera*, for the Season; it may be no unpleasant Speculation, to reflect a little upon this *Dramatick Piece*, so singular in the Subject and Manner, so much an Original, and which hath frequently given so very agreeable an Entertainment.

ALTHOUGH an evil *Taste* be very apt to prevail, both here and in *London*; yet there is a Point which whoever can rightly touch, will never fail of pleasing a very great Majority; so great, that the Dislikers, out of Dulness or Affectation, will be silent, and forced to fall in with the Herd: The Point I mean, is what we call *Humour*; which, in its Perfection, is allowed to be much preferable to *Wit*; if it be not rather the most useful, and agreeable Species of it.

I AGREE with Sir *William Temple*, that the Word is peculiar to our *English Tongue*; but I differ from him in the Opinion, that the Thing it self is peculiar to the *English Nation*, because the contrary may be found in many *Spanish*, *Italian*, and *French* Productions: And particularly, whoever hath a *Taste* for *true Humour*, will find an Hundred Instances of it, in those Volumes printed in *France*, under the name of *Le Theatre Italien:* To say nothing of *Rabelais*, *Cervantes*, and many others.

NOW I take the *Comedy*, or *Farce*, (or whatever Name the *Criticks* will allow it) called the *Beggar's Opera*, to excel in this

32

Article of *Humour*; and upon that Merit to have met with such prodigious Success, both here and in *England*.

As to *Poetry*, *Eloquence*, and *Musick*, which are said to have most Power over the Minds of Men; it is certain, that very few have a *Taste* or *Judgment* of the Excellencies of the two former; and if a Man succeed in either, it is upon the Authority of those *few Judges*, that lend their *Taste* to the Bulk of Readers, who have none of their own. I am told, there are as few good Judges in *Musick*; and that among those who crowd the *Opera's*, Nine in Ten go thither merely out of *Curiosity*, *Fashion*, or *Affectation*.

But a *Taste* for *Humour*, is in some Manner fixed to the very Nature of Man, and generally obvious to the Vulgar, except upon Subjects too refined, and superior to their Understanding.

And, as this *Taste* of *Humour* is purely natural, so is *Humour* it self; neither is it a *Talent* confined to Men of *Wit*, or *Learning*; for we observe it sometimes among common Servants, and the meanest of the People, while the very Owners are often ignorant of the Gift they possess.

I know very well, that this happy *Talent* is contemptibly treated by *Criticks*, under the Name of *low Humour*, or *low Comedy*; but I know likewise, that the *Spaniards* and *Italians*, who are allowed to have the most Wit of any *Nation* in *Europe*, do most excel in it, and do most esteem it.

By what Disposition of the Mind, what Influence of the Stars, or what Situation of the *Climate*, this Endowment is bestowed upon Mankind, may be a Question fit for *Philosophers* to discuss. It is certainly the best Ingredient towards that Kind of Satyr, which is most useful, and gives the least Offence; which, instead of lashing, laughs Men out of their Follies, and Vices; and is the Character that gives *Horace* the Preference to *Juvenal*.

And, although some Things are too serious, solemn, or sacred to be turned into Ridicule, yet the Abuses of them are certainly not; since it is allowed, that Corruptions in *Religion*, *Politicks*, and *Law*, may be proper *Topicks* for this Kind of *Satyr*.

F

THERE are two Ends that Men propose in writing Satyr; one of them less noble than the other, as regarding nothing further than the private Satisfaction, and Pleasure of the Writer; but without any View towards *personal Malice:* The other is a *publick Spirit*, prompting Men of *Genius* and Virtue, to mend the World as far as they are able. And as both these Ends are innocent, so the latter is highly commendable. With regard to the former, I demand, whether I have not as good a Title to laugh, as Men have to be ridiculous; and to expose Vice, as another hath to be vicious. If I ridicule the Follies and Corruptions of a *Court*, a *Ministry*, or a *Senate*, are they not amply paid by *Pensions*, *Titles*, and *Power*; while I expect, and desire no other Reward, than that of laughing with a few Friends in a Corner? Yet, if those who take Offence, think me in the Wrong, I am ready to change the Scene with them, whenever they please.

BUT, if my Design be to make Mankind better; then I think it is my Duty; at least, I am sure it is the Interest of those very *Courts* and *Ministers*, whose Follies or Vices I ridicule, to reward me for my good Intentions: For if it be reckoned a high Point of Wisdom to get the Laughers on our Side; it is much more easy, as well as wise, to get those on our Side, who can make Millions laugh when they please.

MY Reason for mentioning *Courts*, and *Ministers*, (*whom I never think on, but with the most profound Veneration*) is, because an Opinion obtains, that in the *Beggar's Opera*, there appears to be some Reflection upon *Courtiers* and *Statesmen*, whereof I am by no Means a Judge.

IT is true, indeed, that Mr. GAY, the Author of this Piece, hath been somewhat singular in the Course of his Fortunes; for it hath happened, that after Fourteen Years attending the *Court*, with a large Stock of real Merit, a modest and agreeable Conversation, a *Hundred Promises*, and *five Hundred Friends*, he hath failed of Preferment; and upon a very weighty Reason. He lay under the Suspicion of having written a Libel, or Lampoon against a great * Minister. It is true, that great Minister was demonstratively convinced, and publickly owned

* Sir Robert Walpole.

his Conviction, that Mr. GAY was not the Author; but having lain under the Suspicion, it seemed very just, that he should suffer the punishment; because in this most reformed Age, the Virtues of a Prime Minister are no more to be suspected, than the Chastity of *Cæsar*'s Wife.

IT must be allowed, That the *Beggar's Opera* is not the first of Mr. GAY's Works, wherein he hath been faulty, with Regard to *Courtiers* and *Statesmen*. For to omit his other Pieces; even in his Fables, published within two Years past, and dedicated to the Duke of CUMBERLAND, for which he was *promised* a Reward, he hath been thought somewhat too bold upon the *Courtiers*. And although it be highly probable, he meant only the *Courtiers* of former Times, yet he acted unwarily, by not considering that the Malignity of some People might misinterpret what he said, to the Disadvantage of present *Persons* and Affairs.

BUT I have now done with Mr. GAY as a Politician; and shall consider him henceforward only as Author of the *Beggar's Opera*, wherein he hath by a Turn of *Humour*, entirely new, placed Vices of all Kinds in the strongest and most odious Light; and thereby, done eminent Service, both to *Religion* and *Morality*. This appears from the unparallelled Success he hath met with. All *Ranks*, *Parties*, and *Denominations* of Men, either crowding to see his *Opera*, or reading it with Delight in their Closets; even *Ministers* of State, whom he is thought to have most offended (next to those whom the Actors represent) appearing frequently at the *Theatre*, from a Consciousness of their own Innocence, and to convince the World how unjust a Parallel, *Malice*, *Envy*, and *Disaffection to the Government have made*.

I AM assured that several worthy *Clergy-Men* in this *City*, went privately to see the *Beggar's Opera* represented; and that the *fleering Coxcombs* in the *Pit*, amused themselves with making Discoveries, and spreading the Names of those Gentlemen round the Audience.

I SHALL not pretend to vindicate a *Clergy-Man*, who would appear openly in his Habit at a *Theatre*, with such a vicious Crew, as might probably stand round him, at such *Comedies*, and profane *Tragedies* as are often represented. Besides, I know very well, that Persons of their Function are bound to avoid the Appearance of Evil, or of giving Cause of Offence. But when the *Lords Chancellors*, who are Keepers of the King's Conscience; when the *Judges* of the Land, whose Title is *Reverend*; when *Ladies*, who are bound by the Rules of their Sex to the strictest Decency, appear in the *Theatre* without Censure; I cannot understand, why a young *Clergy-Man*, who comes concealed, out of Curiosity to see an innocent and moral Play, should be so highly condemned: Nor do I much approve the Rigour of a great Prelate, who said, *he hoped none of his Clergy were there*. I am glad to hear there are no weightier Objections against that Reverend Body planted in this City, and I wish there never may. But I should be very sorry, that any of them should be so weak, as to imitate a **Court-Chaplain* in ENGLAND, who preached against the *Beggar's Opera*; which will probably do more Good, than a thousand Sermons of so stupid, so injudicious, and so prostitute a Divine.

IN this happy Performance of Mr. GAY's, all the Characters are just, and none of them carried beyond Nature, or hardly beyond Practice. It discovers the whole System of that Common-Wealth, or that *Imperium in Imperio* of Iniquity, established among us, by which neither our Lives nor our Properties are secure, either in the High-ways, or in publick Assemblies, or even in our own Houses. It shews the miserable Lives and the constant Fate of those abandoned Wretches: For how little they sell their Lives and Souls; betrayed by their *Whores*, their *Comrades*, and the *Receivers* and *Purchasers* of those Thefts and Robberies. This *Comedy* contains likewise a *Satyr*, which, without enquiring whether it affects the present Age, may possibly be useful in Times to come. I mean, where the Author takes the Occasion of comparing those *common Robbers of the Publick*, and their several Stratagems of betraying, undermining and hanging each other, to the several Arts of *Politicians* in Times of Corruption.

THIS *Comedy* likewise exposeth with great Justice, that unnatural Taste for *Italian* Musick among us, which is wholly

* Dr. Herring, *Chaplain to the Society at Lincoln's Inn.*

unsuitable to our Northern *Climate*, and the *Genius* of the *People*, whereby we are over-run with *Italian Effeminacy*, and *Italian* Nonsense. An old Gentleman said to me, that many Years ago, when the Practice of an unnatural Vice grew frequent in *London*, and many were prosecuted for it, he was sure it would be a Fore-runner of *Italian* Opera's and Singers; and then we should want nothing but Stabbing or Poisoning, to make us perfect *Italians*.

Upon the whole, I deliver my Judgment, That nothing but servile Attachment to a Party, Affectation of Singularity, lamentable Dullness, mistaken Zeal, or studied Hypocrisy, can have the least reasonable Objection against this excellent moral Performance of the *Celebrated Mr.* Gay.

THE
INTELLIGENCER

NUMBERS V AND VII

Describ'd it's thus: Defin'd would you it have?
Then the World's honest Man's an arrant Knave.
                                        Ben Jonson

THERE is no *Talent* so useful towards rising in the World, or which puts Men more out of the Reach of Fortune, than that Quality generally possessed by the dullest Sort of People, in common Speech called *Discretion*; a Species of lower Prudence, by the Assistance of which, People of the meanest Intellectuals, without any other Qualification, pass through the World in great Tranquility, and with universal good Treatment, neither giving nor taking Offence. *Courts* are seldom unprovided of Persons under this Character; on whom, if they happen to be of great Quality, most Employments, even the greatest, naturally fall, when Competitors will not agree; and in such Promotions, no body rejoices or grieves. The Truth of this I could prove by several Instances, within my own Memory, (for I say nothing of present Times).

AND, indeed, as Regularity and Forms are of great Use in carrying on the Business of the World, so it is very convenient, that Persons endued with this Kind of Discretion, should have the Share which is proper to their Talents, in the Conduct of Affairs; but, by no Means, meddle in Matters which require *Genius, Learning, strong Comprehension, Quickness of Conception, Magnanimity, Generosity, Sagacity*, or any other superior Gift of human Minds. Because, this Sort of *Discretion*, is usually attended with a strong Desire of Money, and few Scruples about the Way of obtaining it; with servile Flattery and Submission; with a Want of all publick Spirit or Principle; with a perpetual wrong Judgment, when the Owners come into

Power and high Place, how to dispose of Favour and Prefer-ment; having no Measure for Merit and Virtue in others, but those very Steps by which themselves ascended; nor the least Intention of doing Good, or Hurt to the Publick; farther, than either one or t'other, is likely to be subservient to their own Security, or Interest. Thus, being void of all Friendship and Enmity, they never complain or find Fault with the Times; and indeed never have Reason.

MEN of eminent Parts and Abilities, as well as Virtues, do sometimes rise in *Courts*, sometimes in the *Law*, and sometimes even in the *Church*. Such were the Lord *Bacon*, the Earl of *Strafford*, Archbishop *Laud* in the Reign of King *Charles* I. and others in our own Times, whom I shall not name. But these, and many more, under different Princes, and in different Kingdoms, were *disgraced*, or *banished*, or *suffered Death*, merely in Envy to their Virtues and superior *Genius*, which embol-dened them in great Exigencies and Distresses of State, (want-ing a reasonable Infusion of this Aldermanly Discretion) to attempt the Service of their Prince and Country, out of the common Forms.

THIS evil Fortune, which generally attends extraordinary Men in the Management of great Affairs, hath been imputed to divers Causes, that need not be here set down, when so obvious a One occurs; if what a * certain Writer observes, be true; that *when a great Genius appears in the World, the Dunces are all in Confederacy against him.* And, if this be his Fate, when he employs his *Talents* wholly in his Closet, without interfering with any Man's Ambition, or Avarice; what must he expect when he ventures out to seek for Preferment in a Court, but universal Opposition, when he is mounting the Ladder, and every Hand ready to turn him off, when he is at the Top? And in this Point, Fortune generally acts directly contrary to Nature; for in Nature we find, that Bodies full of Life and Spirit mount easily, and are hard to fall; whereas heavy Bodies are hard to rise, and come down with greater Velocity, in Propor-tion to their Weight: But we find Fortune every Day acting just the Reverse of this.

* Vide *the Author's Thoughts on various Subjects.*

THIS Talent of *Discretion*, as I have described it in its several Adjuncts and Circumstances, is no where so serviceable as to the *Clergy*; to whose Preferment nothing is so fatal as the Character of Wit, Politeness in Reading, or Manners, or that Kind of Behaviour, which we contract by having too much conversed with Persons of high Station and Eminency; these Qualifications being reckoned by the *Vulgar* of *all Ranks*, to be Marks of *Levity*, which is the last Crime the World will pardon in a *Clergy-Man:* To this I may add a free Manner of speaking in mixt Company, and too frequent an Appearance in Places of much Resort, which are equally noxious to Spiritual Promotion.

I HAVE known, indeed, a few Exceptions to some Parts of these Observations. I have seen some of the dullest Men alive aiming at Wit; and others, with as little Pretensions, affecting Politeness in Manners and Discourse; but never being able to persuade the World of their Guilt, they grew into considerable Stations, upon the firm Assurance which all People had of their *Discretion*; because they were a Size too low, to deceive the World to their own Disadvantage. But this, I confess, is a Tryal too dangerous often to engage in.

THERE is a known Story of a *Clergyman*, who was recommended for a Preferment by some great Man at Court, to an † Archbishop. His Grace said, he had heard that the *Clergyman* used to play at *Whisk* and *Swobbers:* That as to playing now and then a sober Game at *Whisk* for Pastime, it might be pardoned; but he could not digest those wicked *Swobbers*; and it was with some Pains that my Lord *Summers* could undeceive him. I ask, by what Talents we may suppose that great Prelate ascended so high; or what Sort of Qualifications he would expect in those whom he took into his Patronage, or would probably recommend to Court, for the Government of *distant Churches*.

TWO *Clergymen*, in my Memory, stood Candidates for a small *Free-School* in *Yorkshire*; where a Gentleman of Quality and Interest in the Country, who happened to have a better Understanding than his Neighbours, procured the Place for

† *Dr.* Tenison, *late Archbishop of* Canterbury.

him who was the better Scholar, and more gentlemanly Person of the two; very much to the Regret of all the Parish. The other being disappointed, came up to *London*, where he became the greatest Pattern of this lower *Discretion* that I have known, and possessed with as heavy Intellectuals; which, together with the Coldness of his Temper, and Gravity of his Deportment, carried him safe through many Difficulties: And he lived and died in a great Station, while his Competitor is too obscure for Fame to tell us what became of him.

THIS Species of *Discretion*, which I so much celebrate, and do most heartily recommend, hath one Advantage not yet mentioned; that it will carry a Man safe through all the Malice and Variety of Parties, so far, that whatever Faction happens to be uppermost, his Claim is usually allowed for a Share of what is going. And the Thing seems to be highly reasonable: For in all great Changes, the prevailing Side is usually so tempestuous, that it wants the Ballast of those, whom the World calls *moderate Men*, and I call *Men of Discretion*; whom People in Power may with little Ceremony load as heavy as they please, drive them through the hardest and deepest Roads without Danger of foundering, or breaking their Backs; and will be sure to find them neither resty nor vicious.

I WILL here give the Reader a short History of two *Clergymen* in *England*, the Characters of each, and the Progress of their Fortunes in the World: By which the Force of this Discretion, and the bad Consequences from the Want of that Virtue, will strongly appear.

CORUSODES, an *Oxford* Student, and a Farmer's Son, was never absent from Prayers or Lecture; nor once out of his *College* after *Tom* had tolled. He spent, every Day, ten Hours in his Closet, in reading his Courses, dozing, clipping Papers, or darning his Stockings; which last he performed to Admiration. He could be soberly drunk at the Expence of others, with *College*-Ale, and at those seasons was always most devout. He wore the same Gown five Years, without dragling or tearing. He never once looked into a Play-book, or a Poem. He read *Virgil* and *Ramus* in the same Cadence, but with a very different Taste. He never understood a Jest, or had the least Conception of Wit.

For one Saying he stands in Renown to this Day. Being with some other Students over a Pot of Ale, one of the Company said so many pleasant Things, that the rest were much diverted, only *Corusodes* was silent and unmoved. When they parted, he called this merry Companion aside, and said, *Sir, I perceived by your often speaking, and our Friends laughing, that you spoke many Jests, and you could not but observe my Silence. But, Sir, this is my Humour, I never make a Jest myself, nor ever laugh at another Man's.*

CORUSODES thus endowed, and got into Holy Orders; having by the most extreme Parsimony saved Thirty-four Pounds, out of a very beggarly Fellowship; went up to *London*, where his Sister was Waiting-Woman to a Lady, and so good a Solicitor, that by her Means he was admitted to read Prayers in the Family twice a Day, at Ten Shillings a Month. He had now acquired a low, obsequious, awkward Bow, and a Talent of gross Flattery, both in and out of Season; he would shake the Butler by the Hand; he taught the Page his *Catechism*; and was sometimes admitted to dine at the Steward's Table. In short, he got the good Word of the whole Family; and was recommended, by my Lady, for Chaplain to some other noble Houses, by which his Revenue (beside Vales) amounted to about Thirty Pounds a Year. His Sister procured him a Scarf from my Lord, (who had a small Design of Gallantry upon her;) and by his Lordship's Sollicitation, he got a Lectureship in Town of Sixty Pounds a Year; where he preached constantly in Person, in a grave Manner, with an audible Voice, a Style Ecclesiastick, and the Matter (such as it was) well suited to the Intellectuals of his Hearers. Some Time after, a Country Living fell in my Lord's Disposal; and his Lordship, who had now some Encouragement given him of Success in his Amour, bestowed the Living on *Corusodes*, who still kept his Lectureship and Residence in Town, where he was a constant Attendant at all Meetings relating to Charity, without ever contributing further than his frequent pious Exhortations. If any Women of better Fashion in the Parish happened to be absent from Church, they were sure of a Visit from him in a Day or two, to chide and to dine with them.

HE had a select Number of Poor, constantly attending at the Street Door of his Lodgings, for whom he was a common Solicitor to his former Patroness, dropping in his own Half-Crown among the Collections, and taking it out when he disposed of the Money. At a Person of Quality's House, he would never sit down till he was thrice bid, and then upon the Corner of the most distant Chair. His whole Demeanor was formal and starched, which adhered so close, that he could never shake it off in his highest Promotion.

His Lord was now in great Employment at Court, and attended by him with the most abject Assiduity; and his Sister being gone off with Child to a private Lodging, my Lord continued his Graces to *Corusodes*; got him to be a Chaplain in Ordinary, and in due Time a Parish in Town, and a *Dignity in the Church*.

HE paid his *Curates* punctually, at the lowest Salary, and partly out of the Communion-Money; but gave them good Advice in Abundance. He married a Citizen's Widow, who taught him to put out small Sums at *Ten per Cent.* and brought him acquainted with Jobbers in '*Change-Alley*. By her Dexterity, he sold the Clerkship of his Parish, when it became vacant.

HE kept a miserable House, but the Blame was laid wholly upon *Madam*; for the good Doctor was always at his *Books*, or visiting the Sick, or doing other Offices of Charity and Piety in his Parish.

HE treated all his Inferiors of the Clergy with a most sanctified Pride; was rigorously and universally censorious upon all his Brethren of the Gown, on their first Appearance in the World, or while they continued meanly preferred; but gave large Allowance to the Laity of high Rank, or great Riches; using neither Eyes nor Ears for their Faults: He was never sensible of the least Corruption in *Courts*, *Parliaments*, or *Ministries*; but made the most favourable Constructions of all publick Proceedings: And Power, in whatever Hands, or whatever Party, was always secure of his most charitable Opinion. He had many wholsome Maxims ready to excuse all Miscarriages of

State; *Men are but Men*; *Erunt vitia donec homines*; and *Quod supra nos, nihil ad nos:* With several others of equal Weight.

IT would lengthen my Paper beyond Measure, to trace out the whole System of his Conduct; his dreadful Apprehensions of *Popery*; his great Moderation towards Dissenters of all Denominations; with hearty Wishes, that by yielding somewhat on both Sides, there might be a general Union among Protestants; his short, inoffensive Sermons in his Turns at Court, and the Matter exactly suited to the present Juncture of prevailing Opinions; the Arts he used to obtain a Mitre in which he succeeded, by writing against Episcopacy; and the Proofs he gave of his Loyalty, by palliating or defending the Murder of a martyred Prince.

ENDOWED with all these Accomplishments, we leave him in the full Career of Success, mounting fast towards the Top of the Ladder Ecclesiastical, which he hath a fair Probability to reach, without the Merit of one single Virtue; moderately stocked with the least valuable Parts of Erudition: utterly devoid of all *Taste*, *Judgment*, or *Genius*; and in his Grandeur naturally chusing to hawl up others after him, whose Accomplishments most resemble his own; except his beloved Sons, Nephews, or other Kindred be not in Competition; or lastly, except his Inclinations be diverted by those who have Power to mortify or further advance him.

EUGENIO set out from the same University, and about the same Time with *Corusodes:* He had the Reputation of an arch Lad at School, and was unfortunately possessed with a *Talent* for *Poetry*, on which Account he received many chiding Letters from his Father, and grave Advice from his Tutor. He did not neglect his College-Learning; but his chief Study was the Authors of Antiquity, with a perfect knowledge in the *Greek* and *Roman Tongues*. He could never procure himself to be chosen Fellow; for it was objected against him, that he had written Verses, and particularly some wherein he glanced at a certain Reverend Doctor, famous for Dullness; That he had been seen bowing to Ladies as he met them in the Street; and it was proved, that once he had been found dancing in a private Family, with half a Dozen of both Sexes.

HE was the younger Son to a Gentleman of a good Birth, but small Estate; and his Father dying, he was driven to *London*, to seek his Fortune: He got into Orders, and became Reader in a Parish-Church, at twenty Pounds a Year; was carried by an *Oxford* Friend to *Will's Coffee-House*, frequented in those Days by the Men of Wit; where in some Time he had the bad Luck to be distinguished. His scanty Salary compelled him to run deep in Debt for a new Gown and Cassock; and now and then forced him to write some Paper of Wit or Humour, or preach a Sermon for ten Shillings, to supply his Necessities. He was a thousand Times recommended by his poetical Friends to great Persons, as a young Man of excellent Parts, who deserved Encouragement; and received a thousand Promises: But his Modesty, and a generous Spirit, which disdained the Slavery of continual Application and Attendance, always disappointed him; making room for vigilant Dunces, who were sure to be never out of Sight.

HE had an excellent Faculty in preaching, if he were not sometimes a little too refined, and apt to trust too much to his own Way of thinking and reasoning.

WHEN upon the Vacancy of Preferment he was hardly drawn to attend upon some promising Lord; he received the usual Answer, *that he came too late, for it had been given to another the very Day before*. And he had only the Comfort left, that every Body said, it was a thousand Pities, some thing could not be done for poor Mr. *Eugenio*.

THE Remainder of this Story will be dispatched in a few Words. Wearied with weak Hopes, and weaker Pursuits, he accepted a Curacy in *Derbyshire*, of thirty Pounds a Year; and when he was five and forty, had the great Felicity to be preferred by a Friend of his Father's, to a Vicaridge worth annually sixty Pounds, in the most desert Parts of *Lincolnshire*; where, his Spirit quite sunk with those Reflections that Solitude and Disappointments bring; he married a Farmer's Widow, and is still alive, utterly undistinguished and forgotten; only some of the Neighbours have accidentally heard, *that he had been a* notable Man *in his Youth*.

THE

INTELLIGENCER

Number IX

FROM frequently reflecting upon the Course and Method of educating Youth in this and a neighbouring Kingdom, with the general Success and Consequence thereof, I am come to this Determination; That, Education is always the *worse* in Proportion to the *Wealth* and *Grandeur* of the Parents: Nor do I doubt in the least, that if the whole World were now under the Dominion of *one Monarch* (provided I might be allowed to chuse *where* he should fix the Seat of his Empire) the only Son and Heir of that Monarch, would be the worst educated Mortal that ever was born since the Creation: And I doubt, the same Proportion will hold through all Degrees and Titles, from an Emperor downwards, to the common Gentry.

I do not say, that this hath been always the Case; for in better Times it was directly otherwise; and a Scholar may fill half his *Greek* and *Roman* Shelves with Authors of the noblest Birth, as well as highest Virtue. Nor, do I tax all Nations at present with this Defect; for I know there are some to be excepted, and particularly *Scotland*, under all the Disadvantages of its Climate and Soil; if that Happiness be not rather owing even to those very Disadvantages. What is then to be done, if this Reflection must fix on two Countries, which will be most ready to take Offence, and which of all others it will be least prudent or safe to offend?

But there is one Circumstance yet more dangerous and lamentable: For if, according to the *Postulatum* already laid down, the higher Quality any Youth is of, he is in greater Likelihood to be worse educated; it behoves me to dread, and keep far from the Verge of *Scandalum Magnatum*.

Retracting therefore that hazardous *Postulatum*; I shall

venture no further at present, than to say, that perhaps *some* Care in educating the Sons of Nobility and principal Gentry, might not be ill employed. If this be not delivered with Softness enough, I must for the future be silent.

IN the mean Time, let me ask only two Questions, which relate to a neighbouring Kingdom, from whence the Chief among us are descended, and whose manners we most affect to follow. I ask first, how it comes about, that for above sixty Years past, the chief Conduct of Affairs in that Kingdom hath been generally placed in the Hands of *New-men*, with few Exceptions? The noblest Blood of *England* having been shed in the grand Rebellion, many great Families became extinct, or supplied by Minors. When the King was restored, very few of those Lords remained, who began, or at least had improved their Education, under the happy Reign of King *James*, or King *Charles* I. of which Lords the two principal were the Marquis of *Ormond*, and the Earl of *Southampton*. The Minors having, during the Rebellion and Usurpation, either received too much Tincture of bad Principles from those fanatick Times; or coming to Age at the Restoration, fell into the Vices of that dissolute Reign.

I DATE from this Æra, the corrupt Method of Education among us, and the Consequence thereof, in the Necessity the Crown lay under of introducing *New-men* into the highest Employments of State, or to the Office of what we now call Prime Ministers; Men of Art, Knowledge, Application and Insinuation, merely for Want of a Supply among the Nobility. They were generally (though not always) of good Birth, sometimes younger Brothers, at other times such, who although inheriting ample Fortunes, yet happened to be well educated, and provided with Learning. Such under that King, were *Hyde*, *Bridgeman*, *Clifford*, *Osborn*, *Godolphin*, *Ashley-Cooper*: Few or none under the short Reign of King *James* II. Under King *William*; *Sommers*, *Montague*, *Churchil*, *Vernon*, *Harry Boyle*, and many others. Under the Queen; *Harley*, *St. John*, *Harcourt*, *Trevor*, who indeed were Persons of the best private Families, but unadorned with Titles. So in the last Reign, Mr. *Robert Walpole*, was for many Years Prime

Minister, in which Post he still HAPPILY continues: His Brother
Horace is Ambassador Extraordinary to *France*. Mr. *Addison*
and Mr. *Craggs*, without the least Alliance to support them,
have been Secretaries of State.

IF the Facts have been thus for above sixty Years past,
(whereof I could, with a little further Recollection, produce
many more Instances) I would ask again, how it hath happened,
that in a Nation plentifully abounding with Nobility, so great
a Share in the most important Parts of publick Management,
hath been for so long a Period chiefly intrusted to Commoners; unless some Omissions or Defects of the highest
Import, may be charged upon those, to whom the Care of
educating our noble Youth hath been committed? For, if
there be any Difference between human Creatures in the Point
of *natural parts*, as we usually call them; it should seem, that
the Advantage lies on the Side of Children born from noble
and wealthy Parents; the same traditional Sloth and Luxury,
which render their Bodies weak and effeminate, perhaps refin-
ing and giving a freer Motion to the Spirits, beyond what can
be expected from the gross, robust Issue of meaner Mortals.
Add to this, the peculiar Advantages, which all young Noblemen possess, by the Privileges of their Birth; such as a free
Access to Courts, and a Deference paid to their Persons.

BUT as my Lord *Bacon* chargeth it for a Fault in Princes,
that they are impatient to compass *Ends*, without giving
themselves the Trouble of consulting or executing the *Means:*
So perhaps it may be the Disposition of young Nobles, either
from the Indulgence of Parents, Tutors and Governors, or their
own Inactivity, that they expect the *Accomplishments* of a good
Education, without the least Expence of *Time* or *Study*, to
acquire them.

WHAT I said last, I am ready to retract. For the Case is
infinitely worse; and the very Maxims set up to direct *modern*
Education, are enough to destroy all the Seeds of Knowledge,
Honour, Wisdom and Virtue among us. The current Opinion
prevails, that the Study of *Greek* and *Latin* is Loss of Time;
that the publick Schools by mingling the Sons of Noblemen
with those of the Vulgar, engage the former in bad Company;

that Whipping breaks the Spirits of Lads well born; that Universities make young Men Pedants; that to dance, fence, speak *French*, and know how to behave your self among great Persons of both Sexes, comprehends *the whole Duty of a Gentleman*.

I CANNOT but think this wise System of Education, hath been much cultivated among us by those Worthies of the Army, who during the last War, returning from *Flanders* at the Close of each Campaign, became the Dictators of Behaviour, Dress, and Politeness, to all those Youngsters, who frequent Chocolate-Coffee-Gaming-Houses, Drawing-Rooms, Opera's, Levees and Assemblies; where a Colonel, by his Pay, Perquisites, and Plunder, was qualified to out-shine many Peers of the Realm; and by the Influence of an *exotick* Habit and Demeanor, added to other foreign Accomplishments, gave the Law to the whole Town; and was copied as the Standard-Pattern of whatever was refined in Dress, Equipage, Conversation, or Diversions.

I REMEMBER in those Times, an admired Original of that Vocation, sitting in a Coffee-House near two Gentlemen, whereof one was of the Clergy, who were engaged in some Discourse that savoured of Learning; this Officer thought fit to interpose; and professing to deliver the Sentiments of his Fraternity, as well as his own, (and probably did so of too many among them) turning to the Clergy-Man, spoke in the following Manner. *D—n me, Doctor, say what you will, the Army is the only School for Gentlemen. Do you think my Lord* Marlborough *beat the* French *with* Greek *and* Latin. *D—n me, a Scholar when he comes into good Company, what is he but an Ass? D—n me, I would be glad, by G—d, to see any of your Scholars with his Nouns, and his Verbs, and his Philosophy, and Trigonometry, what a Figure he would make at a Siege or Blockade, or reconoitring——D—n me*, &c. After which he proceeded with a Volley of Military Terms, less significant, sounding worse, and harder to be understood than any that were ever coined by the Commentators upon *Aristotle*. I would not here be thought to charge the Soldiery with Ignorance and Contempt of Learning, without allowing Exceptions, of which

I have known a few: But however, the worse Example, especially in a great Majority, will certainly prevail.

I HAVE heard, that the late Earl of *Oxford*, in the Time of his Ministry, never passed by *White's Chocolate-House* (the common Rendezvous of infamous Sharpers, and noble Cullies) without bestowing a Curse upon that famous Academy, as the Bane of half the *English Nobility*. I have likewise been told another Passage concerning that great Minister; which, because it gives a humorous Idea of one principal Ingredient in modern Education, take as followeth. *Le Sac*, the famous *French* Dancing-Master, in great Admiration, asked a Friend, whether it were true, that Mr. *Harley* was made an Earl and Lord-Treasurer? And finding it confirmed, said; * *Well, I wonder what the Devil the Queen could see in him; for I attended him two Years, and he was the greatest Dunce that ever I taught.*

ANOTHER Hindrance to good Education, and I think the greatest of any; is that pernicious Custom in rich and noble Families, of entertaining *French* Tutors in their Houses. These wretched *Pedagogues* are enjoyned by the Father, to take special Care that the Boy shall be perfect in his *French*; by the Mother, that *Master* must not walk till he is hot, nor be suffered to play with other Boys, nor be wet in his Feet, nor daub his Cloaths: And to see that the Dancing-Master attends constantly, and does his Duty: She further insists, that the Child be not kept too long poring on his Book, because he is subject to sore Eyes, and of a weakly Constitution.

By these Methods, the young Gentleman is in every Article as fully accomplished at eight Years old, as at eight and twenty; Age adding only to the Growth of his Person and his Vices; so that if you should look at him in his Boyhood through the magnifying End of a Perspective, and in his Manhood through the other, it would be impossible to spy any Difference; the same Airs, the same Strut, the same Cock of his Hat, and Posture of his Sword, (as far as the Change of Fashions will allow) the same Understanding, the same Compass of Knowledge, with the very same Absurdity, Impudence, and Impertinence of Tongue.

* *The Author's Friends have heard him tell this Passage as from the Earl himself.*

He is taught from the Nursery, that he must inherit a great Estate, and hath no Need to mind his Book; which is a Lesson he never forgets to the End of his Life. His chief Solace is to steal down, and play at Span-Fathing with the Page, or young Black-a-moore, or little favourite Foot-boy; one of which is his principal Confident and Bosom-Friend.

There is one young * Lord in this Town, who by an unexampled Piece of good Fortune, was miraculously snatched out of the Gulph of Ignorance; confined to a publick School for a due Term of Years; well whipped when he deserved it; clad no better than his Comrades, and always their Play-fellow on the same Foot; had no Precedence in the School, but what was given him by his Merit, and lost it whenever he was negligent. It is well known how many Mutinies were bred at this unprecedented Treatment; what Complaints among his *Relations*, and other *Great Ones* of both Sexes; that his Stockings with Silver Clocks were ravished from him; that he wore his own Hair; that his Dress was undistinguished; that he was not fit to appear at a Ball or Assembly, nor suffered to go to either: And it was with the utmost Difficulty, that he became qualified for his present Removal to the University; where he may probably be farther persecuted, and possibly with Success, if the Firmness of a Governor, and his own good Dispositions will not preserve him. I confess, I cannot but wish he may go on in the Way he began; because, I have a Curiosity to know by so *singular* an Experiment, whether Truth, Honour, Justice, Temperance, Courage, and good Sense, acquired by a *School* and *College* Education, may not produce a very tolerable Lad; although he should happen to fail in one or two of those Accomplishments, which in the general Vogue are held so important to the finishing of a Gentleman.

It is true, I have known an Academical Education to have been exploded in publick Assemblies; and have heard more than one or two Persons of high rank declare, they could learn nothing more at *Oxford* and *Cambridge*, than to drink Ale, and smoke Tobacco; wherein I firmly believed them, and could

* *The Author is supposed to mean the Lord Viscount Montcassels of Ireland.*

have added some Hundred Examples from my own Observation in one of those Universities: But they all were of young Heirs sent thither only for Form; either from Schools, where they were not suffered by their careful Parents to stay above three Months in the Year; or from under the Management of *French* Family-Tutors, who yet often attended them in their *College*, to prevent all Possibility of their Improvement: But, I never yet knew any one Person of Quality, who followed his Studies at the University, and carried away his just Proportion of Learning, who was not ready upon all Occasions to celebrate and defend that Course of Education, and to prove a Patron of learned Men.

THERE is one Circumstance in a learned Education, which ought to have much Weight, even with those who have no Learning at all. The Books read at *Schools* and *Colleges*, are full of Incitements to Virtue, and Discouragements from Vice, drawn from the wisest Reasons, the strongest Motives, and the most influencing Examples. Thus, young Minds are filled early with an Inclination to Good, and an Abhorrence of Evil; both which increase in them, according to the Advances they make in Literature: And, although they may be, and too often are, drawn by the Temptations of Youth, and the Opportunities of a large Fortune, into some Irregularities, when they come forward into the great World; it is ever with Reluctance and Compunction of Mind, because their Byass to Virtue still continues. They may stray sometimes out of Infirmity or Complyance, but they will soon return to the right Road, and keep it always in view. I speak only of those Excesses, which are too much the Attendants of Youth and warmer Blood: for, as to the Points of Honour, Truth, Justice, and other noble Gifts of the Mind, wherein the Temperature of the Body hath no Concern, they are seldom or never known to be misled.

I HAVE engaged my self very unwarily in too copious a Subject for so short a Paper. The present Scope I would aim at, is to prove, that some Proportion of human Knowledge appears requisite to those, who, by their Birth or Fortune, are called to the making of Laws, and in a subordinate Way to the Execution of them; and that such Knowledge is not to be obtained without a Miracle; under the frequent, corrupt, and sottish Methods, of educating those, who are born to Wealth or Titles. For, I would have it remembered, that I do by no Means confine these Remarks to young Persons of noble Birth; the same Errors running through all Families, where there is Wealth enough to afford, that their Sons (at least the Eldest) may be good for nothing. Why should my Son be a Scholar, when it is not intended that he should live by his Learning? By this Rule, if what is commonly said be true, that Money answereth all Things, why should my Son be honest, temperate, just, or charitable, since he hath no Intention to depend upon any of these Qualities for a Maintenance?

WHEN all is done, perhaps upon the whole, the Matter is not so bad as I would make it: And GOD, who worketh Good out of Evil, acting only by the ordinary Course and Rule of Nature, permits this continual Circulation of human Things for his own unsearchable Ends. The Father grows rich by Avarice, Injustice, Oppression; he is a Tyrant in the Neighbourhood over Slaves and Beggars, whom he calleth his Tenants. Why should he desire to have Qualities infused into his Son, which himself never possessed, or knew, or found the Want of in the Acquisition of his Wealth? The Son bred in Sloth and Idleness, becomes a Spendthrift, a Cully, a Profligate; and goes out of the World a Beggar, as his Father came in: Thus the former is punished for his own Sins, as well as for those of the latter. The Dunghil having raised a huge Mushroom of short Duration, is now spread to enrich other Mens Lands. It is, indeed, of worse Consequence, where noble Families are gone to Decay; because their Titles and Privileges outlive their Estates: And, Politicians tell us, that nothing is more dangerous to the Publick, than a numerous Nobility without Merit or Fortune. But even here, GOD hath likewise prescribed some Remedy in the Order of Nature; so many great Families coming to an End by the Sloth, Luxury, and abandoned Lusts, which enervated their Breed through every Succession, producing gradually a more effeminate Race, wholly unfit for Propagation.

THE

INTELLIGENCER

Number XIX

N. B. *In the following Discourse the* Author *personates a Country Gentleman in the North of* Ireland. *And this Letter is supposed as directed to the* Drapier.

Having on the 12th *of* October *last, received a* LETTER, *signed* Andrew Dealer, *and* Patrick Pennyless; *I believe the following* PAPER, *just come to my Hands, will be a sufficient Answer to it.*

Sic vos, non vobis, vellera fertis oves.

Written in the Year 1728.

SIR,

I AM a Country Gentleman, and a Member of *Parliament*, with an Estate of about 1400*l*. a Year; which, as a *Northern* Landlord, I receive from above two Hundred Tenants: And my Lands having been let near twenty Years ago, the Rents, until very lately, were esteemed to be not above half Value; yet by the intolerable Scarcity of *Silver*, I lye under the greatest Difficulties in receiving them; as well as in paying my Labourers; or buying any Thing necessary for my Family from *Tradesmen*, who are not able to be long out of their *Money*. But the Sufferings of me, and those of my Rank, are Trifles in Comparison of what the meaner Sort undergo; such as the *Buyers* and *Sellers*, at *Fairs* and *Markets*; the *Shopkeepers* in every *Town*; the *Farmers* in general; all those who travel with *Fish*, *Poultry*, *Pedlary-ware*, and other Conveniences to sell:

54

But more especially *Handycrafts-men*, who work for us by the Day; and common Labourers whom I have already mentioned. Both these Kinds of People I am forced to employ until their Wages amount to a *Double Pistole*, or a *Moidore*, (for we hardly have any *Gold* of lower Value left us) to divide it among themselves as they can: And this is generally done at an *Ale-house*, or *Brandy-shop*; where, besides the Cost of getting *Drunk*, (which is usually the Case) they must pay *Ten Pence* or a *Shilling*, for changing their *Piece* into *Silver*, to some *Huckstering Fellow*, who follows that *Trade*. But, what is infinitely worse, those poor Men for want of due Payment, are forced to take up their *Oat-meal*, and other Necessaries of Life, at almost double Value; and, consequently, are not able to discharge half their Score; especially under the Scarceness of *Corn*, for two Years past; and the melancholly Disappointment of the present *Crop*.

The Causes of this, and a Thousand other Evils, are clear and manifest to you, and all thinking Men; although hidden from the Vulgar: These indeed complain of hard Times, the Dearth of Corn, the Want of Money, the Badness of Seasons; that their Goods bear no Price, and the Poor cannot find work; but their weak Reasonings never carry them to the Hatred and Contempt born us by our Neighbours and Brethren, without the least Grounds of Provocation; who rejoyce at our Sufferings, although sometimes to their own Disadvantage. They consider not the dead Weight upon every beneficial Branch of our Trade; that half our Revenues are annually sent to *England*; with many other Grievances peculiar to this unhappy Kingdom; which keep us from enjoying the common Benefits of Mankind; as you and some other Lovers of their Country have so often observed, with such good Inclinations, and so little Effect.

It is true indeed, that under our Circumstances in general; this Complaint for the Want of *Silver*, may appear as ridiculous, as for a Man to be impatient about a *Cut-Finger*, when he is struck with the *Plague*: And yet a poor Fellow going to the *Gallows*, may be allowed to feel the Smart of *Wasps* while he is upon *Tyburn-Road*. This Misfortune is so urging, and vexatious in every Kind of small Traffick; and so hourly pressing upon all Persons in the Country whatsoever; that a Hundred Inconveniences, of perhaps greater Moment in themselves, have been tamely submitted to, with far less Disquietude and Murmurs. And the Case seems yet the harder, if it be true, what many skilful Men assert, that nothing is more easy than a Remedy; and, that the Want of *Silver*, in Proportion to the little *Gold* remaining among us, is altogether as unnecessary, as it is inconvenient. A Person of Distinction assured me very lately, that, in discoursing with the * *Lord Lieutenant*, before his last Return to *England*; his *Excellency* said, *He had pressed the Matter often, in proper Time and Place, and to proper Persons*; *and could not see any Difficulty of the least Moment, that could prevent us from being made easy upon this Article.*

WHOEVER carries to *England* twenty seven *English* Shillings, and brings back one *Moidore* of full Weight, is a Gainer of Nine Pence *Irish*: In a *Guinea*, the Advantage is Three Pence; and Two Pence in a *Pistole*. The BANKERS, who are generally Masters of all our *Gold* and *Silver*, with this Advantage, have sent over as much of the latter, as came into their Hands. The Value of One Thousand *Moidores* in *Silver*, would thus amount in clear Profit, to 37*l.* 10*s.* The *Shopkeepers*, and other *Traders*, who go to *London* to buy Goods, followed the same Practice; by which we have been driven into this insupportable Distress.

TO a common Thinker, it should seem, that nothing would be more easy, than for the *Government* to redress this Evil, at any Time they shall please. When the Value of *Guineas* was lowered in *England* from 21*s.* and 6*d.* to only 21*s.* the Consequences to this Kingdom were obvious, and manifest to us all: And a sober Man may be allowed at least to wonder, although he dare not complain, why a new Regulation of *Coin* among us, was not then made; much more, why it hath never been since. It would surely require no very profound Skill in *Algebra*, to reduce the Difference of *Nine Pence in Thirty Shillings*; or *Three Pence* in a *Guinea* to less than a *Farthing*; and so small a Fraction could be no Temptation, either to *Bankers* to hazard their

* *The Lord* Carteret.

Silver at Sea, or Tradesmen to load themselves with it, in their Journeys to *England*. In my humble Opinion it would be no unseasonable Condescension, if the *Government* would graciously please to signify to the *poor loyal Protestant Subjects* of *Ireland*, either that this miserable Want of *Silver*, is not possible to be remedied in any Degree, by the nicest Skill in *Arithmetick*; or else, that it doth not stand with the good Pleasure of *England*, to suffer any *Silver* at all among us. In the former Case, it would be Madness to expect Impossibilities; and in the other, we must submit: For, Lives and Fortunes are always at the Mercy of the CONQUEROR.

THE Question hath been often put in *printed Papers*, by the DRAPIER and others, or, perhaps, by the same WRITER, under different Styles; why this Kingdom should not be permitted to have a *Mint* of its own, for the Coinage of *Gold*, *Silver*, and *Copper*; which is a Power exercised by many *Bishops*, and every petty Prince in *Germany*? But this Question hath never been answered; nor the least Application, that I have heard of, made to the *Crown* from hence, for the Grant of a *Publick Mint*; although it stands upon Record, that several Cities and Corporations here, had the Liberty of *Coining Silver*. I can see no Reasons, why we alone of all Nations, are thus restrained; but such as I dare not mention: Only thus far, I may venture; that *Ireland* is the first Imperial Kingdom, since *Nimrod*, which ever wanted Power, to *Coin* their own *Money*.

I KNOW very well, that in *England*, it is lawful for any Subject to petition either the *Prince* or the *Parliament*, provided it be done in a dutiful and regular Manner: But what is lawful for a Subject of *Ireland*, I profess I cannot determine: Nor will undertake, that your *Printer* shall not be prosecuted, in a *Court of Justice*, for publishing my *Wishes*, that a poor Shop-keeper might be able to change a *Guinea*, or a *Moidore*, when a Customer comes for a *Crown*'s Worth of Goods. I have known less Crimes punished with the utmost Severity, under the Title of *Disaffection*. And I cannot but approve the Wisdom of the *Antients*, who, after *Astrea* had fled from the Earth, at least took Care to provide *three upright Judges for Hell*. Mens Ears, among us, are indeed grown so nice, that whoever happens to think out of Fashion, in what relates to the Welfare of this Kingdom, dare not so much as complain of the *Tooth-ach*; lest our weak and busy Dablers in Politicks, should be ready to swear against him for *Disaffection*.

THERE was a Method practised by Sir *Ambrose Crawley*, the great Dealer in *Iron-works*; which I wonder the Gentlemen of our Country, under this great Exigence, have not thought fit to imitate. In the several Towns and Villages where he dealt, and many Miles round; he gave *Notes* instead of *Money*, from *Two Pence* to *Twenty Shillings*; which passed current in all Shops and Markets, as well as in Houses, where Meat or Drink was sold. I see no Reason, why the like Practice may not be introduced among us, with some Degree of Success; or at least may not serve as a poor Expedient, in this our *blessed Age of Paper*; which, as it dischargeth all our greatest Payments, may be equally useful in the smaller; and may just keep us alive, until an *English Act of Parliament shall forbid it*.

I HAVE been told, that among some of our poorest *American* Colonies, upon the Continent, the People enjoy the Liberty of cutting the little *Money* among them into Halves and Quarters, for the Conveniences of small Traffick. How happy should we be, in Comparison of our present Condition, if the like Privilege were granted to us, of employing the Sheers, for want of a *Mint*, upon our *foreign Gold*; by clipping it into *Half-Crowns*, and *Shillings*, and even lower Denominations; for Beggars must be content to live upon Scraps; and it would be our Felicity, that these Scraps could never be exported to other Countries, while any Thing better was left.

IF neither of these Projects will avail, I see nothing left us, but to truck and barter our Goods, like the *wild Indians*, with each other; or with our too powerful Neighbours; only with this Disadvantage on our Side, that the *Indians* enjoy the Product of their own Land; whereas the better half of ours is sent away, without so much as a Recompence in *Bugles* or *Glass* in return.

IT must needs be a very comfortable Circumstance, in the present Juncture, that some Thousand Families are gone, or going, or preparing to go from hence, and settle themselves in *America*. The poorer Sort, for want of Work; the Farmers whose beneficial Bargains are now become a Rack-Rent too hard to be born. And those who have any *ready Money*, or can purchase any, by the Sale of their Goods or Leases; because they find their Fortunes hourly decaying, that their Goods will bear no Price, and that few or none have any *Money* to buy the very Necessaries of Life, are hastening to follow their departed Neighbours. It is true, *Corn* among us carries a very high Price; but it is for the same Reason, that *Rats*, and *Cats*, and dead *Horses*, have been often bought for *Gold* in a Town besieged.

THERE is a Person of Quality in my Neighbourhood, who Twenty Years ago, when he was just come to Age, being unexperienced, and of a generous Temper, let his Lands, even as Times went then, at a low Rate to able Tenants; and consequently by the Rise of Land since that Time, looked upon his Estate to be set at half Value: But Numbers of these Tenants, or their Descendants, are now offering to sell their Leases by Cant, even those which were for Lives, some of them renewable for ever, and some Fee-Farms, which the Landlord himself hath bought in at half the Price they would have yielded seven Years ago. And some Leases let at the same Time for Lives, have been given up to him, without any Consideration at all.

THIS is the most favourable Face of Things at present among us; I say, among us of the *North*, who are esteemed the only thriving People of the Kingdom. And how far, and how soon this Misery and Desolation may spread, is easy to foresee.

THE vast Sums of *Money* daily carried off, by our numerous Adventurers to *America*, have deprived us of our *Gold* in these Parts, almost as much as of our *Silver*.

AND the good Wives who come to our Houses, offer us their Pieces of Linen, upon which their whole Dependence lies, for so little Profit, that it can neither half pay their Rents, not half support their Families.

IT is remarkable, that this Enthusiasm spread among our *Northern* People, of sheltering themselves in the Continent of

America, hath no other Foundation, than their present insupportable Condition at home. I have made all possible Enquiries, to learn what Encouragement our People have met with, by any Intelligence from those Plantations, sufficient to make them undertake so tedious and hazardous a Voyage, in all Seasons of the Year; and so ill accommodated in their Ships, that many of them have died miserably in their Passage; but could never get one satisfactory Answer. Somebody, they know not who, had written a Letter to his Friend or Cousin from thence, inviting him, by all Means, to come over; that it was a fine fruitful Country, and to be held for ever at a *Penny* an Acre. But the Truth of the Fact is this: The *English* established in those Colonies, are in great Want of Men to inhabit that Tract of Ground, which lies between them and the *wild Indians*, who are not reduced under their Dominion. We read of some barbarous People, whom the *Romans* placed in their Armies, for no other Service than to blunt their Enemies Swords, and afterwards to fill up Trenches with their dead Bodies. And thus our People, who transport themselves, are settled in those interjacent Tracts, as a Screen against the Assaults of the *Savages*; and may have as much Land as they can clear from the Woods at a very reasonable Rate, if they can afford to pay about a *Hundred* Years Purchase, by their Labour. Now, besides the *Fox*'s Reasons, which inclines all those who have already ventured thither, to represent every Thing in a false Light, as well for justifying their own Conduct, as for getting Companions in their Misery: The governing People in those Plantations, have also wisely provided, that no Letters shall be suffered to pass from thence hither, without being first viewed by the Council; by which, our People here are wholly deceived, in the Opinions they have of the happy Condition of their Friends gone before them. This was accidentally discovered some Months ago, by an honest Man; who having transported himself and Family thither, and finding all Things directly contrary to his Hope, had the Luck to convey a private Note, by a faithful Hand, to his Relation here; entreating him not to think of such a Voyage, and to discourage all his Friends from attempting it. Yet this, although it be a

Truth well known, hath produced very little Effect, which is no Manner of Wonder; for as it is natural to a Man in a *Fever* to turn often, although without any Hope of Ease; or when he is pursued, to leap down a Precipice, to avoid an Enemy just at his Back; so, Men in the extremest Degree of Misery and Want, will naturally fly to the first Appearance of Relief, let it be ever so vain or visionary.

You may observe, that I have very superficially touched the Subject I began with, and with the utmost Caution: For I know how criminal the least Complaint hath been thought, however seasonable, or just, or honestly intended; which hath forced me to offer up my daily Prayers, that it may never, at least in my Time, be interpreted by *Inuendo's* as a false, scandalous, seditious and disaffected Action, for a Man to roar under an acute Fit of the *Gout*; which, beside the Loss and the Danger, would be very inconvenient to one of my Age, so severely afflicted with that Distemper.

I wish you good Success; but I can promise you little, in an ungrateful Office you have taken up, without the least View, either to Reputation or Profit. Perhaps your Comfort is, that none but *Villains* and *Betrayers* of their Country, can be your *Enemies*. Upon which I have little to say, having not the Honour to be acquainted with many of that Sort; and therefore, as you easily may believe, am compelled to lead a very retired Life.

I am, SIR,
>*Your most obedient,*
>*Humble Servant,*

>>A. NORTH.

County of *Down,*
>*Dec.* 2, 1728.

A Letter to the Archbishop of Dublin, concerning the Weavers

A LETTER TO THE ARCHBISHOP
OF DUBLIN, CONCERNING
THE WEAVERS.

My Lord,

THE Corporation of Weavers in the woollen Manufacture, who have so often attended Your Grace and called upon me with their Schemes and proposalls were with me on Thursday last, when he who spoke for the rest and in the name of his absent brethren said it was the opinion of the whole body, that if somewhat were written at this time by an able hand to persuade the People of the Kingdom to wear their own woollen Manufactures it might be of good use to the Nation in generall, and preserve many hundreds of their Trade from starving. To which I answered that it was hard for any man of common Spirit to turn his thoughts to such Speculations, without discovering a Resentment which people are too delicate to bear. For, I will not deny to your Grace, that I cannot reflect on the singular condition of this Country, different from all others upon the face of the Earth, without some Emotion, and without often examining as I pass the streets whether those animals which come in my way with two legs and human faces, clad, and erect, be of the same species with what I have seen very like them in England, as to the outward Shape, but differing in their notions, natures, and intellectualls more than any two kinds of Brutes in a forest, which any men of common prudence would immediately discover, by persuading them to define what they mean by Law, Liberty, Property, Courage, Reason, Loyalty or Religion.

One thing, my Lord, I am very confident of; that if God Almighty for our sins would most justly send us a Pestilence, whoever should dare to discover his grief in publick for such a visitation, would certainly be censured for disaffection to the Government. For I solemnly profess, that I do not know one calamity we have undergone this many years, whereof any man whose opinions were not in fashion dared to lament without being openly charged with that imputation. And this is the harder, because although a Mother when she hath corrected her child may sometimes force it to kiss the rod, yet she will never give that power to the foot-boy or the scullion.

My Lord, there are two things for the People of this Kingdom to consider. First their present evil condition; and secondly what can be done in some degree to remedy it.

I shall not enter into a particular Description of our present misery. It hath been already done in severall Papers, and very fully in one, entitled, A short view of the State of Ireland. It will be enough to mention the entire want of Trad, The Navigation Act executed with utmost rigor, The remission of a million every year to England, The ruinous importation of forein Luxury and vanity, The oppression of Landlords, and discouragement of Agriculture.

Now all these evils are without the possibility of a Cure except that of Importations, and to fence against ruinous folly will be always in our power in Spight of the Discouragements, mortifications, contempt, hatred, and oppression we can ly under. But our Trad will never mend, the Navigation Act never be softned, our Absentees never return, our endless forein Payments never be lessened, or our Landlords ever be less exacting.

All other Scheams for preserving this Kingdom from utter ruin are idle and visionary, consequences drawn from wrong reasoning, and from generall Topicks which for the same Causes that they may be true in all Nations are certainly false in ours; as I have told the publick often enough, but with as little effect as what I shall say at present is likely to produce.

I am weary [of] so many abortive Projects for the advancement of Trade, of so many crude Proposals in letters sent me from unknown hands, of so many contradictory Speculations about raising or sinking the value of gold and silver. I am not in the least sorry to hear of the great Numbers going to America, though very much so for the Causes that drive them from us, since the uncontrolled Maxim that People are the Riches of a Nation is no maxim here under our Circumstances.

We have neither [manufactures] to employ them about, nor food to support them.

If a private Gentleman's income be sunk irretrievably for ever from a hundred Pounds to fifty, and that he hath no other method to supply the Deficiency, I desire to know, My Lord, whether such a Person hath any other course to take than to sink half his expenses in every article of Oeconomy, to save himself from Ruin and the Jayl. Is not this more than doubly the case of Ireland, where the want of money, the irrecoverable ruin of Trade, with the other evils above mentioned, and many more too well known and felt, and too numerous or invidious to relate, have been gradually sinking us for above a dozen years past, to a degree that we are at least by two thirds in a worse condition than was ever known since the Revolution? Therefore instead of Dreams and projects for advancing of Trade, we have nothing left but to find out some expedient whereby we may reduce our expences to our Incomes.

Yet this procedure allowed so necessary in all private familys and in its own nature so easy to be put in practice may meet with strong opposition by the cowardly slavish indulgence of the men to the intolerable pride, arrogance, vanity and Luxury of the Women, who strictly adhering to the rules of modern education seem to employ their whole stock of Invention in contriving new arts of profusion, faster than the most parsimonious husband can afford; and to compass this work the more effectually, their universal maxim is to despise and detest everything of the growth and manufacture of their own Country, and most to value whatever comes from the very remotest parts of the globe. And I am convinced, that if the Virtuosi could once find out a world in the Moon, with a passage to it, our women would wear nothing but what came directly from thence.

The prime cost of Wine yearly imported to Ireland is valued at thirty thousand poinds, and the Tea (including Coffee and Chocolate) at five times that sum. The Lace Silks Callicoes and all other unnecessary ornaments for women including English Cloaths and stuffs, added to the former Articles make

up (to compute grossly), about four hundred thousand
Pounds.

Now; if we should allow the thirty thousand Pounds for
wine, wherein the women have their share, and which is all
we have to comfort us, and deduct seventy thousand Pounds
more for over-reckoning, there would still remain three
hundred thousand Pounds, annually spent for unwholesome
drugs, and unnecessary finery. Which prodigious sum would
be wholly saved, and many thousands of our miserable shopkeepers and manufacturers comfortably supported.

Let speculative people busy their Brains as much as they
please, there is no other way to prevent this Kingdom from
sinking for ever than by utterly renouncing all forein dress
and Luxury.

It is absolutely so in fact that every husband of any fortune
in the Kingdom is nourishing a poisonous, devouring serpent
in his Bosom with all the mischief but with none of its wisdom.

If all the women were clad with the growth of their own
Country, they might still vye with each other in the cause of
Foppery, and still have room left to vye with each other, and
equally shew their wit and Judgment in deciding upon the
variety of Irish Stuffs; And if they could be contented with
their native wholesome slops for breakfast, we should hear
no more of their Spleen, Hystericks, Cholicks, Palpitations and
Asthmaes. They might still be allowed to ruin each other
and their husbands at play, because the money lost would only
circulate among our selves.

My Lord; I freely own it a wild Imagination that any words
will cure the sottishness of men, or the vanity of women, but
the Kingdom is in a fair way of producing the most effectuall
remedy, when there will not be money left for the common
course of buying and selling the very necessaryes of life in our
markets, unless we absolutely change the whole method of our
Proceedings.

This Corporation of Weavers in Woollen and Silks, who
have so frequently offered Proposalls both to Your Grace
and to me, are the hottest and coldest generation of Men
that I have known. About a Month ago they attended Your

Grace when I had the honor to be with you, and designed me
then the same favour. They desired you would recommend
to your Clergy to wear Gowns of Irish Stuffs, which might
probably spread the Example among all their Brethren in
the Kingdom, and perhaps among the Lawyers and Gentlemen
of the University and among the Citizens of those Corporations
who appear in Gowns on solemn occasions. I then mentioned
a kind of stuff, not above eight pence a yard, which I heard
had been contrived by some of the Trade and was very
convenient. I desired they would prepare some of that or
any sort of black stuff on a certain day when your Grace
would appoint as many Clergymen as could readyly be found
to meet at your Palace, and there give their Opinions; and
that your Graces Visitations approaching you could then have
the best opportunity of seeing what could be done in a matter
of such consequence as they seemed to think to the woollen
manufacture. But instead of attending, as was expected; They
came to me a fortnight after, with a new Proposal; that something should be writ by an acceptable and able hand to promote
in generall the wearing of home manufacture, and their
civilityes would seem to fix that work upon me. I asked
whether they had prepared the Stuffs, as they had promised,
and Your Grace expected; but they had not made the least step
in the matter, nor as it appears thought of it more.

I did some years ago propose to the Masters and principall
Dealers in the home Manufactures of silk and wool, that they
should meet together, and after mature Consideration, publish Advertisements to the following Purpose. That in order
to encourage the wearing of Irish Manufactures in silk and
woollen, they gave notice to the Nobility and Gentry of the
Kingdom, that they the undersigned would enter into Bonds
for themselves and for each other, to sell the severall sorts of
Stuffs, Cloths and Silks, made to the best perfection they were
able, for certain fixed prices, and in such a manner, that if a
child were sent to any of their shops, the buyer might be
secure of the value and goodness, and measure of the Ware,
and lest this might be thought to look like a Monopoly any
other member of the Trade might be admitted upon such

conditions as should be agreed on. And if any Person whatsoever should complain that he was ill used in the value or
goodness of what he bought: The matter should be examined;
the person injured be fully satisfied, by the whole corporation
without delay, and the Dishonest Seller be struck out of the
Society, unless it appeared evidently that the failure proceeded
only from Mistake.

The mortal danger is, that if these Dealers could prevail
by the goodness and cheapness of their Cloths and Stuffs to
give a turn to the principal People of Ireland in favor of their
goods, they would relapse into the knavish practice peculiar
to this Kingdom, which is apt to run through all Trades even
so low as a common Ale-seller, who as soon as he gets a vogue
for his Liquor, and outsells his Neighbors, thinks his Credit
will put off the worst he can buy; till his Customers will come
no more. Thus I have known at London in a generall mourning, the Drapiers dye black all their old Damaged goods, and
sell them at double rates, and then complain and petition the
Court, that they are ready to starve by the continuance of the
mourning.

Therefore I say, those principal weavers who would enter
in such a compact as I have mentioned, must give sufficient
Security against all such practices; for, if once the women can
persuade their Husbands that forein goods besides the finery
will be as cheap, and do more Service, our last state will be
worse than the first.

I do not here pretend to digest perfectly the method by
which these principal Shopkeepers shall proceed in such a
Proposall; but my meaning is clear enough; and cannot
reasonably be objected against.

We have seen what a destructive Loss the Kingdom received
by the detestable fraud of the Merchants, or Northern weavers,
or both, notwithstanding all the care of the Governors at that
Board; when we had an offer of commerce with the Spaniards,
to the value as I am told of three hundred thousand Pounds a
year. But while we deal like Pedlars, we shall practice like
Pedlars; and sacrifice all honesty to the present urging advantage.

What I have said may serve as an answer to the desire made me by the Corporation of Weavers, that I would offer my notions to the publick. As to anything further, let them apply themselves to the Parliament in their next Session. Let them prevail in the House of Commons to grant one very reasonable request: And I shall think there is still some spirit left in the Nation, when I read a vote to this Purpose: Resolved, *nemine contradicente*, That this House will, for the future, wear no cloaths but such as are made of Irish growth or of Irish manufacture, nor will permit their Wives or Children to wear any other: and that they will to the utmost endeavor to prevayl with their Friends, Relations, Dependants and Tenants to follow their Example. And if at the same time they could banish Tea and Coffee and Chinaware out of their Familyes, and force their wives to chat their Scandal over an Infusion of sage, or other wholesom Domestick vegetables, we might possibly be able to subsist, and pay our Absentees, Pensioners, Generalls, civil officers, Appeals, Colliers, temporary Travellers Students, Schoolboys, spleenatick Visitors of Bath, Tunbridge, and Epsom, with all other smaller Drayns, by sending our crude unwrought goods to England, and receiving from thence and all other Countryes nothing but what is fully manufactured, and keep a few Potatoes and Oatmeal for our own subsistence.

I have been for a dozen years past wisely prognosticating the present condition of this Kingdom, which every human creature of common sense could foretell with as little sagacity as myself. My meaning is that a consumptive body must needs dye, which hath spent all its spirits and received no nourishment; Yet I am often tempted to pity when I hear the poor farmer and Cottager lamenting the hardness of the times, and imputing them either to one or two ill Seasons, which better Clymats than ours are more exposed to, or to the scarcity of Silver which to a Nation of Liberty would be onely a sleight and temporary inconveniency, to be removed at a months warning.

Answer to Several Letters from Unknown Persons

ANSWER TO SEVERAL LETTERS FROM UNKNOWN PERSONS.

GENTLEMEN,

I AM inclined to think that I received a Letter from you two last summer, directed to Dublin, while I was in the Country, whither it was sent me; and I ordered an answer to it to be printed, but It seems it had little effect, and I suppose this will have not much more. But, the heart of this People is waxed gross, and their Ears are dull of hearing, and their eyes they have closed. And, Gentlemen, I am to tell you another thing: That the world is so regardless of what we write for the publick good, that after we have delivered our thoughts, without any prospect of advantage, or of Reputation, which latter is not to be had but by subscribing our names, we cannot prevayl upon a Printer to be at the charge of sending it into the World, unless we will be at all or half the expence; And although we are willing enough to bestow our labors, we think it unreasonable to be out of pocket; because it probably may not consist with the Scituation of our Affairs.

I do very much approve your good intentions, and in a great measure your manner of declaring them, and I do imagine you intended that the world should not onely know your Sentiments, but my Answer, which I shall impartially give.

That great Prelate, in whose cover you directed your Letter, sent it to me this morning, and I begin my answer to-night, not knowing what Interruption I may meet with.

I have ordered your Letter to be printed, as it ought to be, along with my answer, because I conceive it will be more acceptable and informing to the Kingdom.

I shall therefore now go on to answer your Letter in all manner of Sincerity.

Although your letter be directed to me, yet I take myself to be onely an imaginary Person; for although I conjecture

I had formerly one from you, yet I never answered it otherwise than in print; Neither was I at a loss to know the Reasons why so many People of this Kingdom were transporting themselves to America. And, if this Encouragement were owing to a pamphlet written, giving an Account of the Country of Pensilvania, to tempt People to go thither, I do declare that those who were tempted by such a Narrative to such a Journey, were fools, and the Author a most impudent Knave; at least, if it be the same Pamphlet I saw when it first came out, which is above 25 years ago, dedicated to Will Pen (whom by a mistake you call 'Sir William Pen') and styling him by authority of the Scripture, Most noble Governor. For, I was very well acquainted with Pen, and did some years after talk with him upon that Pamphlet, and the Impudence of the Author, who spoke so many things in Praise of the Soyl and Clymat, which Pen himself did absolutely contradict. For he did assure me that his Country wanted the shelter of mountains, which left it open to the Northern winds from Hudson's bay and the frozen sea, which destroyed all Plantations of Trees, and was even pernicious to all common vegetables. But indeed, New York, Virginia, and other parts less northward; or more defended by Mountains, are described as excellent Countryes but, upon what Conditions of advantage Foreigners go thither, I am yet to seek.

What Evils do our People avoyd by running from hence, is easyer to be determined. They conceive themselves to live under the Tyranny of most cruel exacting Landlords, who have no view further than encreasing their rent-rolls. Secondly, you complain of the want of Trade whereof you seem not to know the reason. Thirdly, you lament most justly the money spent by absentees in England. Fourthly, you complain that your Linnen Manufacture declines. Fifthly, that your Tythcollectors oppress you. Sixthly, that your Children have no hopes of Preferment in the Church, the Revenue, or the Army; to which You might have added the Law, and all civill Employments whatsoever. Seventhly, you are undone for silver, and want all other money.

I could easily add some other motives, which to men of

Spirit who desire and expect and think they deserve the common Privileges of human nature, would be of more force than any you have yet named, to drive them out of this Kingdom; but as these Speculations may probably not much affect the Brains of your people, I shall chuse to let them pass unmentioned. Yet I cannot but observe, that my very good and virtuous friend, his excellency Burnet, (*O fili, nec tali indigne parente!*) hath not hitherto been able to persuade his Vassals by his oratory in the style of a command, to settle a Revenue on his Vice-royal person. I have been likewise assured that in one of those Colonyes on the Continent which Nature hath so far favored as by the Industry of the Inhabitants to produce a great quantity of excellent Rice, the Stubbornness of the People, who having been told that the world is wide, took it into their heads that they might sell their own Rice at whatever forein markets they pleased, and seem by their practice very unwilling to quit that Opinion.

But, to return to my Subject: I must confess to you both, that if one reason of your Peoples deserting us be the Despair of things growing better in their own Country; I have not one Syllable to answer, because that would be to hope for what is impossible, and so I have been telling the publick these ten years. For there are three events which must precede any such blessing: First, a Liberty of Trade, Secondly, a Share of Preferments in all kinds to the British Natives, and Thirdly, a return of those absentees, who take away almost one half of the Kingdoms Revenues. As to the first, there is nothing left us but despair, and for the third, it will never happen till the Kingdom hath no money to send them; for which in my own particular I should not be sorry.

The exaction of Landlords hath indeed been a grievance of above twenty years standing. But as to what you object about the severe Clauses relating to Improvement, the fault lyes wholly on the other side: For the Landlords either by their Ignorance, or greedyness, of making large rent-rolls, have performed this matter so ill, as we see by experience, that there is not one Tenant in five hundred who hath made any improvement worth mentioning. For which I appeal to any man who rides through the Kingdom, where little is to be found among the Tenants but Beggary and Desolation; the Cabbins of the Scotch themselves in Ulster being as dirty and miserable as those of the wildest Irish. Whereas, good firm penal Clauses for Improvement, with a tolerable easy rent, and a reasonable Period of time would in twenty years have encreased the Rents of Ireland at least a third part in the intrinsick value.

I am glad to hear you speak with some decency of the Clergy, and to impute the exactions you lament, to the Managers or Farmers of the Tythes. But you entirely mistake the Fact; for I defy the wickedest and most powerfull Clergy-men in the kingdom to oppress the meanest Farmer in the Parish; and I likewise defy the same Clergy-man to prevent himself from being cheated by the same Farmer, whenever that Farmer shall be disposed to be knavish or peevish. For although the Ulster tithing-table is more advantageous to the Clergy than any other in the Kingdom, yet the Minister can demand no more than his tenth; and where the Corn much exceeds the small Tyths, as except in some Districts, I am told, it always doth, he is at the mercy of every stubborn Farmer, especially of those whose sect as well as interest incline them to opposition. However, I take it, that your People bent for America do not shew the best part of their prudence, in making this one part of their Complaint; yet, they are so far wise as not to make the Payment of Tythes a Scruple of Conscience, which is too gross for any protestant Dissenter except a Quaker to pretend. But, do your people indeed think, that if Tythes were abolished, or delivered into the hands of the Landlord, after the blessed manner in the Scotch spiritual Oeconomy, that the Tenant would sit easyer in his Rent under the same Person, who must be Lord of the Soyl and of the Tyth together?

I am ready enough to grant, that the oppression of Landlords, the utter ruin of Trade, with its necessary consequence the want of money, half the revenues of the Kingdom spent abroad, the continued Dearth of three years, and the strong delusion in your People by false allurement from America may be the chief motives of their eagerness after such an Expedition; [but, there is likewise another temptation, which is not of inconsiderable weight; which is their itch of living in a Country where their Sect is predominant, and where their eyes and consciences will not be offended by the stumbling-block of Ceremonyes, habits, and spiritual Titles.]

But, I was surprised to find, that those Calamityes whereof we are innocent have been sufficient to drive many familyes out of their country, who had no reason to complain of oppressive Landlords. For while I was last year in the Northern parts, a Person of Quality, whose estate was let above 20 years ago, and then at a very reasonable rent, some for Leases of Lives, and some perpetuityes, did in a few months purchase eleven of those Leases at a very inconsiderable price, although they were two years ago reckoned to pay but half value. From whence it is manifest, that our present miserable condition and the dismal prospect of worse, with other reasons above assigned are sufficient to put men upon trying this desperate experiment of changing the scene they are in although Landlords should by a miracle become less inhuman.

There is hardly a Scheme proposed for improving the trade of this Kingdom, which doth not manifestly shew the Stupidity and ignorance of the Proposer; and I laugh with contempt at those weak wise heads, who proceed upon general Maxims, or advise us to follow the Examples of Holland and England. These Empiricks talk by rote, without understanding the Constitution of the Kingdom; as if a Physician knowing that Exercise contributed much to health should prescribe to his Patient under a severe fit of the gout, to walk ten miles every morning. The Directions for Ireland are very short and plain, to encourage agriculture and home consumption, and utterly discard all Importations which are not absolutely necessary for health or Life. And how few necessityes, conveniencyes, or even comforts of Life are denyed us by Nature, or not to be attained by Labor and Industry. Are those detestable Extravagancies of Flanders Lace, English Cloth of our own wooll, and other Goods, Italian or Indian Silks, Tea, Coffee, Chocolate, China-ware, and that profusion of Wines, by the knavery of Merchants growing dearer every Season, with a hundred unnecessary Fopperyes, better known to others than me;

Are these I say fit for us, any more than for the beggar who could not eat his Veal without Oranges. Is it not the highest Indignity to human nature, that men should be such poltrons as to suffer the Kingdom and themselves to be undone, by the Vanity, the Folly, the Pride, and Wantonness of their Wives, who under their present Corruptions seem to be a kind of animal suffered for our sins to be sent into the world for the Destruction of Familyes, Societyes, and Kingdoms; and whose whole study seems directed to be as expensive as they possibly can in every useless article of living, who by long practice can reconcile the most pernicious forein Drugs to their health and pleasure, provided they are but expensive; as Starlings grow fat with henbane: who contract a Robustness by meer practice of Sloth and Luxury: who can play deep severall hours after midnight, sleep beyond noon, revel upon Indian poisons, and spend the revenue of a moderate family to adorn a nauseous unwholesom living Carcase. Let those few who are not concerned in any part of this accusation, suppose it unsaid; let the rest take it among them. Gracious God in His mercy look down upon a nation so shamefully besotted.

If I am possessed of an hundred pounds a year, and by some misfortune it sinks to fifty, without a possibility of ever being retrieved; Does it remain a question in such an exigency, what I am to do: Must not I retrench one-half in every article of expence? or retire to some cheap distant part of the Country where necessaryes are at half-value?

Is there any mortal who can shew me under the circumstances we stand with our neighbors, under their Inclinations towards us, under Laws never to be repealed, under the Desolation caused by absentees, under many other circumstances not to be mentioned, that this Kingdom can ever be a Nation of Trade, or subsist by any other method than that of a reduced family, by the utmost parsimony, in the manner I have already prescribed.

I am tired with Letters from many unreasonable well-meaning People, who are daily pressing me to deliver my Thoughts in this deplorable Juncture, which upon many others I have so often done in vain. What will it import that half a score people in a Coffee-house may happen to read this paper, and even the Majority of those few differ in every sentiment from me. If the Farmer be not allowed to sow his Corn; If half the little money among us be sent to pay rents to Irish absentees, and the rest for forreign Luxury and Dress for the women, what will our charitable Dispositions avayl, when there is nothing left to be given, when contrary to all custom and example all necessaryes of Life are so exorbitant, when money of all kinds was never known to be so scarce. So that Gentlemen of no contemptible Estates are forced to retrench in every article, (except what relates to their wives,) without being able to shew any bounty to the Poor.

An Answer to Several Letters sent me from Unknown Hands

AN

A N S W E R

TO SEVERAL

LETTERS sent me from unknown Hands.

Written in the Year 1729.

I AM very well pleased with the good opinion you express of me, and wish it were any way in my power to answer your expectations, for the service of my country. I have carefully read your several schemes and proposals, which you think should be offered to the parliament. In answer, I will assure you, that, in another place, I have known very good proposals rejected with contempt by public assemblies, merely because they were offered from without doors; and yours perhaps might have the same fate, especially if handed into the public by me, who am not acquainted with three members, nor have the least interest with one. My printers have been twice prosecuted, to my great expence, on account of discourses I writ for the public service, without the least reflection on parties or persons; and the success I had in those of the Drapier was not owing to my abilities, but to a lucky juncture, when the fuel was ready for the first hand that would be at the pains of kindling it. It is true both those envenomed prosecutions were the workmanship of a judge, who is now gone to his own place*. But, let that be as it will, I am determined henceforth never to be the instrument of leaving an innocent man at the mercy of that bench.

It is certain, there are several particulars relating to this kingdom, (I have mentioned a few of them in one of my Drapier's letters) which it were heartily to be wished that the Parliament would take under their consideration, such as will

* Lord Chief-Justice Whitshed.

nowise interfere with England, otherwise than to its advantage.

The first I shall mention is touched at in a letter which I received from one of you, Gentlemen, about the highways; which, indeed, are almost every where scandalously neglected. I know a very rich man in this city, a true lover and saver of his money, who, being possessed of some adjacent lands, hath been at great charge in repairing effectually the roads that lead to them; and hath assured me, that his lands are thereby advanced four or five shillings an acre, by which he gets treble interest. But, generally speaking, all over the kingdom, the roads are deplorable; and, what is more particularly barbarous, there is no sort of provision made for travellers on foot; no, not near this city, except in a very few places, and in a most wretched manner: Whereas the English are so particularly careful in this point, that you may travel there an hundred miles with less inconvenience than one mile here. But, since this may be thought too great a reformation, I shall only speak of roads for horses, carriages, and cattle.

Ireland is, I think, computed to be one third smaller than England; yet, by some natural disadvantages, it would not bear quite the same proportion in value, with the same encouragement. However, it hath so happened, for many years past, that it never arrived to above one eleventh part in point of riches; and, of late, by the continual decrease of trade, and increase of absentees, with other circumstances not here to be mentioned, hardly to a fifteenth part; at least, if my calculations be right, which I doubt are a little too favourable on our side.

Now, supposing day-labour to be cheaper by one half here than in England, and our roads, by the nature of our carriages and the desolation of our country, to be not worn and beaten above one eighth part so much as those of England, which is a very moderate computation; I do not see why the mending of them would be a greater burthen to this kindgom than to that.

There have been, I believe, twenty acts of parliament, in

six or seven years of the late king*, for mending long tracts of impassable ways in several counties of England, by erecting turnpikes, and receiving passage-money in a manner that every body knows. If what I have advanced be true, it would be hard to give a reason against the same practice here, since the necessity is as great, the advantage in proportion perhaps much greater, the materials of stone and gravel as easy to be found, and the workmanship at least twice as cheap. Besides, the work may be done gradually, with allowances for the poverty of the nation, by so many perch a year; but with a special care to encourage skill and diligence, and to prevent fraud in the undertakers, to which we are too liable, and which are not always confined to those of the meaner sort: But against these, no doubt, the wisdom of the nation may, and will provide.

Another evil, which, in my opinion, deserves the public care, is the ill-management of the bogs, the neglect whereof is a much greater mischief to this kingdom than most people seem to be aware of.

It is allowed indeed, by those who are esteemed most skilful in such matters, that the red swelling mossy bog, whereof we have so many large tracts in this island, is not by any means to be fully reduced; but the skirts, which are covered with a green coat, easily may, being not an accretion, or annual growth of moss, like the other. Now the landlords are generally too careless that they suffer their tenants to cut their turf in these skirts, as well as the bog adjoined, whereby there is yearly lost a considerable quantity of land throughout the kingdom, never to be recovered.

But this is not the greatest part of the mischief. For the main bog, although perhaps not reducible to natural soil, yet, by continuing large, deep, straight canals through the middle, cleaned at proper times, as low as the channel or gravel, would become a secure summer-pasture; the margins might, with great profit and ornament, be filled with quickins, birch, and other trees proper for such a soil, and the canals be convenient for water-carriage of the turf, which is now drawn

* King George I.

upon sled-cars with great expence, difficulty, and loss of time, by reason of the many turf-pits scattered irregularly through the bog, wherein great numbers of cattle are yearly drowned. And it hath been, I confess, to me a matter of the greatest vexation as well as wonder, to think how any landlord could be so absurd as to suffer such havock to be made.

All the acts for encouraging plantations of forest-trees are, I am told, extremely defective; which, with great submission, must have been owing to a defect of skill in the contrivers of them. In this climate, by the continual blowing of the West-south-west wind, hardly any tree of value will come to perfection that is not planted in groves, except very rarely, and where there is much land-shelter. I have not, indeed, read all the acts; but, from enquiry, I cannot learn that the planting in groves is enjoined. And, as to the effects of these laws, I have not seen the least, in many hundred miles riding, except about a very few gentlemens houses, and even those with very little skill or success. In all the rest, the hedges generally miscarry, as well as the larger slender twigs planted upon the tops of ditches, merely for want of common skill and care.

I do not believe that a greater and quicker profit could be made, than by planting large groves of ash, a few feet asunder, which in seven years would make the best kind of hop-poles, and grow in the same, or less time, to a second crop from their roots.

It would likewise be of great use and beauty in our desert scenes, to oblige all tenants and cottagers to plant ash or elm before their cabbins, and round their potatoe-gardens, where cattle either do not, or ought not to come to destroy them.

The common objections against all this, drawn from the laziness, the perverseness, or thievish disposition of the poor native Irish, might be easily answered, by shewing the true reasons for such accusations, and how easily those people may be brought to a less savage manner of life: But my printers have already suffered too much for my speculations. However, supposing the size of a native's understanding just equal to that of a dog or horse, I have often seen those two animals to be civilized by rewards, at least as much as by punishments.

It would be a noble achievement to abolish the Irish language in this kingdom, so far at least as to oblige all the natives to speak only English on every occasion of business, in shops, markets, fairs, and other places of dealing: Yet I am wholly deceived if this might not be effectually done in less than half an age, and at a very trifling expence, for such I look upon a tax to be, of only six thousand pounds a year, to accomplish so great a work. This would, in a great measure, civilize the most barbarous among them, reconcile them to our customs and manner of living, and reduce great numbers to the national religion, whatever kind may then happen to be established. The method is plain and simple; and, although I am too desponding to produce it, yet I could heartily wish some public thoughts were employed to reduce this uncultivated people from that idle, savage, beastly, thievish manner of life, in which they continue sunk to a degree, that it is almost impossible for a country gentleman to find a servant of human capacity, or the least tincture of natural honesty; or who does not live among his own tenants in continual fear of having his plantations destroyed, his cattle stolen, and his goods pilfered.

The love, affection, or vanity of living in England, continuing to carry thither so many wealthy families, the consequences thereof, together with the utter loss of all trade, except what is detrimental, which hath forced such great numbers of weavers and others to seek their bread in foreign countries, the unhappy practice of stocking such vast quantities of land with sheep and other cattle, which reduceth twenty families to one: These events, I say, have exceedingly depopulated this kingdom for several years past. I should heartily wish, therefore, under this miserable dearth of money, that those who are most concerned would think it adviseable to save a hundred thousand pounds a year, which is now sent out of this kingdom to feed us with corn. There is not an older or more uncontroverted maxim in the politics of all wise nations, than that of encouraging agriculture. And, therefore, to what kind of wisdom a practice so directly contrary among us may be reduced, I am by no means a judge. If labour and people make the true riches of a nation, what must be the issue where one part of the people are forced away, and the other part have nothing to do?

If it should be thought proper by wiser heads, that his Majesty might be applied to in a national way, for giving the kingdom leave to coin halfpence for its own use; I believe no good subject will be under the least apprehension that such a request could meet with refusal, or the least delay. Perhaps we are the only kingdom upon earth, or that ever was or will be upon earth, which did not enjoy that common right of civil society, under the proper inspection of its prince, or legislature, to coin money of all usual metals for its own occasions. Every petty prince in Germany, vassal to the Emperor, enjoys this privilege. And I have seen in this kingdom several silver pieces, with the inscription of *Civitas Waterford, Droghedagh*, and other towns.

A Letter on Maculla's Project about Halfpence

A LETTER ON MACULLA'S PROJECT ABOUT HALFPENCE & A NEW ONE PROPOSED, 1729

SIR,

YOU desire to know my opinion concerning Mr. Maculla's Project, of circulating notes stamped on copper, that shall pass for the value of halfpence and pence. I have some knowledge of the man; and about a month ago he brought me his book, with a couple of his half-penny notes: but I was then out of order, and he could not be admitted. Since that time I called at his house, where I discoursed the whole affair with him as thorowly as I could. I am altogether a stranger to his character. He talked to me in the usual style, with a great profession of zeal for the publick good; which is the common cant of all projectors in their bills, from a first minister of state down to a corn-cutter. But I stopped him short, as I would have done a better man; because it is too gross a pretence to pass at any time, and especially in this age, where we all know one another so well. Yet, whoever proposeth any scheam which may prove to be a publick benefit, I shall not quarrel, if it prove likewise very beneficial to the contriver. It is certain that, next to the want of silver, our greatest distress in point of coin is the want of small change, which may be some poor relief for the defect of the former; since the Crown will not please to take that work upon them here as they do in England. One thing in Mr. Maculla's book is certainly right, that no law hinders me from giving a payable note upon leather, wood, copper, brass, iron, or any other material (except gold and silver) as well as upon paper. The question is, whether I can sue him on a copper bond, when there is neither his hand nor seal nor witnesses to prove it. To supply this he hath proposed, that the materials upon which his note is written shall be in some degree of value equal to the debt. But that is one principall matter to be enquired into.

His scheam is this: He gives you a piece of copper for a halfpenny, or penny, stampt with a promissary note, to pay you twenty pence for every pound of the said copper notes whenever you shall return them: eight and fourty of these halfpenny pieces are to weigh a pound, and he sells you that pound, coyned and stamped, for two shillings; by which he clearly gains 20*l. per Cent.* that is to say, four pence for laying out twenty pence; allowing his copper at fourteen pence, and the coinage at six pence *per* pound.

This will certainly arise to a great sum, if he should circulate as large a quantity of his notes as the Kingdom, under the great dearth of silver, may very probably require: Enough indeed to make any Irish tradesman's fortune; which, however, I should not repine at in the least, if we could be sure of his fair dealing.

It was obvious for me to raise the common objection, why Mr. Maculla would not give security to pay the whole sum to any man who returned him his copper notes, as my Lord Dartmouth and Col. Moore were by their patents obliged to do. To which he gave me some answers plausible enough. First, he conceived that his coins were much nearer to the intrinsic value than any of those coined by patents, the bulk and goodness of the metal fully equalling the best English halfpence made by the Crown. That he apprehended the ill-will of envious and designing people, who, if they found him to have a great vent for his notes, since he wanted the protection of a patent, might make a run upon him which he could not be able to support. And, lastly, that his copper, as is already said, being equal in value and bulk to the English halfpence, he did not apprehend they should ever be returned, unless a combination, proceeding from spight and envy, might be formed against him.

But there are some points in his proposal, which I cannot well answer for, nor do I know whether he would be able to do it himself. The first is, whether the copper he gives us will be as good as what the Crown provided for the English halfpence and fathings. And, secondly, whether he will always continue to give us as good? And, thirdly, when he will think fit to stop his hand, and give us no more. For, I should be as sorry to lie at the mercy of Mr. Maculla, as of Mr. Wood.

There is another difficulty of the last importance. It is known enough that the Crown is supposed to be neither gainer nor loser by the coinage of any metal: For they subtract, or ought to subtract, no more from the intrinsick value than what will just pay the charges of the Mint; and how much that will amount to is the question. By what I could gather from Mr. Maculla, good copper is worth fourteen pence *per* pound. By this computation, if he sells his copper notes for two shillings the pound, and will pay twenty pence back, then the expence of coinage for one pound of copper must be sixpence, which is 30 *per cent*. The world should be particularly satisfied on this article before he vends his notes: For the discount of 30 *per cent*. is prodigious, and vastly more than I can conceive it ought to be. For, if we add to that proportion the 20 *per cent*. which he owneth to keep for his own profit, there will be a discount of 50 *per cent*. Or, to reckon, I think, a fairer way, whoever buys a pound of Mr. Maculla's coin at two shillings, carries home only the real value of fourteen pence, which is a pound of copper; and thus he is a loser of ten pence in every two shillings. But, however, this high discount of 30 *per cent*. will be no objection against Maculla's proposal; because, if the charge of coinage will honestly amount to so much, and we suppose his copper notes may be returned upon him, he will be the greater sufferer of the two; because the buyer can lose but four pence in a pound, and Maculla must lose sixpence, which was the charge of the coinage. But Maculla hath still 30 *per cent*. by the same, if they be returned.

Upon the whole, there are some points which must be settled to the general satisfaction, before we can safely take Mr. Maculla's copper notes for value received; and how he will give that satisfaction, is not within my knowledge or conjecture.

The first point is, that we shall be always sure of receiving good copper, equal in bulk and in fineness to the best English halfpence.

The second point is, to know what allowance he makes to himself, either out of the weight or mixture of his copper, or both, for the charge of his coinage. As to the weight, the matter is easy by his own scheme: For, as I have said before, he proposes forty-eight to weigh a pound, which he gives you for two shillings, and receives it by the pound at twenty pence: So that, supposing pure copper to be fourteen pence a pound, he makes you pay 30 *per cent.* for the labour of coining, as I have already observed, besides 20 *per cent.* when he sells it. But, if to this he adds any alloy, to debase the metal, although it be not above 10 *per cent.* then Mr. Maculla's promissary notes will, to the intrinsick value of the metal, be above 55 *per cent.* discount.

For subtracting ten *per cent.* of 50*l.* worth of copper, it will be 5 *per cent.* in the whole £100

which added to	–	–	–	–	–	50
						5
will be per cent.	–	–	–	–	–	55

That we are under great distress for change, and that Mr. Maculla's copper notes, on supposition of the metal being pure, is less liable to objection than the project of Wood, may be granted; but such a discount, where we are not sure even of our twenty pence a pound, appears hitherto a dead weight on his scheme.

Since I writ this, calling to mind that I had some copper halfpence by me, I weighed them with those of Mr. Maculla, and observed as follows.

First, I weighed Mr. Maculla's halfpenny against an English one of King Charles the Second, which outweighed Maculla's above a fifth part, or 20 *per cent.*

I likewise weighed an Irish Patrick and David halfpenny, which out-weighed Mr. Maculla's twelve and a half *per cent.* It had a very fair and deep impression, and was milled very skilfully round.

I found that even a common Harp halfpenny, well preserved,

weighed equal to Maculla's. And even some of Wood's half-pence were near equal in weight to his. Therefore, if it be true that he doth not think Wood's copper to have been faulty, he may probably give us no better.

I have laid these loose thoughts together with little order, to give you and others, who may read them, opportunity of digesting them better. I am no enemy to Mr. Maculla's project, but I would have it put upon a better foot. I own, that this halfpenny of King Charles the Second which I weighed against Mr Maculla's, was of the finest kind I had seen. However, it is plain, the Crown could afford it without being a loser: For, the benefit of defrauding the Crown never accrueth to the publick, but is wholly turned to the advantage of those whom the Crown employeth. But it is probable, that the officers of the Mint were then more honest than they have since thought fit to be. For I confess not to have met those of any other year so weighty, or in appearance of so good metal, among all the copper coins of the three last reigns. Yet these, however, out-weigh those of Mr. Maculla; for I have tried the experiment on a hundred of them. I have indeed seen accidentally one or two very light, but it must certainly have been done by chance, or rather, I suppose them to be counterfeits. Be that as it will, it is allowed on all hands, that * good copper was never known to be cheaper than it is at present. I am ignorant of the price, further than from his informing me that it is only fourteen pence a pound; by which I observe he charges the coinage at 30 *per cent.* and therefore I cannot but think his demands are exorbitant. But, to say the truth, the dearness or cheapness of the metal do not properly enter into the question. What we desire is, that it should be of the best kind, and as weighty as can be afforded; that the profit of the contriver should be reduced from 20 to 8 *per cent.* and the charge of coinage, if possible, from 30 to 10 or 15 at most.

Mr. Maculla must also give good security that he will coin only a determinate sum, not exceeding twenty thousand

* *This letter was written in the year* 1729, *when copper was* 14d. *a pound, but in this year* 1759, *it is* 16d. *halfpenny.*

K

pounds; by which, although he should deal with all upright-
ness imaginable, and make his coin as good as that I weighed
of King Charles the Second; he will at 20 *per cent.* gain four
thousand pounds: a very good additional job to a private
tradesman's fortune.

I must advise him also to employ better workmen, and make
his impressions deeper and plainer, by which a rising rim may
be left about the edge of his coin, to preserve the letters from
wearing out too soon. He hath no wardens nor masters, or
other officers of the Mint to suck up his profit; and, therefore,
can afford to coin cheaper than the Crown, if he will but find
good materials, proper implements and skilful workmen.

Whether this project will succeed in Mr. Maculla's hands
(which, if it be honestly executed, I should be glad to see;)
one thing I am confident of, that it might be easily brought
to perfection by a society of nine or ten honest gentlemen of
fortune, who wish well to their country, and would be content
to be neither gainers nor losers, further than the bare interest
of their money. And Mr. Maculla, as being the first starter
of the scheme, might be considered and rewarded by such a
society; whereof, although I am not a man of fortune, I should
think it an honour and happiness to be one, even with borrowed money, upon the best security I could give. And,
first, I am confident, without any skill but by general reason,
that the charge of coining copper would be very much less
than 30 *per cent.* Secondly, I believe ten thousand pounds in
half-pence and farthings would be sufficient for the whole
Kingdom, even under our great and most *unnecessary distress*
for the want of silver; and that, without such a distress, half
that sum would suffice.

For I compute and reason thus: The City of Dublin, by a
gross computation, contains ten thousand families; and, I am
told by shopkeepers, that if silver were as plenty as usual,
two shillings in copper would be sufficient, in the course of
business, for each family; but, in consideration of the want of
silver, I would allow five shillings to each family, which would
amount to 2500*l.*; and to help this, I would recommend a
currency of all the genuine undefaced harp-halfpence, which

are left of Lord Dartmouth's and Mr. Moor's patents under King Charles the Second; and the small Patrick and David for farthings. To the rest of the Kingdom I would assign the 7500*l.* remaining; reckoning Dublin to answer one fourth of the Kingdom, as London is judged to answer) if I mistake not) one third of England; I mean in the view of money only.

To compute our want of small change by the number of souls in the Kingdom, besides being perplexed, is, I think, by no means just. They have been reckoned at a million and a half, whereof a million at least are beggars, in all circumstances, except that of wandering about for alms, and that circumstance may arrive soon enough, when it will be time to add another ten thousand pounds in copper. But, without doubt, the families of Ireland, who lie chiefly under the difficulties of wanting small change, cannot be above forty or fifty thousand; which the sum of ten thousand pounds, with the addition of the fairest old halfpence, would tolerably supply. For, if we give too great a loose to any projector to pour in upon us what he pleases, the Kingdom will be (how shall I express it under our present circumstances?) more than undone.

And hence appears, in a very strong light, the villainy of Wood, who proposed the coinage of one hundred and eight thousand pounds in copper, for the use of Ireland; whereby every family in the Kingdom would be loaden with ten or a dozen shillings, although Wood might not transgress the bounds of his patent, and although no counterfeits, either at home or abroad, were added to the number; the contrary to both which would indubitably have happened. So ill informed are great men on the other side, who talk of a million with as little ceremony as we do of half a crown.

But, to return to the proposal I have made: Suppose ten gentlemen, lovers of their country, should raise 200 *l.* a-piece; and, from the time the money is deposited as they shall agree, should begin to charge it with seven *per cent.* for their own use: That they should as soon as possible provide a Mint and good workmen, and buy copper sufficient for coining two thousand pounds, subtracting a fifth part of the interest of ten thousand pounds for the charges of the tools, and fitting up a place for the Mint; the other four parts of the same interest to be subtracted equally out of the four remaining coinages of 2000 *l.* each, with a just allowance for other necessary incidents. Let the charge of coinage be fairly reckoned, and the Kingdom informed of it, as well as of the price of copper. Let the coin be as well and deeply stamped as it ought. Let the metal be as pure as can consist to have it rightly coined, (wherein I am wholly ignorant) and the bulk as large as that of King Charles the Second. And let this club of ten gentlemen give their joint security to receive all the coins they issue out for seven or ten years, and return gold and silver without any defalcation.

Let the same club or company, when they have issued out the first two thousand pounds, go on the second year, if they find a demand, and that their scheme hath answered to their own intention as well as to the satisfaction of the publick. And, if they find 7 *per cent.* not sufficient, let them subtract 8, beyond which I would not have them go. And, when they have in five years coined ten thousand pounds, let them give publick notice that they will proceed no farther, but shut up their Mint, and dismiss their workmen; unless the real, universal, and unsolicited declaration of the nobility and gentry of the Kingdom, shall signify a desire that they should go on for a certain sum farther. This company may enter into certain regulations among themselves, one of which should be, to keep nothing concealed, and duly to give an account to the world of their methods of acting.

Give me leave to compute, wholly at random, what charge the Kingdom will be at, by the loss of intrinsic value in the coinage of 10,000 *l.* in copper, under the management of such a society of gentlemen.

First, it is plain, that instead of 20 *per cent.* as demanded by Mr. Maculla, this society desires but 8 *per cent.*

Secondly, whereas Mr. Maculla charges the expence of coinage at 30 *per cent.* I hope and believe this society will be able to perform it at 10.

Thirdly, whereas it doth not appear that Mr. Maculla

can give any security for the goodness of his copper, because not one in ten thousand have the skill to distinguish; the society will be all engaged that theirs shall be of the best standard.

Fourthly, that whereas Mr. Maculla's halfpence are above one-fifth lighter, than that kind coined in the time of King Charles the Second; these gentlemen will oblige themselves to the publick, to give their coin of the same weight and goodness with those half-pence, unless they shall find they cannot afford it; and, in that case, they shall beforehand inform the publick, shew their reasons, and signify how large they can make them without being losers; and so give over or pursue their scheme, as they find the opinion of the world to be. However, I do not doubt but they can afford them as large, and of as good metal, as the best English halfpence that have been coined in the three last reigns, which very much outweigh those of Mr. Maculla. And this advantage will arise in proportion, by lessening the charge of coinage from 30 *per cent.* to 10, or 15, or 20, at most.

But I confess myself in the dark on that article; only I think it impossible it should amount to any proportion near 30 *per cent.* otherwise the coiners of those counterfeit halfpence, called *Raps*, would have little encouragement to follow their trade.

But the indubitable advantages by having the management in such a society would be, the paying 8 *per cent.* instead of 20, the being sure of the goodness and just weight of the coin, and the period to be put to any further coinage than what was absolutely necessary to supply the wants and desires of the Kingdom: And all this under the security of ten gentlemen of credit, and fortune, who would be ready to give the best security and satisfaction, that they had no design to turn the scheme into a job.

As to any mistakes I have made in computation, they are of little moment; and I shall not descend so low as to justify them against any caviller.

The strongest objection against what I offer, and which

perhaps may make it appear visionary, is the difficulty to find half a score gentlemen, who, out of a publick spirit, will be at the trouble, for no more profit than one *per cent.* above the legal interest, to be overseers of a Mint for five years; and perhaps, without any justice, raise the clamour of the people against them. Besides, it is most certain that many a squire is as fond of a job, and as dextrous to make the best of it, as Mr. Maculla himself, or any of his level. However, I do not doubt, but there may be ten such persons in this town, if they had only some visible mark to know them at sight. Yet I just foresee another inconveniency: That knavish men are fitter to deal with others of their own denomination; while those who are honest and best intentioned, may be the instruments of as much mischief to the publick, for want of cunning, as the greatest knaves; and more, because of the charitable opinion which they are apt to have of others. Therefore, how to join the prudence of the serpent with the innocency of the dove in this affair, is the most difficult point. It is not so hard to find an honest man, as to make this honest man active, and vigilant, and skilful; which I doubt will require a spur of profit greater than my scheme will afford him, unless he will be contented with the honour of serving his country, and the reward of a good conscience.

After reviewing what I had written, I see very well that I have not given any allowance for the first charge of preparing all things necessary for coining, which I am told will amount to about 200*l.* besides 20*l. per annum*, for five years rent of a house to work in.

I can only say, that this making in all but 300*l.* it will be an addition of no more than 3 *per cent.* out of 10,000*l.*

But the great advantages to the publick, by having the coinage placed in the hands of ten gentlemen, such as I have already described (if such are to be found) are these:

First, They propose no other gain to themselves than one *per cent* above the legal interest for the money they advance; which will hardly afford them coffee when they meet at their Mint-house.

Secondly, They bind themselves to make their coins of as good copper, as the best English halfpence; and as well coined, and of equal weight: and do likewise bind themselves to charge the publick with not one farthing for the expence of coinage, more than it shall really stand them in.

Thirdly, They will, for a limited term of seven or ten years, as shall be thought proper upon mature consideration, pay gold and silver, without any defalcation, for all their own coin that shall be returned upon their hands.

Fourthly, They will take care that the coins shall have a deep impression, leaving a rising rim on both sides, to prevent their being defaced in a long time; and the edges shall still be milled.

I suppose they need not be very apprehensive of counterfeits, which will be difficult to make so as not to be discovered: For it is plain that those bad halfpence, called *Raps*, are so easily distinguished, even from the most worn genuine halfpenny, that nobody will now take them for a farthing, although under the great present want of change.

I shall here subjoin some computations relating to Mr. Maculla's copper notes. They were sent to me by a person well skilled in such calculations, and therefore I refer them to the reader, it being a matter wholly out of my trade.

Mr. Maculla charges good copper at fourteen pence *per* pound, but I know not whether he means Avoirdupois, or Troy weight.

Avoirdupois is 16 ounces to a pound, equal to	6960 Grains
A pound Troy weight is — — —	5760 Grains
Mr. Maculla's copper is 14d. *per* pound avoirdupois.	
Two of Maculla's penny-notes, one with another weigh — — — — —	524 Grains
By which computation 2*s*. of his notes, which he sells for a pound weight, will weigh —	6288 Grains
But a pound avoirdupois weighs as above —	6960 Grains
	672

This difference makes ten *per cent*. to Mr. Maculla's profit in point of weight.

The Old Patrick and David halfpenny weighs	149 Grains
Maculla's halfpenny weighs — — —	131 Grains
The difference is — —	18

Which is equal to 10½ *per cent*.

The English halfpenny of King Charles II. weighs — — — — —	167 Grains
Maculla's halfpenny weighs — — —	131 Grains
The difference — —	36

which difference allowed a fifth part, is 20 *per cent*.

Another COMPUTATION.

Mr. Maculla allows his pound of copper (coinage included) to be worth twenty pence for which he demands 2*s*.

His coinage he computes at six pence *per* pound weight.

Therefore, he laying out only twenty pence, and gaining four pence, he makes *per cent*. profit.	20
The six pence *per* pound wt. allowed for coinage, makes *per cent*.	30
The want of weight in his halfpence, compared as above, is *per cent*. — — —	10
By all which, (viz. coinage, profit, and of weight) the publick loses *per cent*. — —	60

If Mr. Maculla's coins will not pass, and he refuses to receive them back, the owner cannot sell them at above twelve pence *per* pound weight; whereby, with the defect of weight of 10 *per cent*. he will lose 60 *per cent*.

The scheme of the society raised as high as it can probably be, will be only thus:

For interest of their money *per cent*.— — — — 8
For coinage, instead of 10, suppose at most *per cent*. — 20
For 300*l*. laid out for tools, a Mint, and house-rent, charge *per cent*. upon the coinage of 10,000*l*. — — 3
Charges in all upon interest, coinage, &c. *per cent*. — — 31

Which, with all the advantages above-mentioned of the goodness of the metal, the largeness of the coin, the deepness and fairness of the impression, the assurance of the society confining itself to such a sum as they undertake, or as the Kingdom shall approve; and lastly, their paying in gold or silver for all their coin returned upon their hands, without any defalcation, would be of mighty benefit to the Kingdom; and with a little steadiness and activity, could, I doubt not, be easily compassed.

I would not in this scheme recommend the method of promissory notes after Mr. Maculla's manner; but, as I have seen in old Irish coins, the words *Civitas Dublin* on one side, with the year of our Lord, and the Irish Harp, on the reverse.

A Modest Proposal

A MODEST
PROPOSAL

For preventing the

CHILDREN

OF

POOR PEOPLE

From being a

𝔅𝔲𝔯𝔱𝔥𝔢𝔫 𝔱𝔬 𝔱𝔥𝔢𝔦𝔯 𝔓𝔞𝔯𝔢𝔫𝔱𝔰,

OR THE

COUNTRY,

AND

For making them Beneficial to the
PUBLICK.

By Dear Swift

DUBLIN:
Printed by *S. Harding*, opposite the *Hand and Pen* near *Fishamble-Street*, on the *Blind Key*.
MDCCXXIX.

Facing Page 109

A MODEST

PROPOSAL

FOR

Preventing the Children of poor People in Ireland, *from being a Burden to their Parents or Country; and for making them beneficial to the Publick.*

Written in the Year 1729

IT is a melancholly Object to those, who walk through this great Town, or travel in the Country; when they see the *Streets*, the *Roads*, and *Cabbin-doors* crowded with *Beggars* of the Female Sex, followed by three, four, or six Children, *all in Rags*, and importuning every Passenger for an Alms. These *Mothers*, instead of being able to work for their honest Livelyhood, are forced to employ all their Time in stroling to beg Sustenance for their *helpless Infants*; who, as they grow up, either turn *Thieves* for want of Work; or leave their *dear Native Country, to fight for the Pretender in* Spain, or sell themselves to the *Barbadoes*.

I THINK it is agreed by all Parties, that this prodigious Number of Children in the Arms, or on the Backs, or at the *Heels* of their *Mothers*, and frequently of their *Fathers*, is *in the present deplorable State of the Kingdom*, a very great additional Grievance; and therefore, whoever could find out a fair, cheap, and easy Method of making these Children sound and useful Members of the Commonwealth, would deserve so well of the Publick, as to have his Statue set up for a Preserver of the Nation.

BUT my Intention is very far from being confined to provide only for the Children of *professed Beggars*: It is of a much greater

Extent, and shall take in the whole Number of Infants at a certain Age, who are born of Parents, in effect as little able to support them, as those who demand our Charity in the Streets.

As to my own Part, having turned my Thoughts for many Years, upon this important Subject, and maturely weighed the several *Schemes of other Projectors*, I have always found them grosly mistaken in their Computation. It is true a Child, *just dropt from its Dam*, may be supported by her Milk, for a Solar Year with little other Nourishment; at most not above the Value of two Shillings; which the Mother may certainly get, or the Value in *Scraps*, by her lawful Occupation of *Begging*: And, it is exactly at one Year old, that I propose to provide for them in such a Manner, as, instead of being a Charge upon their *Parents*, or the *Parish*, or *wanting Food and Raiment* for the rest of their Lives; they shall, on the contrary, contribute to the Feeding, and partly to the Cloathing, of many Thousands.

THERE is likewise another great Advantage in my *Scheme*, that it will prevent those *voluntary Abortions*, and that horrid Practice of *Women murdering their Bastard Children*; alas! too frequent among us; sacrificing the *poor innocent Babes*, I doubt, more to avoid the Expence than the Shame; which would move Tears and Pity in the most Savage and inhuman Breast.

THE Number of Souls in *Ireland* being usually reckoned one Million and a half; of these I calculate there may be about Two hundred Thousand Couple whose Wives are Breeders; from which Number I subtract thirty thousand Couples, who are able to maintain their own Children; although I apprehend there cannot be so many, under *the present Distresses of the Kingdom*; but this being granted, there will remain an Hundred and Seventy Thousand Breeders. I again subtract Fifty Thousand, for those Women who miscarry, or whose Children die by Accident, or Disease, within the Year. There only remain an Hundred and Twenty Thousand Children of poor Parents, annually born: The Question therefore is, How this Number shall be reared, and provided for? Which, as I have already said, under the present Situation of Affairs, is utterly impossible, by all the Methods hitherto proposed: For we can *neither employ them in Handicraft* or *Agriculture*; we neither build Houses, (I mean in the Country) nor cultivate Land: They can very seldom pick up a Livelyhood *by Stealing* until they arrive at six Years old; except where they are of towardly Parts; although, I confess, they learn the Rudiments much earlier; during which Time, they can, however, be properly looked upon only as *Probationers*; as I have been informed by a principal Gentleman in the County of *Cavan*, who protested to me, that he never knew above one or two Instances under the Age of six, even in a Part of the Kingdom *so renowned for the quickest Proficiency in that Art.*

I AM assured by our Merchants, that a Boy or a Girl before twelve Years old, is no saleable Commodity; and even when they come to this Age, they will not yield above Three Pounds, or Three Pounds and half a Crown at most, on the Exchange; which cannot turn to Account either to the Parents or the Kingdom; the Charge of Nutriment and Rags, having been at least four Times that Value.

I SHALL now therefore humbly propose my own Thoughts; which I hope will not be liable to the least Objection.

I HAVE been assured by a very knowing *American* of my Acquaintance in *London*; that a young healthy Child, well nursed, is, at a Year old, a most delicious, nourishing, and wholesome Food; whether *Stewed, Roasted, Baked,* or *Boiled*; and, I make no doubt, that it will equally serve in a *Fricasie*, or *Ragoust.*

I DO therefore humbly offer it to *publick Consideration*, that of the Hundred and Twenty Thousand Children, already computed, Twenty thousand may be reserved for Breed; whereof only one Fourth Part to be Males; which is more than we allow to *Sheep, black Cattle,* or *Swine*; and my Reason is, that these Children are seldom the Fruits of Marriage, *a Circumstance not much regarded by our Savages*; therefore, *one Male* will be sufficient to serve *four Females*. That the remaining Hundred thousand, may, at a Year old, be offered in Sale to the *Persons of Quality* and *Fortune*, through the Kingdom; always advising the Mother to let them suck plentifully in the last Month, so as to render them plump, and fat for a good

Table. A Child will make two Dishes at an Entertainment for Friends; and when the Family dines alone, the fore or hind Quarter will make a reasonable Dish; and seasoned with a little Pepper or Salt, will be very good Boiled on the fourth Day, especially in *Winter*.

I HAVE reckoned upon a Medium, that a Child just born will weigh Twelve Pounds; and in a solar Year, if tolerably nursed, encreaseth to twenty eight Pounds.

I GRANT this Food will be somewhat dear, and therefore very *proper for Landlords*; who, as they have already devoured most of the Parents, seem to have the best Title to the Children.

INFANTS Flesh will be in Season throughout the Year; but more plentiful in *March*, and a little before and after: For we are told by a grave * Author, an eminent *French* Physician, that *Fish being a prolifick Dyet*, there are more Children born in *Roman Catholick Countries* about Nine Months after *Lent*, than at any other Season: Therefore reckoning a Year after *Lent*, the Markets will be more glutted than usual; because the Number of *Popish Infants*, is, at least, three to one in this Kingdom; and therefore it will have one other Collateral Advantage, by lessening the Number of *Papists* among us.

I HAVE already computed the Charge of nursing a Beggar's Child (in which List I reckon all *Cottagers*, *Labourers*, and Four fifths of the *Farmers*) to be about two Shillings *per Annum*, Rags included; and I believe, no Gentleman would repine to give Ten Shillings for the *Carcase of a good fat Child*; which, as I have said, will make four Dishes of excellent nutritive Meat, when he hath only some particular Friend, or his own Family, to dine with him. Thus the Squire will learn to be a good Landlord, and grow popular among his Tenants; the Mother will have Eight Shillings net Profit, and be fit for Work until she produceth another Child.

THOSE who are more thrifty (*as I must confess the Times require*) may flay the Carcase; the Skin of which, artificially dressed, will make admirable *Gloves for Ladies*, and *Summer Boots for fine Gentlemen*.

As to our City of *Dublin*; Shambles may be appointed for

* Rabelais.

this Purpose, in the most convenient Parts of it; and Butchers we may be assured will not be wanting; although I rather recommend buying the Children alive, and dressing them hot from the Knife, as we do *roasting Pigs*.

A very worthy Person, *a true Lover of his Country*, and whose Virtues I highly esteem, was lately pleased, in discoursing on this Matter, to offer a Refinement upon my Scheme. He said, that many Gentlemen of this Kingdom, having of late destroyed their Deer; he conceived, that the Want of Venison might be well supplied by the Bodies of young Lads and Maidens, not exceeding fourteen Years of Age, nor under twelve; so great a Number of both Sexes in every County being now ready to starve, for Want of Work and Service: And these to be disposed of by their Parents, if alive, or otherwise by their nearest Relations. But with due Deference to so excellent a Friend, and so deserving a Patriot, I cannot be altogether in his Sentiments. For as to the Males, my *American* Acquaintance assured me from frequent Experience, that their Flesh was generally tough and lean, like that of our School-boys, by continual Exercise, and their Taste disagreeable; and to fatten them would not answer the Charge. Then, as to the Females, it would, I think, with humble Submission, *be a Loss to the Publick*, because they soon would become Breeders themselves: And besides it is not improbable, that some scrupulous People might be apt to censure such a Practice (although indeed very unjustly) as a little bordering upon Cruelty; which, I confess, hath always been with me the strongest Objection against any Project, how well soever intended.

But in order to justify my Friend; he confessed, that this Expedient was put into his Head by the famous *Salmanaazor*, a Native of the Island *Formosa*, who came from thence to *London*, above twenty Years ago, and in Conversation told my Friend, that in his Country, when any young Person happened to be put to Death, the Executioner sold the Carcase to *Persons of Quality*, as a prime Dainty; and that, in his Time, the Body of a plump Girl of fifteen, who was crucified for an Attempt to poison the Emperor, was sold to his Imperial

L

Majesty's prime Minister of State, and other great *Mandarins* of the Court, *in Joints from the Gibbet*, at Four hundred Crowns. Neither indeed can I deny, that if the same Use were made of several plump young girls in this Town, who, without one single Groat to their Fortunes, cannot stir Abroad without a Chair, and appear at the *Play-house*, and *Assemblies* in foreign Fineries, which they never will pay for; the Kingdom would not be the worse.

SOME Persons of a desponding Spirit are in great Concern about that vast Number of poor People, who are Aged, Diseased, or Maimed; and I have been desired to employ my Thoughts what Course may be taken, to ease the Nation of so grievous an Incumbrance. But I am not in the least Pain upon that Matter; because it is very well known, that they are every Day *dying*, and *rotting*, by *Cold* and *Famine*, and *Filth*, and *Vermin*, as fast as can be reasonably expected. And as to the younger Labourers, they are now in almost as hopeful a Condition: They cannot get Work, and consequently pine away for Want of Nourishment, to a Degree, that if at any Time they are accidentally hired to common Labour, they have not Strength to perform it; and thus the Country, and themselves, are in a fair Way of being soon delivered from the Evils to come.

I HAVE too long digressed; and therefore shall return to my Subject. I think the Advantages by the Proposal which I have made, are obvious, and many, as well as of the highest Importance.

FOR, *First*, as I have already observed, it would greatly lessen the *Number of Papists*, with whom we are yearly over-run; being the principal Breeders of the Nation, as well as our most dangerous Enemies; and who stay at home on Purpose, with a Design to *deliver the Kingdom to the Pretender*; hoping to take their Advantage by the Absence *of so many good Protestants*, who have chosen rather to leave their Country, than stay at home, and pay Tithes against their Conscience, to an idolatrous *Episcopal Curate*.

SECONDLY, The poorer Tenants will have something valuable of their own, which, by Law, may be made liable to

Distress, and help to pay their Landlord's Rent; their Corn and Cattle being already seized, and *Money a Thing unknown*.

THIRDLY, Whereas the Maintenance of an Hundred Thousand Children, from two Years old, and upwards, cannot be computed at less than ten Shillings a Piece *per Annum*, the Nation's Stock will be thereby encreased Fifty Thousand Pounds *per Annum*; besides the Profit of a new Dish, introduced to the Tables of all *Gentlemen of Fortune* in the Kingdom, who have any Refinement in Taste; and the Money will circulate among ourselves, the Goods being entirely of our own Growth and Manufacture.

FOURTHLY, The constant Breeders, besides the Gain of Eight Shillings *Sterling per Annum*, by the Sale of their Children, will be rid of the Charge of maintaining them after the first Year.

FIFTHLY, This Food would likewise bring great *Custom to Taverns*, where the Vintners will certainly be so prudent, as to procure the best Receipts for dressing it to Perfection; and consequently, have their Houses frequented by all the *fine Gentlemen*, who justly value themselves upon their Knowledge in good Eating; and a skilful Cook, who understands how to oblige his Guests, will contrive to make it as expensive as they please.

SIXTHLY, This would be a great Inducement to Marriage, which all wise Nations have either encouraged by Rewards, or enforced by Laws and Penalties. It would encrease the Care and Tenderness of Mothers towards their Children, when they were sure of a Settlement for Life, to the poor Babes, provided in some Sort by the Publick, to their annual Profit instead of Expence. We should soon see an honest Emulation among the married Women, *which of them could bring the fattest Child to the Market*. Men would become as *fond* of their Wives, during the Time of their Pregnancy, as they are now of their *Mares* in Foal, their *Cows* in Calf, or *Sows* when they are ready to farrow; nor offer to beat or kick them, (as it is too *frequent* a Practice) for fear of a Miscarriage.

MANY other Advantages might be enumerated. For instance, the Addition of some Thousand Carcasses in our

Exportation of barrelled Beef: The Propagation of *Swines Flesh*, and Improvement in the Art of making good *Bacon*; so much wanted among us by the great Destruction of *Pigs*, too frequent at our Tables, and are no way comparable in Taste, or Magnificence, to a well-grown fat yearling Child; which, roasted whole, will make a considerable Figure at a *Lord Mayor's Feast*, or any other publick Entertainment. But this, and many others, I omit; being studious of Brevity.

Supposing that one Thousand Families in this City, would be constant Customers for Infants Flesh; besides others who might have it at *merry Meetings*, particularly *Weddings* and *Christenings*; I compute that *Dublin* would take off, annually, about Twenty Thousand Carcasses; and the rest of the Kingdom (where probably they will be sold somewhat cheaper) the remaining Eighty Thousand.

I can think of no one Objection, that will possibly be raised against this Proposal; unless it should be urged, that the Number of People will be thereby much lessened in the Kingdom. This I freely own; and it was indeed one principal Design in offering it to the World. I desire the Reader will observe, that I calculate my Remedy *for this one individual Kingdom of* Ireland, *and for no other that ever was, is, or I think ever can be upon Earth.* Therefore, let no man talk to me of other Expedients: *Of taxing our Absentees at five Shillings a Pound: Of using neither Cloaths, nor Houshold Furniture except what is of our own Growth and Manufacture: Of utterly rejecting the Materials and Instruments that promote foreign Luxury: Of curing the Expensiveness of Pride, Vanity, Idleness, and Gaming in our Women: Of introducing a Vein of Parsimony, Prudence and Temperance: Of learning to love our Country, wherein we differ even from* Laplanders, *and the Inhabitants of* Topinamboo: *Of quitting our Animosities, and Factions; nor act any longer like the* Jews, *who were murdering one another at the very Moment their City was taken: Of being a little cautious not to sell our Country and Consciences for nothing: Of teaching Landlords to have, at least, one Degree of Mercy towards their Tenants.* Lastly, *Of putting a Spirit of Honesty, Industry, and Skill into our Shop-keepers; who, if a Resolution could now be taken to buy only our native Goods, would immediately unite to cheat and exact upon us in the Price, the Measure, and the Goodness; nor could ever yet be brought to make one fair Proposal of just Dealing, though often and earnestly invited to it.*

THEREFORE I repeat, let no Man talk to me of these and the like Expedients; till he hath, at least, a Glimpse of Hope, that there will ever be some hearty and sincere Attempt to put *them in Practice.*

BUT, as to my self; having been wearied out for many Years with offering vain, idle, visionary Thoughts; and at length utterly despairing of Success, I fortunately fell upon this Proposal; which, as it is wholly new, so it hath something *solid* and *real*, of no Expence, and little Trouble, full in our own Power; and whereby we can incur no Danger in *disobliging* ENGLAND: For, this Kind of Commodity will not bear Exportation; the Flesh being of too tender a Consistence, to admit a long Continuance in Salt; *although, perhaps, I could name a Country, which would be glad to eat up our whole Nation without it.*

AFTER all, I am not so violently bent upon my own Opinion, as to reject any Offer proposed by wise Men, which shall be found equally innocent, cheap, easy, and effectual. But before something of that Kind shall be advanced, in Contradiction to my Scheme, and offering a better; I desire the Author, or Authors, will be pleased maturely to consider two Points. *First*, As Things now stand, how they will be able to find Food and Raiment, for a Hundred Thousand useless Mouths and Backs? And *secondly*, There being a round Million of Creatures in human Figure, throughout this Kingdom; whose whole Subsistence, put into a common Stock, would leave them in Debt two Millions of Pounds *Sterling*; adding those, who are Beggars by Profession, to the Bulk of Farmers, Cottagers, and Labourers, with their Wives and Children, who are Beggars in Effect; I desire those Politicians, who dislike my Overture, and may perhaps be so bold to attempt an Answer, that they will first ask the Parents of these Mortals, Whether they would not, at this Day, think it a great Happiness to have been sold for Food at a Year old, in the Manner I prescribe; and thereby have avoided such a perpetual Scene of Misfortunes, as they have since gone through; by the *Oppres-*

sion of Landlords; the Impossibility of paying Rent, without Money or Trade; the Want of common Sustenance, with neither House nor Cloaths, to cover them from the Inclemencies of Weather; and the most inevitable Prospect of intailing the like, or greater Miseries upon their Breed for ever.

I PROFESS, in the Sincerity of my Heart, that I have not the least personal Interest, in endeavouring to promote this necessary Work; having no other Motive than the *publick Good of my Country, by advancing our Trade, providing for Infants, relieving the Poor, and giving some Pleasure to the Rich*. I have no Children, by which I can propose to get a single Penny; the youngest being nine Years old, and my Wife past Child-bearing.

A Proposal

that all the Ladies and Women of Ireland should
appear constantly in Irish Manufactures

A

PROPOSAL

THAT

All the Ladies and Women of Ireland should appear constantly
in Irish Manufactures.

Written in the Year 1729.

THERE was a treatise written about nine years ago to persuade the people of Ireland to wear their own manufactures.* This treatise was allowed to have not one syllable in it of party or disaffection, but was wholly founded upon the growing poverty of the nation, occasioned by the utter want of trade in every branch, except that ruinous importation of all foreign extravagancies from other countries. This treatise was presented, by the Grand-jury of the city and county of Dublin, as a scandalous, seditious, and factious pamphlet. I forget who was the foreman of the city Grand-jury, but the foreman for the county was one Doctor Seal, register to the Archbishop of Dublin, wherein he differed much from the sentiments of his Lord. The Printer was tried before the late Mr. Whitshed, that famous Lord Chief-Justice; who, on the bench, laying his hand on his heart, declared upon his salvation that the Author was a Jacobite, and had a design to beget a quarrel between the two nations. In the midst of this prosecution, about 1500 weavers were forced to beg their bread, and had a general contribution made for their relief, which just served to make them drunk for a week; and then they were forced to turn rogues, or strolling beggars, or to leave the kingdom.

* See Vol. ix, p. 13.

The Duke of Grafton, who was then Lieutenant, being perfectly ashamed of so infamous and unpopular a proceeding, obtained from England a *noli prosequi* for the Printer. Yet the Grand-jury had solemn thanks given them from the Secretary of State.

I mention this passage (perhaps too much forgotten) to shew how dangerous it hath been for the best meaning person to write one syllable in the defence of his country, or discover the miserable condition it is in.

And, to prove this truth, I will produce one instance more; wholly omitting the famous case of the Drapier, and the proclamation against him, as well as the perverseness of another jury against the same Mr. Whitshed, who was violently bent to act the second part in another scene.

About two years ago there was a small paper printed, which was called *A Short View of the State of Ireland,** relating the several causes whereby any country may grow rich, and applying them to Ireland. Whitshed was dead, and consequently the printer was not troubled. Mist, the famous journalist, happened to reprint this paper in London, for which his press-folks were prosecuted for almost a twelvemonth; and, for ought I know, are not yet discharged.

This is our case; insomuch, that, although I am often without money in my pocket, I dare not own it in some company, for fear of being thought disaffected.

But since I am determined to take care, that the author of this paper shall not be discovered, (following herein the most prudent practice of the Drapier) I will venture to affirm, that the three seasons wherein our corn hath miscarried, did no more contribute to our present misery, than one spoonful of water thrown upon a rat already drowned would contribute to his death; and that the present plentiful harvest, although it should be followed by a dozen ensuing, would no more restore us, than it would the rat aforesaid to put him near the fire, which might indeed warm his fur-coat, but never bring him back to life.

The short of the matter is this: The distresses of the

* See above, p. 1.

kingdom are operating more and more every day, by very large degrees, and so have been doing for above a dozen years past.

If you demand from whence these distresses have arisen, I desire to ask the following question.

If two thirds of any kingdom's revenue be exported to another country, without one farthing of value in return, and if the said kingdom be forbidden the most profitable branches of trade wherein to employ the other third, and only allowed to traffic in importing those commodities which are most ruinous to itself, how shall that kingdom stand?

If this question were formed into the first proposition of an hypothetical syllogism, I defy the man born in Ireland, who is now in the fairest way of getting a collectorship, or a cornet's post, to give a good reason for denying it.

Let me put another case. Suppose a gentleman's estate of 200*l.* a year should sink to one hundred, by some accident, whether by an earthquake or inundation it matters not, and suppose the said gentleman utterly hopeless and unqualified ever to retrieve the loss; how is he otherwise to proceed in his future oeconomy, than by reducing it on every article to one half less, unless he will be content to fly his country, or rot in jail? This is a representation of Ireland's condition, only with one fault, that it is a little too favourable. Neither am I able to propose a full remedy for this, that shall ever be granted, but only a small prolongation of life, until God shall miraculously dispose the hearts of our neighbours, our kinsmen, our fellow protestants, fellow subjects, and fellow rational creatures, to permit us to starve without running further in debt. I am informed that our national debt (and God knows how we wretches came by that fashionable thing a national debt) is about 250,000*l*; which is, at least, one third of the whole kingdom's rents, after our absentees and other foreign drains are paid, and about 50,000*l.* more than all the cash.

It seems there are several schemes for raising a fund to pay the interest of this formidable sun, (not the principal, for this is allowed impossible). The necessity of raising such a fund is strongly and regularly pleaded from the late deficiencies in the duties and customs. And is it the fault of Ireland that these funds are deficient? If they depend on trade, can it possibly be otherwise, while we have neither liberty to trade, nor money to trade with; neither hands to work, nor business to employ them, if we had? Our diseases are visible enough, both in their causes and effects; and the cures are well known, but impossible to be applied.

If my steward comes and tells me, that my rents are sunk so low that they are very little more than sufficient to pay my servants their wages, have I any other course left, than to cashier four in six of my rascally footmen, and a number of other varlets in my family, of whose insolence the whole neighbourhood complains. And I should think it extremely severe in any law, to force me to maintain a household of fifty servants, and fix their wages, before I had offered my rent-roll upon oath to the legislators.

To return from digressing: I am told one scheme for raising a fund to pay the interest of our national debt, is by a further duty of forty shillings a ton upon wine. Some gentlemen would carry this matter much further by raising it to twelve pounds; which, in a manner, would amount to a prohibition. Thus weakly arguing from the practice of England.

I have often taken notice, both in print and in discourse, that there is no topic so fallacious, either in talk or in writing, as to argue how we ought to act in Ireland from the example of England, Holland, France, or any other country, whose inhabitants are allowed the common rights and liberties of humankind. I could undertake to name six or seven of the most uncontrolled maxims in government, which are utterly false in this kingdom.

As to the additional duty on wine, I think any person may deliver his opinion upon it, until it shall have passed into a law; and, till then, I declare mine to be positively against it.

First, because there is no nation yet known, in either hemisphere, where the people of all conditions are more in want of some cordial, to keep up their spirits, than in this of ours. I am not in jest; and, if the fact will not be allowed me, I shall not argue it.

Secondly, It is too well and generally known, that this tax of forty shillings additional on every ton of wine (which will be double at least to the home-consumer) will increase equally every new session of parliament, until perhaps it comes to twelve pounds.

Thirdly, Because, as the merchants inform me, and as I have known many the like instances in England, this additional tax will more probably lessen this branch of the revenue, than encrease it. And therefore Sir John Stanley, a commissioner of the customs, in England, used to say, That the House of Commons were generally mistaken in matters of trade, by an erroneous opinion that two and two make four. Thus, if you should lay an additional duty of one penny a pound on raisins, or sugar, the revenue, instead of rising, would certainly sink; and the consequence would only be, to lessen the number of plum-puddings, and ruin the confectioner.

Fourthly, I am likewise assured by merchants, that, upon this additional forty shillings, the French will at least equally raise their duties upon all commodities we export thither.

Fifthly, If an original extract of the exports and imports be true, we have been gainers upon the balance by our trade with France for several years past; and, although our gain amounts to no great sum, we ought to be satisfied, since we are no losers, with the only consolation we are capable of receiving.

Lastly, The worst consequence is behind. If we raise the duty on wine to a considerable height, we lose the only hold we have of keeping among us the few gentlemen of any tolerable estates. I am confident, there is hardly a gentleman of eight hundred pounds a year and upwards, in this kingdom, who would balance half an hour to consider whether he should live here or in England, if a family could be as cheaply maintained in the one as the other. As to eatables, they are as cheap in many fine counties of England, as in some very indifferent ones here; or, if there be any difference, that vein of thrift, and prudence in oeconomy, which passes there without reproach, (and chiefly in London itself) would amply make up the difference. But the article of French wine is hardly tolerable, in any degree of plenty, to a middling fortune: And this is it which, by growing habitual, wholly turns the scale with those few landed men disengaged from employments, who content themselves to live hospitably with plenty of good wine in their own country, rather than in penury and obscurity in another, with bad, or with none at all.

Having therefore, as far as in me lies, abolished this additional duty upon wine; for I am not under the least concern about paying the interest of the national debt, but leave it, as in loyalty bound, wholly to the wisdom of the Honourable House of Commons: I come now to consider by what methods we may be able to put off, and delay our utter undoing as long as it is possible.

I never have discoursed any reasonable man upon this subject, who did not allow that there was no remedy left us, but to lessen the importation of all unnecessary commodities, as much as it was possible; and likewise, either to persuade our absentees to spend their money at home, which is impossible, or tax them at five shillings in the pound during their absence, with such allowances, upon necessary occasions, as it shall be thought convenient; or, by permitting us a free trade, which is denied to no other nation upon earth. The three last methods are treated by Mr. Prior, in his most useful treatise, added to his list of absentees.

It is to gratify the vanity and pride, and luxury of the women, and of the young fops who admire them, that we owe this insupportable grievance of bringing in the instruments of our ruin. There is annually brought over to this kingdom near ninety thousand pounds worth of silk, whereof the greater part is manufactured: Thirty thousand pounds more is expended in muslin, holland, cambric, and callico. What the price of lace amounts to, is not easy to be collected from the custom-house book, being a kind of goods that takes up little room, and is easily run; but, considering the prodigious price of a woman's head-dress, at ten, twelve, twenty pounds a yard, must be very great. The tea, rated at seven shillings *per* pound, comes to near twelve thousand pounds; but, considering it as the common luxury of every chambermaid, sempstress, and tradesman's wife, both in town and country, however they come by it, must needs cost the kingdom double that sum. Coffee is somewhat above 7000*l*. I have seen no account of chocolate, and some other Indian or American goods. The drapery imported is about 24,000*l*. The whole amounts (with one or two other particulars) to 150,000*l*. The lavishing of all which money is just as prudent and necessary, as to see a man in an embroidered coat begging out of Newgate in an old shoe.

I allow that the thrown and raw silk is less pernicious; because we have some share in the manufacture; but we are not now in circumstances to trifle. It costs us above 40,000*l*. a year: And if the ladies, till better times, will not be content to go in their own country shifts, I wish they may go in rags. Let them vie with each other in the fineness of their native linen: Their beauty and gentleness will as well appear, as if they were covered over with diamonds and brocade.

I believe no man is so weak, as to hope or expect that such a reformation can be brought about by a law. But a thorough, hearty, unanimous vote, in both Houses of Parliament, might perhaps answer as well: Every senator, noble or plebeian, giving his honour, that neither himself, nor any of his family, would, in their dress or furniture of their houses, make use of any thing except what was of the growth and manufacture of this kingdom; and that they would use the utmost of their power, influence and credit, to prevail on their tenants, dependants, and friends, to follow their example.

Maxims controlled in Ireland

Maxims examined.

Decrease of things necessary to Life.   X

Lowness of Interest   X

High purchase of Land.   X

Building ???? to the Metropolis   X

People the Riches of a Nation.   X

Tax per Luxury.

   Rex nolunt diu male administrari

Parliament not minding any thing printed, tis but a Pamphlet
Folly of those who ~~argue~~ from England, told. To
~~Whom~~ wider or ~~~~ ??? Con, that Society is a good
thing. ~~'Tis ~~~~~~ ~~~~~~ they need learn to have
Accidental aid unexpected impediments
To ~~~~ ~~legislate~~ that from a Science to the
~~~~ of ~~Nation~~, and upon the Principle that man being
essentially Creature, they apt to go into Councils &c
Parliament not needing Pamphlets, made me write this
when all was over, that they may judge from effects

MAXIMS

CONTROLLED

IN IRELAND.

*The Truth of some Maxims in State and Government, examined
with reference to Ireland.*

THERE are certain Maxims of State, founded upon long
observation and experience, drawn from the constant
practice of the wisest nations, and from the very principles of government, nor ever controlled by any writer upon
politics. Yet all these Maxims do necessarily pre-suppose a
kingdom, or commonwealth, to have the same natural rights
common to the rest of mankind who have entered into civil
society. For, if we could conceive a nation where each of the
inhabitants had but one eye, one leg, and one hand, it is plain
that, before you could institute them into a republic, an
allowance must be made for those material defects, wherein
they differed from other mortals. Or, imagine a legislator
forming a system for the government of Bedlam, and, proceeding upon the maxim that man is a sociable animal, should
draw them out of their cells, and form them into corporations
or general assemblies; the consequence might probably be,
that they would fall foul on each other, or burn the house
over their own heads.

Of the like nature are innumerable errors, committed by
crude and short thinkers, who reason upon general topics,
without the least allowance for the most important circumstances, which quite alter the nature of the case.

This hath been the fate of those small dealers, who are
every day publishing their thoughts either on paper or in their
assemblies for improving the trade of Ireland, and referring
us to the practice and example of England, Holland, France,
or other nations.

I shall therefore examine certain Maxims of government, which generally pass for uncontrolled in the world, and consider how far they will suit with the present condition of this kingdom.

First, it is affirmed by wise men, that the dearness of things necessary for life, in a fruitful country, is a certain sign of wealth and great commerce; For, when such necessaries are dear, it must absolutely follow that money is cheap and plentiful.

But this is manifestly false in Ireland, for the following reason. Some years ago, the species of money here, did probably amount to six or seven hundred thousand pounds; and I have good cause to believe, that our remittances then did not much exceed the cash brought in to us. But the prodigious discouragements we have since received in every branch of our trade, by the frequent enforcements, and rigorous execution of the navigation-act, the tyranny of under customhouse officers, the yearly addition of absentees, the payments to regiments abroad, to civil and military officers residing in England, the unexpected sudden demands of great sums from the treasury, and some other drains of perhaps as great consequence, we now see ourselves reduced to a state (since we have no friends) of being pitied by our enemies, at least, if our enemies were of such a kind as to be capable of any regards towards us, except of hatred and contempt.

Forty years are now passed since the Revolution, when the contention of the British empire was, most unfortunately for us, and altogether against the usual course of such mighty changes in government, decided in the least important nation, but with such ravages and ruin executed on both sides, as to leave the kingdom a desert, which, in some sort, it still continues. Neither did the long rebellions in 1641 make half such a destruction of houses, plantations, and personal wealth, in both kingdoms, as two years campaigns did in ours, by fighting England's battles.

By slow degrees, and by the gentle treatment we received under two auspicious reigns, we grew able to live without running in debt. Our absentees were but few, we had great indulgence in trade, a considerable share in employments of church and state; and, while the short leases continued, which were let some years after the war ended, tenants paid their rents with ease and chearfulness, to the great regret of their landlords, who had taken up a spirit of oppression that is not easily removed. And although in these short leases, the rent was gradually to encrease after short periods; yet, as soon as the term elapsed, the land was let to the highest bidder, most commonly without the least effectual clause for building or planting. Yet by many advantages, which this island then possessed, and hath since utterly lost, the rents of lands still grew higher upon every lease that expired, until they have arrived at the present exorbitance; when the frog, over-swelling himself, burst at last.

With the price of land, of necessity rose that of corn and cattle, and all other commodities that farmers deal in: Hence likewise, obviously, the rates of all goods and manufactures among shopkeepers, the wages of servants, and hire of labourers. But, although our miseries came on fast with neither trade nor money left, yet neither will the landlord abate in his rent, nor can the tenant abate in the price of what that rent must be paid with, nor any shopkeeper, tradesman, or labourer live at lower expence, for food and clothing, than he did before.

I have been the larger upon this first head, because the same observations will clear up and strengthen a good deal of what I shall affirm upon the rest.

The second Maxim of those who reason upon trade and government, is to assert, that low interest is a certain sign of great plenty of money in a nation, for which, as in many other articles, they produce the examples of Holland and England. But, with relation to Ireland, this Maxim is likewise entirely false.

There are two reasons for the lowness of interest in any country. First, that which is usually alledged, the great plenty of species; and this is obvious. The second is the want of trade, which seldom falls under common observation, although it be equally true. For, where trade is altogether discouraged, there are few borrowers. In those countries where men can employ a large stock, the young merchant, whose fortune may be four or five hundred pounds, will venture to borrow as much more, and can afford a reasonable interest. Neither is it easy at this day to find many of those, whose business reaches to employ even so inconsiderable a sum, except among the importers of wine; who, as they have most part of the present trade in these parts of Ireland in their hands, so they are the most exorbitant, exacting, fraudulent dealers, that ever trafficked in any nation, and are making all possible speed to ruin both themselves and the nation.

From this defect, of gentlemen's not knowing how to dispose of their ready money, ariseth the high purchase of lands, which in all other countries is reckoned a sign of wealth. For, the frugal squires, who live below their incomes, have no other way to dispose of their savings but by mortgage or purchase, by which the rates of land must naturally encrease; and, if this trade continues long under the uncertainty of rents, the landed men of ready money will find it more for their advantage to send their cash to England, and place it in the funds; which I myself am determined to do, the first considerable sum I shall be master of.

It hath likewise been a Maxim among politicians, that the great encrease of buildings in the metropolis argues a flourishing state. But this, I confess, hath been controlled from the example of London; where, by the long and annual parliamentary sessions, such a number of senators, with their families, friends, adherents, and expectants, draw such prodigious numbers to that city, that the old hospitable custom of lords and gentlemen living in their antient seats, among their tenants, is almost lost in England; is laughed out of doors; insomuch that, in the middle of summer, a legal House of Lords and Commons might be brought in a few hours to London from their country villas within twelve miles round.

The case in Ireland is yet somewhat worse: For the absentees of great estates, who, if they lived at home, would have many rich retainers in their neighbourhoods, having learned to rack their lands, and shorten their leases, as much as any residing squire; and the few remaining of these latter, having some vain hope of employments for themselves or their children, and discouraged by the beggarliness and thievery of their own miserable farmers and cottagers, or seduced by the vanity of their wives, on pretence of their children's education, (whereof the fruits are so apparant) together with that most wonderful and yet more unaccountable zeal for a seat in their assembly, though at some years purchase of their whole estates. These and some other motives better let pass, have drawn such a concourse to this beggarly city, that the dealers of the several branches of building have found out all the commodious and inviting places for erecting new houses, while fifteen hundred of the old ones, which is a seventh part of the whole city, are said to be left uninhabited, and falling to ruin. Their method is the same with that which was first introduced by Doctor Barebone at London, who died a bankrupt. The mason, the bricklayer, the carpenter, the slater, and the glazier, take a lot of ground, club to build one or more houses, unite their credit, their stock, and their money, and when their work is finished, sell it to the best advantage they can. But, as it often happens, and more every day, that their fund will not answer half their design, they are forced to undersell it at the first story, and are all reduced to beggary. Insomuch, that I know a certain fanatic brewer*, who is reported to have some hundreds of houses in this town, is said to have purchased the greater part of them at half value from ruined undertakers, hath intelligence of all new houses where the finishing is at a stand, takes advantage of the builder's distress, and, by the advantage of ready money, gets fifty *per cent.* at least for his bargain.

It is another undisputed Maxim in government, that people are the riches of a nation; which is so universally granted, that it will be hardly pardonable to bring it in doubt. And I will grant it to be so far true, even in this island, that, if we had the African custom or privilege, of selling our useless bodies for slaves to foreigners, it would be the most useful branch of our trade, by ridding us of a most unsupportable

* Leeson.

burthen, and bringing us money in the stead. But, in our present situation, at least five children in six who are born lie a dead weight upon us for the want of employment. And a very skilful computer assured me, that above one half of the souls in this kingdom supported themselves by begging and thievery, whereof two thirds would be able to get their bread in any other country upon earth. Trade is the only incitement to labour: where that fails, the poorer native must either beg, steal, or starve, or be forced to quit his country. This hath made me often wish, for some years past, that, instead of discouraging our people from seeking foreign soil, the public would rather pay for transporting all our unnecessary mortals, whether Papists or Protestants, to America, as drawbacks are sometimes allowed for exporting commodities where a nation is over-stocked. I confess myself to be touched with a very sensible pleasure, when I hear of a mortality in any country-parish or village, where the wretches are forced to pay for a filthy cabin and two ridges of potatoes treble the worth, brought up to steal or beg, for want of work, to whom death would be the best thing to be wished for, on account both of themselves and the public.

Among all taxes imposed by the legislature, those upon luxury are universally allowed to be the most equitable and beneficial to the subject; and the commonest reasoner on government might fill a volume with arguments on the subject. Yet here again, by the singular fate of Ireland, this maxim is utterly false; and the putting it in practice may have such a pernicious consequence, as I certainly believe the thoughts of the proposers were not able to reach.

The miseries we suffer by our absentees are of a far more extensive nature than seems to be commonly understood. I must vindicate myself to the reader so far, as to declare solemnly that what I shall say of those lords and squires, doth not arise from the least regard I have for their understandings, their virtues, or their persons. For, although I have not the honour of the least acquaintance with any one among them, (my ambition not soaring so high) yet I am too good a witness of the situation they have been in for thirty years past, the veneration paid them by the people, the high esteem they are in among the prime nobility and gentry, the particular marks of favour and distinction they receive from the court: The weight and consequence of their interest, added to their great zeal and application for preventing any hardships their country might suffer from England, wisely considering that their own fortunes and honours were embarked in the same bottom.

Advertisement by Dr. Swift, in his Defence against Joshua, Lord Allen

ADVERTISEMENT BY DR. SWIFT, IN HIS DEFENCE AGAINST JOSHUA, LORD ALLEN

'WHEREAS Dr. Jonathan Swift, Dean of St. Patrick's, Dublin, hath been credibly informed, that on Friday the 13th of this instant February a certain person did, in a public place and in the hearing of a great number, apply himself to the Right Honourable the Lord Mayor of this city, and some of his brethren, in the following reproachful manner: "My lord, you and your city can squander away the public money, in giving a gold box to a fellow who hath libelled the government!" or words to that effect.

'Now, if the said words, or words to the like effect, were intended against him the said Dean, and as a reflection on the Right Honourable the Lord Mayor, aldermen, and commons, for their decreeing unanimously, and in full assembly, the freedom of this city to the said Dean, in an honourable manner, on account of an opinion they had conceived of some services done by him the said Dean to this city, and to the kingdom in general,—the said Dean doth declare, That the said words, or words to the like effect, are insolent, false, scandalous, malicious, and, in a particular manner, perfidious; the said person, who is reported to have spoken the said or the like words, having, for some years past, and even within some few days, professed a great friendship for the said Dean; and, what is hardly credible, sending a common friend of the Dean and himself, not many hours after the said or the like words had been spoken, to renew his profession of friendship to the said Dean, but concealing the oratory; whereof the said Dean had no account till the following day, and then told it to all his friends.'

The Substance of What was said by the Dean on receiving his Freedom

THE

S U B S T A N C E

OF

What was said by the DEAN of St. PATRICK's to the Lord
Mayor and some of the Aldermen, when his Lordship
came to present the said Dean with his Freedom in a Gold
Box.

WHEN his Lordship had said a few words, and presented the instrument, the Dean gently put it back,
and desired first to be heard. He said, He was much
obliged to his Lordship and the city for the honour they were
going to do him, and which, as he was informed, they had
long intended him: That it was true, this honour was mingled
with a little mortification, by the delay which attended it;
but which, however, he did not impute to his Lordship or
the city: And that the mortification was the less, because he
would willingly hope the delay was founded on a mistake;
for which opinion he would tell his reason. He said, It was
well known, that, some time ago, a * person with a title was
pleased, in two great assemblies, to rattle bitterly some body
without a name, under the injurious appellations of a Tory, a
Jacobite, an enemy to King George, and a libeller of the
government; which character, the Dean said that many people
thought, was applied to him: But he was unwilling to be of
that opinion, because the person who had delivered those
abusive words had, for several years, caressed and courted,
and solicited his friendship more than any man in either kingdom had ever done; by inviting him to his house in town and
country, by coming to the Deanry often, and calling or sending
almost every day when the Dean was sick, with many other

* Joshua, Lord Viscount Allen.

particulars of the same nature, which continued even to a day or two of the time when the said person made those invectives in the Council and House of Lords. Therefore, that the Dean would by no means think those scurrilous words could be intended against him; because such a proceeding would overthrow all the principles of honour, justice, religion, truth, and even common humanity. Therefore the Dean will endeavour to believe, that the said person had some other object in his thoughts, and it was only the uncharitable custom of the world that applied this character to him. However, that he would insist on this argument no longer: But one thing he would affirm and declare, without assigning any name, or making any exception, That, whoever either did or does, or shall hereafter at any time, charge him with the character of a Jacobite, an enemy to King George, or a libeller of the government, the said accusation was, is, and will be false, malicious, slanderous, and altogether groundless. And, he would take the freedom to tell his Lordship and the rest that stood by, that he had done more service to the Hanover-title, and more disservice to the Pretender's cause, than forty thousand of those noisy, railing, malicious, empty zealots, to whom nature hath denied any talent that could be of use to God or their country, and left them only the gift of reviling, and spitting their venom, against all who differ from them in their destructive principles both in church and state. That he confessed it was sometimes his misfortune to dislike some things in public proceedings in both kingdoms, wherein he had often the honour to agree with wise and good men; but this did by no means affect either his loyalty to his prince, or love to his country. But, on the contrary, he protested that such dislikes never arose in him from any other principles, than the duty he owed to the King, and his affection to the kingdom. That he had been acquainted with courts and ministers long enough, and knew too well that the best ministers might mistake in points of great importance; and that he had the honour to know many more able, and at least full as honest as any can be at present. The Dean further said, That, since he had been so falsely represented, he thought it became him to give some account of himself for above twenty years, if it were only to justify his Lordship and the city for the honour they were going to do him. He related briefly how, merely by his own personal credit, without other assistance, and in two journeys at his own expence, he had procured a grant of the first fruits to the clergy, in the late Queen's time; for which he thought he deserved some gentle treatment from his brethren. That, during all the administration of the said ministry, he had been a constant advocate for those who are called the Whigs; had kept many of them in their employments, both in England and here, and some who were afterwards the first to lift up their heels against him. He reflected a little upon the severe treatment he had met with upon his return to Ireland after her Majesty's death, and for some years after. That, being forced to live retired, he could think of no better way to do public service, than by employing all the little money he could save, and lending it, without interest, in small sums to poor industrious tradesmen, without examining their party or their faith. And God had so far pleased to bless his endeavours, that his managers tell him he hath recovered above two hundred families in this city from ruin, and placed most of them in a comfortable way of life. The Dean related how much he had suffered in his purse, and with what hazard to his liberty, by a most iniquitous judge; * who, to gratify his ambition and rage of party, had condemned an innocent book, written with no worse a design, than to persuade the people of this kingdom to wear their own manufactures. How the said judge had endeavoured to get a jury to his mind, but they proved so honest, that he was forced to keep them eleven hours, and send them back nine times, until, at last, they were compelled to leave the printer † to the mercy of the court. And the Dean was forced to procure a *noli prosequi* from a ‡ Noble Person, then secretary of state, who had been his old friend. The Dean then freely confessed himself to be author of those books called the *Drapier's Letters*, spoke gently of the proclamation offering 300*l.* to discover the writer.

---

* Whitshed.   † Mr. Edward Waters.
‡ Charles, 2nd Duke of Grafton, then Lord Lieutenant of Ireland.

He said, That although a certain person was pleased to mention those books in a slight manner at a public assembly, yet he (the Dean) had learned to believe, that there were ten thousand to one in the kingdom who differed from that person; and the people of England, who had ever heard of the matter, as well as in France, were all of the same opinion. The Dean mentioned several other particulars, some of which, those from whom I had the account could not recollect, and others, although of great consequence, perhaps his enemies would not allow him. The Dean concluded with acknowledging to have expressed his wishes, that an inscription might have been graven on the box, shewing some reason why the city thought fit to do him that honour, which was much out of the common forms to a person in a private station; those distinctions being usually made only to chief governors, or persons in very high employments.

A Vindication of His Excellency
Excellency
John, Lord *Carteret*

A
VINDICATION
OF HIS

Ex—y the Lord *C*—,

FROM

The CHARGE of favouring
none but *Toryes*, *High-Churchmen*, and *Jacobites*.

L O N D O N :

Printed, and *D U B L I N* Re-printed in the Year
MDCCXXX.

A

VINDICATION

OF HIS

EXCELLENCY

THE

Lord C———T,

FROM THE

CHARGE

Of favouring none but

TORIES, HIGH-CHURCHMEN and
JACOBITES.

By the Reverend Dr. S———T.

LONDON:

Printed for T. WARNER at the *Black-Boy*
in *Pater-Noster-Row*. MDCCXXX.
(Price 6*d.*)

A

VINDICATION

Of His Excellency

John, Lord *Carteret*,

FROM

The CHARGE of favouring none but *Tories*, *High-Churchmen* and *Jacobites*.

Written in the Year 1730

IN order to treat this important Subject, with the greatest Fairness and Impartiality; perhaps it may be convenient to give some Account of his *Excellency*; in whose Life and Character, there are certain Particulars, which might give a very just Suspicion of some Truth in the Accusation he lies under.

HE is descended from two noble, antient, and most loyal Families, the *Carterets*, and the *Granvilles*: Too much distinguished, I confess, for what they acted, and what they suffered in defending the former Constitution in Church and State, under King *Charles* the Martyr; I mean that very Prince, on Account of whose Martyrdom, *a Form of Prayer, with Fasting, was enjoined by Act of Parliament, to be used on the 30th Day of* January *every Year, to implore the Mercies of God, that the Guilt of that sacred and innocent Blood, might not be visited on us or our Posterity*; as we may read at large in our *Common-Prayer Books*. Which Day hath been solemnly kept, even within the Memory of many Men now alive.

HIS *Excellency* the present Lord, was educated in the University of *Oxford*; from whence, with a Singularity, scarce to be justified, he carried away more *Greek*, *Latin*, and *Philosophy*, than properly became a Person of his Rank; indeed much more of each than most of those who are forced to Live by their Learning, will be at the unnecessary Pains to load their Heads with.

THIS was the Rock he split on, upon his first Appearance in the World, and just got clear of his Guardians. For, as soon as he came to Town, some Bishops, and Clergymen, and other Persons most eminent for Learning and Parts, got him among them; from whom, although he were fortunately dragged by a Lady and the Court, yet he could never wipe off the Stain, nor wash out the Tincture of his University Acquirements and Disposition.

To this, another Misfortune was added; that it pleased God to endow him with great natural Talents, Memory, Judgment, Comprehension, Eloquence, and Wit: And, to finish the Work, all these were fortified, even in his Youth, with the Advantages received by such Employments, as are best fitted both to exercise and polish the Gifts of Nature and Education; having been Ambassador in several Courts, when his Age would hardly allow him to take a Degree; and made principal Secretary of State, at a Period when, according to Custom, he ought to have been busied in losing his Money at a Chocolate-House; or in other Amusements equally laudable and epidemick among Persons of Honour.

I CANNOT omit another weak Side in His Excellency. For it is known, and can be proved upon him, that *Greek* and *Latin* Books might be found every Day in his Dressing-Room, if it were carefully searched; and there is Reason to suspect, that some of the said Books have been privately conveyed to him by *Tory* Hands. I am likewise assured, that he hath been taken in the very Fact of reading the said Books; even in the Midst of a Session, to the great Neglect of publick Affairs.

I OWN, there may be some Grounds for this Charge; because I have it from good Hands, that when His Excellency is at Dinner, with one or two Scholars at his Elbows, he grows a most unsupportable, and unintelligible Companion to all the fine Gentlemen round the Table.

I CANNOT deny that His Excellency lies under another great Disadvantage. For, with all the Accomplishments abovementioned, adding that of a most comely and graceful Person; and during the Prime of Youth, Spirits, and Vigour, he hath in a most unexemplary Manner led a regular domestick Life; discovers a great Esteem, and Friendship, and Love for his Lady, as well as a true Affection for his Children; and when he is disposed to admit an entertaining Evening Companion, he doth not always enough reflect, whether the Person may possibly in former Days, have lain under the Imputation of a *Tory*; nor, at such Times, do the natural or *affected* Fears of *Popery* and the *Pretender*, make any Part of the Conversation; I presume, because neither *Homer*, *Plato*, *Aristotle*, nor *Cicero*, have made any mention of them.

THESE I freely acknowledge to be his Excellency's Failings: Yet, I think it is agreed by Philosophers and Divines; that some Allowance ought to be given to human Infirmity, and to the Prejudices of a wrong Education.

I AM well aware, how much my Sentiments differ from the *orthodox* Opinion of one or two principal Patriots, (at the Head of whom I name with Honour *Pistorides*.) For these have decided the Matter directly against me, by declaring, that no Person who was ever known to lie under the Suspicion of one single *Tory* Principle; or who had been once seen at a great Man's Levee in the *worst of Times*, should be allowed to come within the Verge of the Castle; much less to bow in the Antichamber, appear at the *Assemblies*, or dance at a Birth-Night. However, I dare assert, that this Maxim hath been often controlled; and that on the contrary, a considerable Number of *early Penitents* have been received into Grace, who are now an *Ornament*, *Happiness*, and *Support* to the Nation.

NEITHER do I find any murmuring on some other Points of greater Importance, where this favourite Maxim is not so strictly observed.

To instance only in one. I have not heard that any Care

hath hitherto been taken, to discover whether Madam * *Vio-
lante* be a *Whig* or *Tory* in her Principles; or even that she
trary, I am told that she openly professeth herself to be a
HIGH-FLYER; and it is not improbable, by her *outlandish*
Name she may also be a *Papist* in her Heart; yet we see this
illustrious and dangerous Female, openly caressed by principal
Persons of both Parties; who contribute to support her in a
splendid Manner, without the least Apprehensions from a
Grand-Jury; or even from 'Squire *Hartly Hutcheson* himself,
that *zealous Prosecutor of Hawkers and Libels*. And, as *Hobbes*
wisely observes, *so much Money* being equivalent to *so much
Power*; it may deserve considering, with what Safety such an
Instrument of *Power* ought to be trusted in the Hands of an
Alien, who hath not given any legal Security for her good
Affection to the Government.

I CONFESS, there is one Evil which I could wish our
Friends would think proper to redress. There are many
Whigs in this Kingdom of the *old fashioned Stamp*, of whom we
might make very good Use; they bear the same Loyalty with
us, to the *Hanoverian* Family, in the Person of King *George*
the IId. The same Abhorrence of the *Pretender*, with the
Consequents of *Popery* and *Slavery*; and the same Indulgence to
tender Consciences: But having nothing to ask for themselves,
and therefore the more Leisure to think for the Publick;
they are often apt to entertain Fears, and melancholly Prospects,
concerning the State of their Country, the Decay of Trade,
the Want of Money, the miserable Condition of the People,
with other Topicks of like Nature; all which do equally concern
both *Whig* and *Tory*; who, if they have any Thing to lose, must
be equally Sufferers. Perhaps, one or two of these melancholly Gentlemen, will sometimes venture to publish their
Thoughts in Print: Now I can, by no Means, approve our
usual Custom of cursing and railing at this Species of Thinkers,
under the Names of *Tories*, *Jacobites*, *Papists*, *Libellers*, *Rebels*,
and the like.

THIS was the utter Ruin of that poor, angry, bustling, well-
meaning Mortal *Pistorides*; who lies equally under the Contempt

* A famous Italian *Rope-Dancer*.

of both Parties; with no other Difference, than a Mixture of *Pity* on one Side, and of *Aversion* on the other.

How hath he been pelted, pestered, and pounded by one single Wag, who promiseth never to forsake him, living or dead?

I was much pleased with the Humour of a *Surgeon* in this Town; who, having, in his own Apprehension, received some great Injustice from the Earl of *Galloway*, and despairing of Revenge, as well as Relief; declared to all his Friends, that he had set apart one Hundred Guineas, to purchase the Earl's Carcase from the Sexton, whenever *it* should dye; to make a Skeleton of the Bones, stuff the Hide, and shew them for three Pence; and thus get Vengeance for the Injuries he had suffered by its Owner.

Of the like Spirit, too often, is that implacable Race of Wits; against whom there is no Defence but Innocence, and Philosophy: Neither of which is likely to be at Hand; and therefore, the Wounded have no where to fly for a Cure, but to downright Stupidity, a crazed Head, or a profligate Contempt of Guilt and Shame.

I am therefore sorry for that other miserable Creature *Traulus*; who although of somewhat a different Species, yet seems very far to outdo even the Genius of *Pistorides*, in that miscarrying Talent of railing without Consistency or Discretion, against the most innocent Persons, according to the present Scituation of his Gall and Spleen. I do not blame an *honest* Gentleman for the bitterest Invectives against one, to whom he professeth the greatest Friendship; provided he acts in the Dark, so as not to be discovered: But in the Midst of *Caresses*, *Visits*, and *Invitations*, to run into the Streets, or to *as publick a Place*; and without the least pretended Incitement, sputter out the basest and falsest Accusations; then to wipe his Mouth, come up smiling to his Friend, shake him by the Hand, and tell him in a Whisper, it was *all for his Service*. This Proceeding, I am bold to think a great Failure in Prudence; and I am afraid lest such a Practitioner, with a Body so *open*, so *foul*, and so *full of Sores*, may fall under the Resentment of an incensed political *Surgeon*, who is not in much Renown for his Mercy upon great Provocation: Who, without waiting for his Death, will *flay*, and *dissect* him alive; and to the View of Mankind, lay open all the disordered Cells of his Brain, the Venom of his Tongue, the Corruption of his Heart, and Spots and Flatuses of his Spleen—And all this for *Three-Pence*.

IN such a Case what a Scene would be laid open! And to drop my Metaphor, what a Character of our mistaken Friend might an angry Enemy draw and expose! particularizing that unnatural Conjunction of Vices and Follies, so inconsistent with each other in the same Breast: Furious and fawning, scurrilous and flattering, cowardly and provoking, insolent and abject; most profligately false, with the strongest Professions of Sincerity; positive and variable, tyrannical and slavish.

I APPREHEND that if all this should be set out to the World by an angry Whig of the *old* Stamp; the unavoidable Consequence must be a Confinement of our *Friend* for some Months *more* to his Garret; and thereby depriving the Publick for so long a Time, and in so *important a Juncture*, of his useful Talents in their Service: While he is fed like a wild Beast through a Hole; but I hope with a special Regard to the *Quantity* and *Quality* of his Nourishment.

IN vain would his Excusers endeavour to palliate his Enormities, by imputing them to Madness; Because, it is well known, that Madness only operates by inflaming and enlarging the good or evil Dispositions of the Mind: For the *Curators* of *Bedlam* assure us, that some Lunaticks are Persons of *Honour*, *Truth*, *Benevolence*, and many other Virtues, which appear in their highest Ravings, although after a wild incoherent Manner; while others, on the contrary, discover in every Word and Action, the utmost *Baseness* and Depravity of human Minds; which infallibly they possessed in the same Degree, although perhaps under a better Regulation, before their Entrance into that *Academy*.

BUT it may be objected that there is an Argument of much Force to excuse the Overflowings of that Zeal, which our *Friend* shews or means for our Cause. And it must be confessed, that the *easy and smooth Fluency of his Elocution, bestowed* on him by Nature, and cultivated by continual Practice, added to the Comeliness of his Person, the Harmony of his Voice, the Gracefulness of his Manner, and the Decency of his Dress, are Temptations too strong for such a Genius to resist upon any publick Occasion, of making them appear with *universal Applause:* And if good Men are sometimes accused of loving their *Jest* better than their *Friend*; surely to gain the Reputation of the first *Orator* in the Kingdom, no Man of Spirit would scruple to lose all the *Friends* he had in the World.

I T is usual for Masters to make their Boys declaim on both Sides of an Argument; and as some kinds of Assemblies are called the *Schools of Politicks*, I confess nothing can better improve political Schoolboys, than the Art of making plausible or implausible Harangues; against the very Opinion for which they resolve to Determine.

So Cardinal *Perron* after having spoke for an Hour to the Admiration of all his Hearers, to prove the Existence of God; told some of his Intimates, that he could have spoken another Hour, and much better, to prove the contrary.

I HAVE placed this Reasoning in the strongest Light, that I think it will bear; and have nothing to answer, but that allowing it as much Weight as the Reader shall please, it hath constantly met with ill success in the Mouth of our *Friend*; but whether for Want of good Luck, or good Management, I suspend my Judgment.

To return from this long Digression; if Persons in high Stations have been allowed to chuse *Wenches*, without Regard even to Difference in Religion, yet never incurred the least Reflection on their Loyalty, or their Protestantism; shall the Chief Governor of a great Kingdom be censured for chusing a *Companion*, who may formerly have been suspected for differing from the *Orthodox* in some speculative Opinions of Persons and Things, which cannot affect the fundamental Principles of a sound *Whig*?

BUT let me suppose a very possible Case. Here is a Person sent to govern *Ireland*, whose unfortunate weak Side it happens to be, for several Reasons abovementioned, that he hath encouraged the Attendance of *one* or *two* Gentlemen distinguished

for their Taste, their Wit, and their Learning; who have taken
the Oaths to His Majesty, and pray heartily for him: Yet
because they may, perhaps, be stigmatized as *quondam* Tories
by *Pistorides* and his Gang; his Excellency must be forced to
banish them, under the Pain and Peril of displeasing the
Zealots of his own Party; and thereby be put into a worse
Condition than every common good Fellow; who may be a
sincere *Protestant,* and a loyal Subject; and yet rather chuse to
drink fine Ale at the *Pope*'s *Head,* than muddy at the *King*'s.

LET me then return to my Supposition. It is certain,
the high-flown Loyalists in the *present* Sense of the Word,
have their thoughts, and Studies, and Tongues, so entirely
diverted by political Schemes, that the *Zeal* of their *Principles*
hath *eaten up* their *Understandings*; neither have they Time from
their Employments, their Hopes, and their hourly Labours
for acquiring new Additions of Merit, to amuse themselves
with Philological Converse, or Speculations which are utterly
ruinous to all Schemes of rising in the World. What then
must a great Man do, whose ill Stars have fatally perverted
him to a Love, and Taste, and Possession of Literature,
Politeness, and good Sense? Our thorow-sped Republick
of Whigs, which contains the Bulk of all *Hopers, Pretenders, Ex-
pecters,* and *Professors,* are, beyond all Doubt, most *Highly
useful* to Princes, to Governors, to great Ministers, and to their
Country; but at the same Time, and by necessary Consequence,
the most disagreeable Companions to all who have that unfortunate Turn of Mind peculiar to his Excellency, and perhaps
to five or six more in a Nation.

I DO not deny it possible, that an Original or Proselyte
Favourer of the Times, might have been born to those useless
Talents, which, in former Ages qualified a Man to be a Poet,
or a Philosopher. All I contend for, is that where the true
Genius of Party once enters, it *sweeps the House clean,* and leaves
room for many *other Spirits* to take joint Possession, until the
last State of that Man is exceedingly better *than the first.*

I ALLOW it is great Error in his Excellency, that he adheres
so obstinately to his old *unfashionable* Academick Education:
Yet so perverse is human Nature, that the usual Remedies for

this Evil in others, have produced a contrary Effect in him; to a Degree that I am credibly informed, he will, as I have already hinted, in the middle of a Session, quote Passages out of *Plato*, and *Pindar*, at his own Table, to some *Book-learned* Companion, without blushing, even when Persons of *great Stations* are by.

I WILL venture one Step further; which is, freely to confess, that this mistaken Method of educating Youth in the Knowledge of antient Learning and Language, is too apt to spoil their *Politicks* and *Principles*; because the Doctrine and Examples of the Books they read, teach them Lessons *directly contrary in every Point*, to the *present Practice* of the World: And accordingly, *Hobbes* most judiciously observes, that the Writings of the *Greeks* and *Romans*, made young Men imbibe Opinions against absolute Power in a Prince, or even in a first *Minister*; and to embrace Notions of Liberty and Property.

IT hath been therefore, a great Felicity to these Kingdoms, that the Heirs to Titles and large Estates, have a Weakness in their Eyes, a Tenderness in their Constitutions; are not able to bear the Pain and Indignity of whipping; and, as the Mother rightly expresses it, could never *take to their Books*, yet are well enough qualified to sign a Receipt for Half a Year's Rent, to put their Name (*rightly spelt*) to a Warrant, and to read Pamphlets against *Religion* and *High-flying*; whereby they fill their Niches, and carry themselves through the World, with that Dignity which best becomes a *Senator* and a *'Squire*.

I COULD heartily wish his Excellency would be more condescending to the *Genius* of the Kingdom he governs; to the Condition of the Times, and to the Nature of the Station he fills. Yet if it be true, what I have read in old *English* Story-books, that one *Agesilaus* (no Matter to the Bulk of my Readers, whether I spell the Names right or wrong) was caught by the *Parson of the Parish*, riding on a Hobby-Horse with his Children; that *Socrates*, a Heathen Philosopher, was found dancing by himself at Four-score; that a King called *Cæsar Augustus* (or some such Name) used to play with Boys; whereof some might possibly be Sons of *Tories*; and that two great Men called *Scipio* and *Lelius*, (I forget their *Christian*

Names, and whether they were Poets or Generals,) often played at *Duck and Drake*, with smooth Stones on a River. Now I say, if these Facts be true, (and the Book where I found them is in Print) I cannot imagine why our most zealous Patriots may not a little indulge his Excellency, in an Infirmity which is not morally Evil; provided he gives no publick Scandal (which is by all Means to be avoided) I say, why he may not be indulged twice a Week, to converse with one or two particular Persons; and let him and them conn over their old *exploded* Readings together, after Mornings spent in hearing and prescribing *Ways and Means* from and to his *most obedient* Politicians, for the Welfare of the Kingdom; although the said particular Person, or Persons, may not have made so publick a Declaration of their political Faith in all its Parts, as the Business of the Nation requires: Still submitting my Opinion to that *happy Majority*, which I am confident is *always in the Right*; by whom the *Liberty* of the Subject hath been so frequently, so strenuously, and so successfully asserted; who, by their wise Councils, have made *Commerce* to flourish, *Money* to abound, Inhabitants to encrease, the Value of Lands and Rents to rise; and the whole Island put on a new Face of *Plenty* and *Prosperity*.

BUT, in order to clear his Excellency more fully from this Accusation of shewing his Favours to *High-flyers*, *Tories*, and *Jacobites*; it will be necessary to come to Particulars.

THE first Person of a *Tory* Denomination, to whom his Excellency gave any Marks of his Favour, was Doctor *Thomas Sheridan*. It is to be observed, that this happened so early in his Excellency's Government, as it may be justly supposed he had not been informed of that Gentleman's Character, upon so *dangerous* an Article. The Doctor being well known, and distinguished for his Skill and Success in the Education of Youth, beyond most of his Profession for many Years past; was recommended to his Excellency on the score of his Learning, and particularly for his Knowledge in the *Greek* Tongue; whereof, it seems, his Excellency is a great Admirer, although for what Reasons I could never imagine. However, it is agreed on all Hands, that his Lordship was too easily prevailed on by the Doctor's Request, or indeed rather from the Bias of his own Nature, to hear a Tragedy acted in that *unknown* Language by the Doctor's Lads, which was written by some Heathen Author; but whether it contained any *Tory* or *High-Church* Principles, must be left to the Consciences of the *Boys*, the *Doctor*, and his *Excellency:* The *only* Witnesses in this Case, whose Testimonies can be depended upon.

I⊤ seems, his Excellency (a Thing never to be sufficiently wondered at) was so pleased with his Entertainment, that some Time after he gave the Doctor a Church-living, to the Value of almost one Hundred Pounds a Year, and made him one of his Chaplains; from an *antiquated* Notion, that good School-masters ought to be encouraged in every Nation, professing Civility and Religion. Yet his Excellency did not venture to make this bold Step, without strong Recommendations from Persons of undoubted Principles, *fitted to the Times*; who thought themselves bound in Justice, Honour, and Gratitude, to do the Doctor a good Office, in return for the Care he had taken of their Children, or those of their Friends. Yet the Catastrophe was terrible: For the Doctor, in the Height of his Felicity and Gratitude, going down to take Possession of his Parish, and furnished with a few led-Sermons, whereof, as it is to be supposed, the Number was very small, having never served a Cure in the Church; he stopt at *Cork*, to attend on his Bishop; and going to Church on the *Sunday* following, was, according to the usual Civility of Country Clergymen, invited by the Minister of the Parish to supply the Pulpit. It *happened* to be the First of *August*; and the First of *August happened* that Year to light upon a *Sunday:* And it *happened* that the Doctor's Text was in these Words; *sufficient unto the Day is the Evil thereof:* And lastly, it *happened* that some one Person of the Congregation, whose Loyalty made him watchful upon every Appearance of Danger to his Majesty's Person and Government, when Service was over, gave the Alarm. Notice was immediately sent up to Town; and by the Zeal of one Man *of no large Dimensions of Body or Mind*, such a Clamour was raised, that we in *Dublin* could apprehend no less than an Invasion by the *Pretender*, who must be landed in the

South. The Result was, that the Doctor must be struck out of the Chaplains List, and appear no more at the Castle; yet whether he were then, or be at this Day, a *Whig* or a *Tory,* I think is a Secret; only it is manifest, that he is a zealous *Hanoverian,* at least in Poetry, and a great Adorer of the present Royal Family, through all its Branches. His Friends likewise assert, that he had preached this same Sermon often, under the same Text; that not having observed the Words till he was in the Pulpit, and had opened his Notes; as he is a Person a little abstracted, he wanted Presence of Mind to change them: And that, in the whole Sermon, there was not a Syllable relating to Government or Party, or to the Subject of the Day.

I N this Incident there seems to have been an Union of Events, that will probably never happen again to the End of the World; or, at least, like the grand Conjunction in the Heavens; which, I think, they say can arrive but once in Twenty Thousand Years.

T H E second Gentleman (if I am right in my Chronology) who, under the Suspicion of a *Tory,* received some Favour from his Excellency, is Mr. *James Stopford;* very strongly recommended by the most eminent *Whig in England,* on the Account of his Learning, and Virtue, and other Accomplishments. He had passed the greatest Part of his Youth in close Study, or in Travelling; and was either not at home, or not at Leisure to trouble his Thoughts about Party; which I allow to be a great Omission; although I cannot honestly place him in the List of *Tories;* and therefore think his Excellency may be fairly acquitted for making him Vicar of *Finglass,* worth about one Hundred Pounds a Year.

T H E Third is Doctor *Patrick Delany.* This Divine lies under some Disadvantage; having, in his Youth, received many Civilities from a certain * Person, then in a very high Station here; for which Reason, I doubt the Doctor never drank his Confusion since; and what makes the Matter desperate, it is now too late; unless our *Inquisitors* will be content with drinking *Confusion* to his *Memory:* The aforesaid eminent Person,

---

* Sir Constantine Phipps, *Lord Chancellor of* Ireland, *when Queen* Anne *died.*

who was a Judge of all Merit, except that of *Party*, distinguished the Doctor, among other Juniors in our University, for his Learning, Virtue, Discretion, and good Sense. But the Doctor was then in too good a Situation at his College, to hope or endeavour at a better Establishment, from one who had no power to give it him.

UPON the present Lord Lieutenant's coming over, the Doctor was named to his Excellency by a * *Friend*, among other Clergymen of Distinction, as Persons whose Characters it was proper his Excellency should know: And by the Truth of which the *Giver* would be content to stand or fall in his Excellency's Opinion; since not one of those Persons were in particular Friendship with the *Gentleman* who gave in their Names. By this and some other Incidents, particularly the Recommendation of the late Archbishop of *Dublin*, the Doctor became known to his Excellency, whose fatal Turn of Mind towards *Heathenish* and *outlandish* Books and Languages; finding, as I conceive, a like Disposition in the Doctor, was the Cause of his becoming so domestick, as we are told he is, at the Castle of *Dublin*.

THREE or four Years ago, the Doctor grown weary of an Academick Life, for some Reasons best known to the Managers of the Discipline in that learned Society (which it may not be for their Honour to mention) resolved to leave it; although by the Benefit of his Pupils, and his Senior-Fellowship with all its Perquisites, he received every Year between Nine Hundred and a Thousand Pounds. And a small Northern Living, in the University's Donation, of somewhat better than one Hundred Pounds a Year, falling at the same time with the Chancellor-ship of *Christ-Church*, to about equal Value, in the Gift of his Excellency: The Doctor ventured into the World in a very scanty Condition; having squandered away all his annual Income in a Manner, which, although perhaps proper enough for a Clergyman without a Family, will not be for the Advantage of his Character to discover either on the Exchange, or at a Banker's Shop.

ABOUT two Months ago, his Excellency gave the Doctor

* *The Author.*

a Prebend in St. *Patrick*'s Cathedral; which, being of near the same Value with either of the two former, will add a third Part to his Revenues, after he shall have paid the great Incumbrances upon it: So that he may now be said to possess of Church Preferments, in scattered Tythes, three Hundred Pounds a Year; instead of the like Sum of infallible Rents from a Senior-Fellowship, with the Offices annexed; besides the Advantage of a free Lodging, a great Number of Pupils, and some other Easements.

But since the Doctor hath not, in any of his Writings, his Sermons, his Actions, his Discourse, or his Company, discovered one single Principle of either *Whig* or *Tory*; and that the Lord Lieutenant still continues to admit him; I shall boldly pronounce him *ONE OF US:* But, like a new *Free-Mason*, who hath not yet learned all the Dialect of the Mystery. Neither can he justly be accused of any *Tory* Doctrines; except, perhaps, some among those few, with which that *wicked Party* was charged, during the Heighth of their Power; but have been since transferred for the most *solid Reasons*, to the *whole Body* of our firmest Friends.

I have now done with the Clergy: And upon the strictest Examination have not been able to find above one of that Order, against whom any *Party* Suspicion can lye; which is the unfortunate Gentleman, Doctor *Sheridan*, who by mere Chance-medley shot his own Fortune dead with a single *Text*.

As to the Laity I can hear of but one Person of the *Tory* Stamp, who since the beginning of his Excellency's Government, did ever receive any solid Mark of his Favour: I mean Sir *Arthur Acheson*, reported to be an acknowledged *Tory*; and, what is almost as bad, a *Scholar* into the Bargain. It is whispered about, as a certain Truth, that this Gentleman is to have a Grant of a certain Barrack upon his Estate, within two Miles of his own House; for which the Crown is to be his Tenant, at the Rent of sixty Pounds *per Annum*; he being only at the Expence of about *Five Hundred* Pounds, to put the House in Repair, build Stables, and other Necessaries. I will place this *invidious* Mark of Beneficence, conferred on a *Tory*, in a fair

Light, by computing the Costs and necessary Defalcations: After which it may be seen how much Sir *Arthur* will be annually a clear Gainer by the Publick; notwithstanding his *unfortunate* Principles, and his Knowledge in *Greek* and *Latin*.

For Repairs, *&c.* 500*l.* the Interest whereof *per Ann.*	30	0	0
For all Manner of Poultry to furnish the Troopers; but which the said Troopers must be at the Labour of catching, valued *per Annum*	5	0	0
For straggling Sheep,	8	0	0
For Game destroyed five Miles round,	6	0	0
	49	0	0
Rent paid to Sir *Arthur*, —— —— ——	60	0	0
Deduct —— —— —— ——	49	0	0
Remains clear —— —— ——	11	0	0

THUS, if Sir *Arthur Acheson* shall have the good Fortune to obtain a Grant of this Barrack, he will receive *net* Profit annually from the Crown ELEVEN Pounds, *Sterl.* to help him in entertaining the Officers, and making Provision for his younger Children.

IT is true, there is another Advantage to be expected, which may fully compensate the Loss of Cattle and Poultry; by multiplying the Breed of Mankind, and particularly that of *good Protestants*, in a Part of the Kingdom half depopulated by the wild Humour among the Farmers thereof, leaving their Country. But I am not so skilful in Arithmetick, as to compute the Value.

I HAVE reckoned one *per Cent.* below the Legal Interest for the Money that Sir *Arthur* must expend: And valued the Damage in the other Articles very moderately. However, I am confident he may with good Management be a *Saver* at least;

which is a *prodigious Instance of Moderation* in our Friends towards a professed *Tory*, whatever Merit he may pretend by the Unwillingness he hath shewn to make his Excellency uneasy in his Administration.

THUS I have, with the utmost Impartiality, collected every single Favour, (further than personal Civilities) conferred by his Excellency on *Tories*, and reputed *Tories*, since his first Arrival hither, to this present 13th Day of *April*, in the Year of our Lord 1730, giving all Allowance possible to the Arguments on the other Side of the Question.

And the Account will stand thus.

DISPOSED of Preferments and Employments to *Tories*, or reputed *Tories*, by his Excellency *John*, Lord *Carteret*, Lord Lieutenant of *Ireland*, in about the Space of six Years.

To Doctor *Thomas Sheridan* in a Rectory near *Kinsale, per Ann.*	100	0	0
To Sir *Arthur Acheson*, Baronet, a Barrack, *per Ann.*	11	0	0
	111	0	0

GIVE me leave now to compute in gross the Value of the Favours done by his Excellency to the *true Friends* of their King and Country, and of the *Protestant Religion*.

IT is to be remembred, that although his Excellency cannot be properly said to bestow Bishopricks, Commands in the Army, the Place of a Judge, or Commissioner in the Revenue, and some others; yet they are, for the most Part, disposed upon his Recommendation, except where the Persons are immediately sent from *England* by their Interest at Court; for which I have allowed large Defalcations in the following Accounts. And it is remarkable, that the *only* considerable Station conferred on a reputed *Tory* since his present Excellency's Government, was of this *latter* Kind.

AND indeed it is but too remarkable, that, in a neighbouring Nation (where this dangerous Denomination of Men is incomparably more Numerous, more Powerful, and of consequence more Formidable) *real Tories* can often with much less Difficulty, obtain very high Favours from the Government, than their *reputed* Brethren can arrive to the lowest in ours. I observe this with all possible Submission to the Wisdom of their Policy; which, however, will not, I believe, dispute the Praise of Vigilance with ours.

WHIG Account

To Persons promoted to Bishopricks or removed to more beneficial ones, computed *per Ann.*	10050	0	0
To Civil Employments,	9030	0	0
To Military Commands,	8436	0	0
	27516	0	0

TORY Account.

To *Tories* — — — — —	111	0	0
Ballance — — — —	27405	0	0

I SHALL conclude with this Observation, That, as I think, the *Tories* have sufficient Reason to be *fully satisfied* with the Share of *Trust*, and *Power*, and *Employments*, which they possess under the *Lenity* of the present Government: So, I do not find how his Excellency can be justly censured for favouring none but *High-Church, High-flyers, Termagants, Laudists, Sacheverellians, Tip-top-gallonmen, Jacobites, Tantivyes, Anti-Hanoverians, Friends to Popery and the Pretender, and to Arbitrary Power, Disobligers of* England, *Breakers of* DEPENDENCY, *Inflamers of Quarrels between the two Nations, Publick Incendiaries, Enemies to the King and Kingdoms, Haters of* TRUE *Protestants, Laurelmen, Annists, Complainers of the Nation's Poverty, Ormondians, Iconoclasts, Anti-Glorious-memorists, Anti-Revolutioners, Whiterosalists, Tenth-a-Junians,* and the like: When by a fair State of the Account; the Ballance, I conceive, *seems to lie* on the other Side.

The Answer to the Craftsman

THE

ANSWER

TO THE

CRAFTSMAN.

SIR,

I DETEST reading your Papers, because I am not of your Principles, and because I cannot endure to be convinced. Yet, I was prevailed on to peruse your CRAFTSMAN of *December the 12th, wherein I discover you to be as great an Enemy of this Country, as you are of your own. You are pleased to reflect on a Project I proposed of making the Children of *Irish* Parents to be useful to the Publick instead of being burthensome; and you venture to assert, that your own Scheme is more charitable, of not permitting our Popish Natives to be listed in the Service of any foreign Prince.

PERHAPS Sir, you may not have heard of any Kingdom so unhappy as this, both in their Imports and Exports. We import a Sort of Goods, of no intrinsick Value, which costeth us above Forty Thousand Pounds a Year to dress, and scour, and polish them, which altogether do not yield one Penny Advantage; and we annually export above Seven Hundred Thousand Pounds a Year in another Kind of Goods, for which we receive not one single Farthing in Return: Even the Money paid for the Letters sent in transacting this Commerce being all returned to *England*. But now, when there is a most lucky Opportunity offered to begin a Trade, whereby this Nation will save many Thousand Pounds a Year, and *England* be a prodigious Gainer, you are pleased, without a Call, officiously and maliciously to interpose with very frivolous Arguments.

* So misdated in the first collected edition of the *Craftsman*, 1731.

IT is well known, that, about Sixty Years ago, the Exportation of live Cattle from hence to *England* was of great Benefit to both Kingdoms, until that Branch of Traffick was stopt by an Act of Parliament on your Side, whereof you have had sufficient Reason to repent. Upon which Account, when another Act passed your Parliament, forbidding the Exportation of live Men to any foreign Country, you were so wise to put in a Clause, allowing it to be done by his Majesty's Permission, under his Sign Manual, for which, among other great Benefits granted to *Ireland*, we are infinitely obliged to the *British* Legislature. Yet this very Grace and Favour you, Mr. *D'Anvers*, whom we never disobliged, are endeavouring to prevent; which, I will take upon me to say, is a manifest Mark of your Disaffection to his Majesty, a Want of Duty to the Ministry, and a wicked Design of oppressing this Kingdom, and a traiterous Attempt to lessen the Trade and Manufacture of *England*.

OUR truest and best Ally the most Christian King hath obtained his Majesty's Licence, pursuant to Law, to export from hence some Thousand Bodies of healthy, young, living Men, to supply his *Irish* Regiments. The King of *Spain*, as you assert yourself, hath desired the same Civility, and seemeth to have at least as good a Claim; supposing then that these two Potentates will only desire Leave to carry off Six Thousand Men between them to *France* and *Spain*, then by computing the Maintenance of a tall, hungry, *Irish* Man, in Food and Cloaths, to be only at Five Pounds a Head, here will be Thirty Thousand Pounds *per Annum* saved clear to the Nation, for they can find no other Employment at Home beside begging, robbing, or stealing. But, if Thirty, Forty, or Fifty Thousand, (which we could gladly spare) were sent on the same Errand, what an immense Benefit must it be to us; and, if the two Princes, in whose Service they were, should happen to be at War with each other, how soon would those Recruits be destroyed, then what a Number of Friends would the Pretender lose, and what a Number of Popish Enemies all true Protestants get rid of. Add to this, that then by such a

Practice, the Lands of *Ireland* that want Hands for Tillage, must be employed in Grazing, which would sink the Price of Wool, raw Hides, Butter, and Tallow, so that the *English* might have them at their own Rates; and in Return send us Wheat to make our Bread, Barley to brew our Drink, and Oats for our Horses, without any Labour of our own.

UPON this Occasion, I desire humbly to offer a Scheme, which, in my Opinion, would best answer the true Interests of both Kingdoms: For, although I bear a most tender, filial Affection to *England*, my dear, native Country; yet, I cannot deny but this noble Island hath a great Share in my Love and Esteem, nor can I express how much I desire to see it flourish in Trade and Opulence, even beyond its present happy Condition.

THE profitable Land of this Kingdom is, I think, usually computed at seventeen Millions of Acres, all which I propose to be wholly turned to Grazing. Now, it is found by Experience, that one Grazier and his Family can manage Two Thousand Acres. Thus, Sixteen Millions Eight Hundred Thousnad Acres may be managed by Eight Thousand Four Hundred Families, and the Fraction of Two Hundred Thousand Acres will be more than sufficient for Cabbins, Out-Houses, and Potatoe-Gardens; because, it is to be understood, that Corn of all Sorts must be sent to us from *England*.

THESE Eight Thousand Four Hundred Families may be divided among the four Provinces, according to the Number of Houses in each Province; and, making the equal Allowance of Eight to a Family, the Number of Inhabitants will amount to Sixty Seven Thousand Two Hundred Souls; to these we are to add a Standing Army of Twenty Thousand *English*, which, together with their Trulls, their Bastards, and their Horse-Boys, will, by a gross Computation, very near double the Count, and be very sufficient for the Defence and Grazing of the Kingdom, as well as to enrich our Neighbours, expel Popery, and keep out the Pretender. And lest the Army should be at a Loss for Business, I think it would be very prudent to employ them in collecting the publick Taxes for paying themselves and the Civil List.

I ADVISE, that all the Owners of these Lands should live constantly in *England*, in order to learn Politeness, and qualify themselves for Employments: But, for fear of increasing the Natives in this Island, that an annual Draught, according to the Number born every Year, be exported to whatever Prince will bear the Carriage; or transplanted to the *English* Dominions on the *American* Continent, as a Screen between his Majesty's *English* Subjects and the savage *Indians*.

I ADVISE likewise, that no Commodity whatsoever, of this Nation's Growth, should be sent to any other Country, except *England*, under the Penalty of high Treason; and that all the said Commodities shall be sent in their natural State, the Hides raw, the Wool uncombed, the Flax in the Stub; excepting only Fish, Butter, Tallow and whatever else will be spoiled in the Carriage. On the contrary, that no Goods whatsoever shall be imported hither, except from *England*, under the same Penalty: That *England* should be forced, at their own Rates, to send us over Cloaths ready made, as well as Shirts and Smocks to the Soldiers and their Trulls; all Iron, Wooden, and Earthen Ware; and whatever Furniture may be necessary for the Cabbins of Graziers, with a sufficient Quantity of Gin, and other Spirits, for those who can afford to get drunk on Holydays.

As to the Civil and Ecclesiastical Administration, which I have not yet fully considered, I can say little; only with Regard to the latter, it is plain, that the Article of paying Tythe for supporting speculative Opinions in Religion, which is so insupportable a Burthen to all true Protestants, and to most Churchmen, will be very much lessened by this Expedient; because dry Cattle pay nothing to the spiritual Hireling, any more than imported Corn; so that the industrious Shepherd and Cow-herd may sit, every Man under his own Blackberry Bush, and on his own Potatoe-Bed, whereby this happy Island will become a new *Arcadia*.

I DO likewise propose, that no Money shall be used in *Ireland*, except what is made of Leather, which likewise shall be coined in *England*, and imported; and that the Taxes shall be levied out of the Commodities we export to *England*, and there turned into Money for his Majesty's Use; and the Rents to Landlords discharged in the same Manner. This will be no Manner of Grievance; for we already see it very practicable to live without Money, and shall be more convinced of it every Day. But whether Paper shall still continue to supply that Defect, or whether we shall hang up all those who profess the Trade of Bankers, (which latter I am rather inclined to) must be left to the Consideration of wiser Politicians.

THAT which maketh me more zealously bent upon this Scheme, is my Desire of living in Amity with our neighbouring Brethren; for we have already tried all other Means, without Effect, to that blessed End: And, by the Course of Measures taken for some years past, it should seem that we are all agreed in the Point.

THIS Expedient will be of great Advantage to both King-doms, upon several Accounts: For, as to *England*, they have a just Claim to the Balance of Trade on their Side with the whole World; and therefore our Ancestors and we, who conquered this Kingdom for them, ought, in Duty and Gratitude, to let them have the whole Benefit of that Conquest to themselves; especially, when the Conquest was amicably made, without Bloodshed, by a Stipulation between the *Irish* Princes and *Henry* II. by which they paid him, indeed, not equal Homage with what the Electors of *Germany* do to the Emperor, but very near the same that he did to the King of *France* for his *French* Dominions.

IN Consequence of this Claim from *England*, that Kingdom may very reasonably demand the Benefit of all our Commodities in their natural Growth, to be manufactured by their People, and a sufficient Quantity of them for our Use to be returned hither fully manufactured.

THIS, on the other Side, will be of great Benefit to our Inhabitants the Graziers, when Time and Labour will be too much taken up in manuring their Ground, feeding their Cattle, sheering their Sheep, and sending over their Oxen fit for Slaughter; to which Employments they are turned by

P

Nature, as descended from the *Scythians*, whose Diet they are still so fond of. So *Virgil* describeth it:

Et lac concretum cum sanguine bibit equino.

Which, in *English*, is Bonnyclabber,* mingled with the Blood of Horses, as they formerly did, until about the Beginning of the last Century Luxury, under the Form of Politeness, began to creep in, they changed the Blood of Horses for that of their black Cattle; and, by Consequence, became less warlike than their Ancestors.

ALTHOUGH I proposed that the Army should be Collectors of the publick Revenues, yet I did not thereby intend that those Taxes should be paid in Gold or Silver, but in Kind, as all other Rent: For the Custom of Tenants making their Payments in Money, is a new Thing in the World little known in former Ages, nor generally practised in any Nation at present, except this Island, and the Southern Parts of *Britain*. But, to my great Satisfaction, I foresee better Times; the antient Manner beginneth to be now practised in many Parts of *Connaught*, as well as in the County of *Corke*, where the 'Squires turn Tenants to themselves, divide so many Cattle to their Slaves, who are to provide such a Quantity of Butter, Hides, or Tallow, still keeping up their Number of Cattle; and carry the Goods to *Corke*, or other Port-Towns, and then sell them to the Merchants. By which Invention there is no such Thing as a ruined Farmer to be seen; but the People live with Comfort on Potatoes and Bonnyclabber, neither of which are vendible Commodities Abroad.

* Thick, sour milk.

On the Bill for the Clergy's Residing on their Livings

ON THE BILL FOR THE CLERGY'S
RESIDING ON THEIR LIVINGS

THOSE Gentlemen who have been promoted to Bishop-ricks in this Kingdom for severall years past, are of two sorts; First, certain private Clergymen from England, who by the force of friends, industry, sollicitation, or other means and merits to me unknown, have been raised to that character by the *mero motu* of the Crown.

Of the other sort, are some Clergymen born in this Kingdom, who have most distinguished themselves by their warmth against Popery, their great indulgence to Dissenters, and all true loyal Protestants; by their zeal for the House of Hanover, abhorrence of the Pretender, and an implicit readyness to fall into any measures that will make the Government easy to those who represent his Majesty's person.

Some of the former kind are such as are said to have enjoyed tolerable preferments in England; and it is therefore much to their commendation, that they have condescended to leave their native Country, and come over hither to be Bishops, meerly to promote Christianity among us; and therefore in my opinion, both their Lordships, and the many dependers they bring over, may justly claim the merit of missionaries sent to convert a Nation from Heresy and Heathenism.

Before I proceed farther, it may be proper to relate some particulars wherein the Circumstances of the English Clergy differ from those of Ireland.

The districts of Parishes throughout England continue much the same as they were before the Reformation; and most of the Churches are of the Gothick Architecture, built some hundred years ago; But the Tythes of great Numbers of Churches having been applied by the Pope's pretended authority to several Abbies, and even before the Reformation bestowed by that Sacrilegious Tyrant Henry VIII., on his ravenous favorites, the maintenance of an Incumbent, in most parts of the kingdom, is contemptibly small. And yet a Vicar there of forty pounds a year, can live with more comfort, than one of three times the nominal value with us. For his forty pounds are duly payd him, because there is not one Farmer in a hundred, who is not worth five times the rent he pays to his Landlord, and fifty times the sum demanded for the Tythes; which, by the small compass of his parish, he can easily collect or compound for; And if his behaviour and understanding be supportable, he will probably receive presents now and then from his parishioners, and perhaps from the Squire; who, although he may sometimes be apt to treat his Parson a little superciliously, will probably be softened by a little humble demeanour. The Vicar is likewise generally sure to find upon his admittance to his living, a convenient House and Barn in repair, with a garden, and a field or two to graze a few cows, and one horse for himself and his wife. He hath probably a market very near him, perhaps in his own village. No entertainment is expected from his visitors beyond a pot of ale, and a piece of Cheese. He hath every Sunday the comfort of a full congregation, of plain, cleanly people of both sexes, well to pass, and who speak his own language. The scene about him is fully cultivated (I mean for the general) and well inhabited. He dreads no thieves for anything but his apples, for the trade of universal stealing is not so epidemick there as with us. His wife is little better than goody, in her birth, education, or dress; and as to himself, we must let his parentage alone. If he be the son of a farmer it is very sufficient, and his sister may very decently be chambermaid to the Squire's wife. He goes about on working days in a grazier's coat, and will not scruple to assist his workmen in harvest time. He is usually wary and thrifty, and often more able to provide for a numerous family than some of ours can do with a Rectory called 300*l.* a year. His Daughters shall go to service, or be sent prentices to the semptstress of the next town; and his sons are put to honest trades. This is the usuall course of an English country vicar from twenty to sixty pounds a year.

As to the clergy of our own kingdom, their livings are

generally larger. Not originally, or by the Bounty of Princes, Parliaments, or charitable endowments, for the same Depradations (and as to glebes, a much greater) have been made here, but, by the destruction and desolation in the long wars between the Invaders and the Natives; during which Time a great part of the Bishops' lands, and almost all the glebes, were lost in the confusion. The first Invaders had almost the whole Kingdom divided among them. New Invaders succeeded, and drove out their Predecessors, as native Irish. These were expelled by others who came after, and upon the same pretensions. Thus it went on for several hundred years, and in some degree even to our own memories. And thus it will probably go on, although not in a Martial way, to the end of the world. For not only the purchasers of debentures forfeited in 1641, were all of English birth, but those after the Restoration, and many who came hither even since the Revolution, are looked upon as perfect Irish; directly contrary to the practice of all wise Nations, and particularly of the Greeks and Romans, in establishing their Colonies, by which name Ireland is very absurdly called.

Under these Distractions the Conquerors always seized what lands they could with little ceremony, whether they belonged to the Church or not: Thus the Glebes were almost universally exposed to the first seizers, and could never be recovered, although the grants, with the particular denominations, are manifest, and still in being. The whole Lands of the See of Waterford were wholly taken by one family; the like is reported of other Bishopricks.

King James the First, who deserves more of the Church of Ireland than all other Princes put together, having the forfeitures of vast tracts of Land in the Northern parts (I think commonly called the escheated Counties), having granted some hundred thousand acres of these Lands to certain Scotch and English favourites, was prevailed on by some great Prelates to grant to some Sees in the North, and to many Parishes there, certain parcels of land for the augmentation of poor Bishopricks, did likewise endow many Parishes with Glebes for the incumbents, whereof a good number escaped

the Depredations of 1641 and 1688. These lands, when they
were granted by King James, consisted mostly of woody
ground, wherewith those parts of this Island were then over-
run. This is well known, universally allowed, and by some in
part remembred; the roots being, in some places not stubbed
out to this day. And the value of the lands was consequently
very inconsiderable; till Scotch colonies came over in swarms
upon great encouragement to make them habitable; at least
for such a race of strong bodyed people, who came hither
from their own bleak barren Highlands, as it were into a
Paradise; who soon were able to get Straw for their bedding,
instead of a Bundle of Heath spread on the ground, and
sprinckled with water. Here, by degrees, they acquired some
degree of politeness and Civility, from such neighboring Irish
as were still left after Tyrone's last rebellion, and are since
grown almost entirely possessors of the North. Thus, at
length, the woods being rooted up, the land was brought in,
and tilled, and the glebes which could not before yield two-
pence an acre, are equal to the best, sometimes affording the
Minister a good demesne, and some land to let.

These wars and desolations in their natural consequences,
were likewise the cause of another effect; I mean that of
uniting several parishes under one Incumbent. For, as the
lands were of little value by the want of inhabitants to cultivate
them, and many of the Churches levelled to the ground,
particularly by the fanatick zeal of those rebellious Saints who
murdered their King, destroyed the Church, and overthrew
Monarchy, (for all which there is a humiliation day appointed
by law, and soon approaching); so, in order to give a tolerable
maintenance to a Minister, and the Country being too poor,
as well as devotion too low, to think of building new churches,
it was found necessary to repair some one Church which had
least suffered, and join sometimes three or more, enough for
a bare support to some clergyman, who knew not where to
provide himself better. This was a case of absolute necessity
to prevent Heathenism, as well as Popery, from overrunning
the Nation. The consequence of these unions was very
different, in different parts; For, in the North, by the Scotch

settlement, their numbers daily increasing by new additions from their own country, and their prolific quality peculiar to Northern people; and lastly by their universally feeding upon oats, (which grain, under its several preparations and denominations, is the only natural luxury of that hardy people) the value of tythes increased so prodigiously, that at this day, I confess, several united parishes ought to be divided, taking in so great a compass, that it is almost impossible for the people to travel timely to their own parish church, or their little churches to contain half their number, though the revenue would be sufficient to maintain two, or perhaps three worthy Clergymen with decency; provided the times mend, or that they were honestly dealt with; which I confess is seldom the case. I shall name only one, and it is the Deanery of Derry; the revenue whereof, if the dean could get his dues, exceeding that of some Bishopricks, both by the compass and fertility of the soil, the number as well as industry of the inhabitants, the conveniency of exporting their corn to Dublin and foreign parts; and, lastly, by the accidental discovery of Marl in many places of the several Parishes. Yet all this revenue is wholly founded upon corn; for I am told there is hardly an acre of Glebe for the Dean to plant and build on.

I am therefore of opinion, that a real un[de]falcated revenue of six hundred pounds a year, is a sufficient income for a country Dean in this kingdom; and since the rents consist wholly of tythes, two parishes, to the amount of that value, should be united, and the Dean reside as Minister in that of Down, and the remaining parishes be divided among worthy Clergymen, to about 300*l*. a year to each. The Deanry of Derry which is a large City might be left worth 800*l*. a year, and Rapho according as it shall be thought proper. These three are the only opulent Deanries in the whole Kingdom; and, as I am informed, consist all of tythes, which was an unhappy expedient in the Church, occasioned by the sacrilegious robberies during the several times of confusion and war; insomuch that at this day there is hardly any remainder left of Dean and chapter lands in Ireland; that delicious morsel swallowed so greedily in England under the fanatick Usurpations.

As to the present Scheme of a bill for obliging the Clergy to residence, now or lately in the privy Councel, I know no more of the particulars than what hath been told me by several Clergymen of distinction; who say that a petition in the name of them all hath been presented by the Lord Lieutenant and Councel, that they might be heard by their council against the Bill, and that the Petition was rejected, with some reasons why it was rejected; for the Bishops are supposed to know best what is proper for the Clergy. It seems the bill consists of two parts. First, a power in the Bishops, with consent of the Archbishop, and the Patron, to take off from every parish whatever it is worth above 300*l.* a year; and this to be done without the Incumbent's consent, which before was necessary in all divisions, The other part of the bill obligeth all Clergymen, from forty pounds a year and upwards, to reside, and build a house in his parish. But those of 40*l.* are remitted till they shall receive 100*l.* out [of] the revenue of first-fruits granted by her late Majesty.

Considerations upon Two Bills, &c.

CONSIDERATIONS

UPON TWO

BILLS

Sent down from the R — H — the

H——— of L———

To the H———ble

H———. of C———

Relating to the

CLERGY

OF

I. * . * . * . * . * . *. *D*.

LONDON.
Printed for A. MOORE, near St. *Paul's*,
and Sold by the Bookſellers of *Weſtminſter*
and *Southwark*, 1732.

ADVERTISEMENT

*I*N the Year 1731, *a Bill was brought into the House of Lords by a great Majority of the Right Reverend the Bishops, for enabling them to divide the Livings of the inferior Clergy; which Bill was approved of in the Privy-Council of* Ireland, *and passed by the Lords in Parliament. It was afterwards sent to the House of Commons for their Approbation; but was rejected by them with a great Majority. The supposed Author of the following Considerations, who hath always been the best Friend to the inferior Clergy of the Church of* England, *as may be seen by many Parts of his Writings, opposed this pernicious Project with great Success; which, if it had passed into Law would have been of the worst Consequence to this Nation.*

CONSIDERATIONS

UPON TWO

BILLS, &c.

I HAVE often, for above a Month past, desired some few Clergymen, who are pleased to visit me, that they would procure an Extract of two Bills, brought into the Council by some of the Bishops, and both of them since passed in the *House of Lords:* But I could never obtain what I desired, whether by the Forgetfulness, or Negligence of those whom I employed, or the Difficulty of the Thing itself. Therefore, if I shall happen to mistake in any Fact of Consequence, I desire my Remarks upon it, may pass for Nothing; for my Information is no better than what I received in Words from several Divines, who seemed to agree with each other. I have not the Honour to be acquainted with any one single *Prelate* of the Kingdom; and am a Stranger to their Characters, further than as common Fame reports them, which is not to be depended on. Therefore, I cannot be supposed to act upon any Principle of Resentment. I esteem their Functions (if I may be allowed to say so without Offence) as truly *Apostolical*, and absolutely necessary to the Perfection of a *Christian Church.*

THERE are no Qualities more incident to the Frailty and Corruptions of human Kind, than an Indifference, or Insensibility for other Mens Sufferings, and a sudden Forgetfulness of their own former humble State, when they rise in the World. These two Dispositions have not, I think, any where so strongly exerted themselves, as in the Order of Bishops, with regard to the inferior Clergy; for which I can find no Reasons, but such as naturally should seem to operate a quite contrary Way. The Maintenance of the *Clergy,* throughout the Kingdom, is precarious and uncertain, collected from a most miserable Race of beggarly Farmers; at whose Mercy every *Minister* lies to be defrauded: His Office, as *Rector*, or *Vicar*, if it be duly executed, is very laborious: As soon as he is promoted to a *Bishoprick*, the Scene is entirely and happily changed; his Revenues are large, and as surely paid as those of the *King*; his whole Business is once a Year to receive the Attendance, the Submission, and the Proxy-Money of all his Clergy, in whatever Part of the Diocese he shall please to think most convenient for himself. Neither is his personal Presence necessary, for the Business may be done by a *Vicar-General*. The Fatigue of Ordination, is just what the Bishops please to make it, and as Matters have been for some Time, and may probably remain, the fewer Ordinations the better. The rest of their visible Office, consists in the Honour of attending Parliaments and Councils, and bestowing Preferments in their own Gift; in which last Employment, and in their Spiritual and Temporal Courts, the Labour falls to their *Vicars-General, Secretaries, Proctors, Apparitors, Seneschals*, and the like. Now, I say, in so quick a Change, where their Brethren, in a few Days, are become their Subjects, it would be reasonable at least, to hope, that the Labour, Confinement, and Subjection from which they have so lately escaped, *like a Bird out of the Snare of the Fowler*, might a little incline them to remember the Condition of those, who were but last Week their Equals, probably their Companions or their Friends, and possibly as reasonable Expectants. There is a known Story of Colonel *Tidcomb*, who, while he continued a Subaltern Officer, was every Day complaining against the Pride, Oppression, and hard Treatment of *Colonels* towards their *Officers*; yet in a very few Minutes after he had received his Commission for a Regiment, walking with a Friend on the *Mall*, he confessed that the Spirit of Colonelship, was coming fast upon him, which Spirit is said to have daily increased to the Hour of his Death.

IT is true, the *Clergy* of this Kingdom, who are promoted to *Bishopricks*, have always some great Advantages; either that of rich *Deaneries*, opulent and multiplied *Rectories* and *Dignities*, strong Alliances by Birth or Marriage, fortified by a superlative Degree of Zeal and Loyalty; but, however, they were all at first no more than young Beginners; and before their great Promotion, were known by their plain *Christian* Names, among their old Companions, the middling Rate of *Clergymen*; nor could, therefore, be Strangers to their Condition, or with any good Grace, forget it so soon, as it hath too often happened.

I CONFESS, I do not remember to have observed any Body of Men, acting with so little Concert as our *Clergy* have done, in a Point where their Opinions appeared to be Unanimous: A Point wherein their whole Temporal Support was concerned, as well as their Power of serving GOD and his Church, in their Spiritual Functions. This hath been imputed to their Fear of disobliging, or hopes of further Favours upon Compliance; because it was observed, that some who appeared at first with greatest Zeal, thought fit suddenly to absent themselves from the usual Meetings; yet, we know what expert Sollicitors the *Quakers*, the *Dissenters*, and even the *Papists* have sometimes found, to drive a Point of Advantage, or prevent an impending Evil.

I HAVE not seen any Extract from the two Bills introduced into the Privy Council by the Bishops; where the Clergy, upon some Failure in Favour, or through the Timorousness of many among their Brethren, were refused to be heard by the Council. It seems, these Bills were both returned, agreed to by the King and Council in *England*; and the *House of Lords* hath, with great Expedition, past them both; and it is said they are immediately to be sent down to the *Commons* for their Consent.

THE Particulars, as they have been imperfectly reported to me, are as follow.

BY one of the Bills, the Bishops have Power to oblige the Country Clergy, to build a Mansion-House upon whatever Part of their Glebes their Lordships shall Command; and if the Living be above 50*l.* a Year, the Minister is bound to build, after three Years, a House that shall cost one Year and an half's Rent of his Income. For Instance, if a Clergyman, with a Wife and seven Children, gets a Living of 55*l. per Annum*, he must after three Years, build a House that shall cost 77*l.* 10*s.*

Q

And must support his Family during the Time the Bishop shall appoint for the Building of it with the Remainder. But, if the Living be under 50*l.* a Year, the Minister shall be allowed 100*l.* out of the first Fruits.

BUT, there is said to be one Circumstance a little Extraordinary; that if there be a single Spot in the Glebe more Barren, more Marshy, more exposed to Winds, more distant from the Church, or Skeleton of a Church, or from any Conveniency of Building: The Rector, or Vicar may be obliged by the Caprice, or Pique of the Bishop, to build, under pain of Sequestration (an Office, which ever falls into the most knavish Hands) upon whatever Point his *Lordship* shall command; although the Farmers have not paid one Quarter of his Dues.

I BELIEVE, under the present Distresses of the Kingdom (which inevitably, without a Miracle, must increase for ever) there are not ten Country Clergymen in *Ireland*, reputed to possess a Parish of 100*l. per Annum*, who, for some Years past, have actually received 60*l.* and that with the utmost Difficulty and Vexation. I am, therefore, at a Loss, what Kind of Valuators the *Bishops* will make use of; and whether the starving *Vicar*, shall be forced to build his House with the Money he never received.

THE other Bill, which passed in two Days after the former, is said to concern the Division of Parishes, into as many Parcels as the *Bishop* shall think fit, only leaving 300*l.* a Year to the Mother Church; which 300*l.* by another *Act* passed some Years ago, they can divide likewise, and crumble as low as their Will and Pleasure will dispose them. So, that instead of six hundred Clergymen, which, I think, is the usual Computation, we may have in a small Compass of Years almost as many Thousands to live with Decency and Comfort, provide for their Children, be charitable to the Poor, and maintain Hospitality.

BUT it is very reasonable to hope, and heartily to be wished by all those who have the least Regard to our Holy Religion, as hitherto established, or to a learned, pious, diligent, conversable *Clergyman*, or even to common Humanity; that the *Honour-*

able House of Commons will, in their great Wisdom, Justice, and Tenderness, to innocent Men, consider these Bills in another Light. It is said, they well knew this Kingdom not to be so over-stocked with neighbouring Gentry; but a discreet, learned *Clergyman*, with a Competency fit for one of his Education, may be an entertaining, a useful, and sometimes a necessary Companion. That, although such a Clergyman may not be able constantly to find BEEF and WINE for his own Family, yet he may be allowed sometimes to afford both to a Neighbour, without distressing himself; and the rather, because he may expect at least as good a Return. It will probably be considered, that in many desolate Parts, there may not be always a sufficient Number of Persons considerable enough to be trusted with *Commissions of the Peace*, which several of the *Clergy* now supply much better than a little, hedge, contemptible, illiterate *Vicar* from twenty to fifty Pounds a Year, the Son of a *Weaver*, *Pedlar*, *Taylor*, or *Miller*, can be presumed to do.

THE Landlords and Farmers by this Scheme can find no Profit, but will certainly be Losers; for Instance, if the large Northern Livings be split into a dozen Parishes, or more, it will be very necessary for the little threadbare *Gownman*, with his Wife, and every Child who can crawl, to watch the Fields at Harvest Time, for fear of losing a single Sheaf, which he could not afford under Peril of a Day's Starving; for according to the *Scotch* Proverb, *a hungry Louse bites sore*. This would of Necessity, breed an infinite Number of Brangles and litigious Suits in the Spiritual Courts; and put the wretched *Pastor* at perpetual Variance with his whole Parish. But, as they have hitherto stood, a Clergyman established in a competent Living is not under the Necessity of being so sharp, vigilant, and exacting. On the contrary, it is well known and allowed, that the Clergy round the Kingdom think themselves well treated, if they lose only one single Third of their legal Demands.

THE Honourable House may, perhaps, be inclined to conceive, that my *Lords* the *Bishops*, enjoy as ample a Power both Spiritual and Temporal, as will fully suffice to answer every

Branch of their Office; That, they want no Laws to regulate the Conduct of those Clergymen, over whom they preside; That, if Non-Residence be a Grievance, it is the Patron's Fault, who makes not a better Choice, or caused the Plurality. That, if the general impartial Character of Persons chosen into the Church, had been more regarded, and the Motive of *Party*, *Alliance*, *Kindred*, *Flatterers*, *Ill-Judgment*, or *Personal Favour* regarded less; there would be fewer Complaints of Non-Residence, Neglect of Cure, blameable Behaviour, or any other Part of Misconduct; not to mention *Ignorance* and *Stupidity*.

I COULD name certain Gentlemen of the *Gown*, whose aukward, spruce, prim, sneering, and smirking Countenances, the very Tone of their Voice, and an ungainly Strut in their Walk, without one single Talent for any one Office, have contrived to get good Preferment by the meer Force of *Flattery* and *Cringing:* For which two Virtues (the only two Virtues they pretend to) they were, however, utterly unqualified. And whom, if I were in Power, although they were my *Nephews* or had married my *Nieces*, I could never in Point of good Conscience or Honour, have recommended to a *Curacy* in *Connaught*.

THE *Honourable House of Commons* may likewise perhaps consider, that the Gentry of this Kingdom differ from all others upon Earth, being less capable of Employments in their own Country, than any others who come from Abroad; and, that most of them have little Expectation of providing for their younger Children, otherwise than by the Church, in which there might be some Hopes of getting a tolerable Maintenance. For, after the Patrons should have settled their *Sons*, their *Nephews*, their *Nieces*, their *Dependents*, and their *Followers*, invited over from the other Side, there would still remain an Overplus of smaller Church Preferments, to be given to such Clergy of the Nation, who shall have their *quantum* of whatever Merit may be then in Fashion. But by these Bills, they will be all as absolutely excluded, as if they had passed under the Denomination of *Tories*; unless they can be contented at the utmost with 5o*l*. a Year; which, by the Difficulties of collecting Tythes in *Ireland*, and the daily increasing Miseries of the People, will hardly rise to half that Sum.

It is observed, that the *Divines* sent over hither to govern this Church, have not seemed to consider the Difference between both Kingdoms, with Respect to the inferior *Clergy*. As to themselves, indeed, they find a large Revenue in Lands let at one quarter Value, which consequently must be paid while there is a Penny left among us; and, the Publick Distress so little affects their Interests, that their Fines are now higher than ever: They content themselves to suppose, that whatever a Parish is said to be worth, comes all into the *Parson*'s Pocket.

The Poverty of great Numbers among the *Clergy* in *England*, hath been the continual Complaint of all Men who wish well to the Church; and many Schemes have been thought on to redress it; yet an *English Vicar* of 40*l.* a Year, lives much more comfortably than one of double the Value in *Ireland*. His Farmers, generally speaking, are able and willing to pay him his full Dues: He hath a decent Church of antient Standing, filled every *Lord*'s *Day* with a large Congregation of plain People, well clad, and behaving themselves as if they believed in God and Christ. He hath a House and Barn in repair, a Field or two to graze his Cows, with a Garden and Orchard. No Guest expects more from him than a Pot of Ale; he lives like an honest plain Farmer, as his Wife is dressed but little better than *Goody*. He is sometimes graciously invited by the Squire, where he sits at humble Distance; if he gets the Love of his People, they often make him little useful Presents: He is happy by being born to no higher Expectation; for he is usually the Son of some ordinary Tradesman, or middling Farmer. His Learning is much of a Size with his Birth and Education; no more of either than what a poor hungry *Servitor* can be expected to bring with him from his *College*. It would be tedious to shew the Reverse of all this in our distant poorer Parishes, through most Parts of *Ireland*, wherein every Reader may make the Comparison.

Lastly, The *Honourable House of Commons* may consider, whether the Scheme of multiplying beggarly *Clergymen*, through the whole Kingdom, who must all have Votes for chusing Parliament Men (provided they can prove their Freeholds to be worth 40*s*. *per Annum*, *ultra reprisas*) may not, by their Numbers, have great Influence upon *Elections*; being entirely under the Dependance of their *Bishops*. For, by a moderate Computation, after all the Divisions and Sub-divisions of Parishes, that, my *Lords*, the *Bishops*, have Power to make by their new Laws, there will, as soon as the present Set of Clergy goes off, be raised an Army of *Ecclesiastical Militants*, able enough for any Kind of Service, except that of the Altar.

I AM, indeed, in some Concern about a Fund for building a thousand or two Churches, wherein these Probationers may read their *Wall-Lectures*; and begin to doubt they must be contented with *Barns*; which *Barns* will be one great advancing Step towards an Accommodation with our *true Protestant Brethren*, the *Dissenters*.

THE Scheme of encouraging *Clergymen* to build Houses by dividing a Living of 500*l*. a Year into ten Parts, is a Contrivance, the Meaning whereof hath got on the wrong Side of my Comprehension; unless it may be argued, that *Bishops* build no Houses, because they are so rich; and therefore, the inferior *Clergy* will certainly build, if you reduce them to Beggary. But I knew a very rich Man of Quality in *England*, who could never be persuaded to keep a *Servant* out of *Livery*; because such Servants would be expensive, and apt in Time, to look like Gentlemen; whereas, the others were ready to submit to the basest Offices, and at a cheaper Pennyworth might increase his Retinue.

I HEAR, it is the Opinion of many wise Men, that before these Bills should pass both Houses, they might be sent back to *England* with the following Clauses inserted.

FIRST, That whereas there may be about a Dozen double *Bishopricks* in *Ireland*, those *Bishopricks* should be split and given to different Persons; and those of a single Denomination be also divided into two, three, or four Parts as Occasion shall require; otherwise there may be a Question started, whether twenty two *Prelates* can effectually extend their paternal Care, and unlimited Power, for the Protection and

Correction of so great a Number of Spiritual *Subjects*. But, this Proposal will meet with such furious Objections, that I shall not insist upon it; for I well remember to have read, what a terrible Fright the *Frogs* were in, upon a Report, that the *Sun* was going to marry.

ANOTHER Clause should be, that none of these twenty, thirty, forty, or fifty Pounders may be suffered to marry, under the Penalty of immediate Deprivation; their Marriages declared *null*, and their Children Bastards: For, some desponding People take the Kingdom to be not in a Condition of encouraging so numerous a Breed of Beggars.

A THIRD Clause will be necessary, that these humble Gentry should be absolutely disqualified from giving Votes in *Elections* for *Parliament Men*.

OTHERS add a Fourth; which is a Clause of Indulgence, that these reduced *Divines* may be permitted to follow any lawful Ways of living, which will not call them too often or too far from their Spiritual Offices: (For, unless I misapprehend, they are supposed to have *Episcopal Ordination*.) For Example, they may be Lappers of Linnen, Bayliffs of the Mannor; they may let Blood, or apply Plaisters for three Miles round: They may get a Dispensation to hold the *Clerkship* and *Sextonship* of their own Parish *in Commendam*. Their Wives and Daughters may make Shirts for the Neighbourhood; or, if a *Barrack* be near, for the *Soldiers*: in Linnen Countries, they may *Card* and *Spin*, and keep a few Looms in the House: They may let Lodgings, and sell a Pot of Ale without Doors, but not at Home, unless to sober Company, and at regular Hours. It is by some thought a little hard, that in an Affair of the last Consequence, to the very Being of the *Clergy*, in the Points of Liberty and Property, as well as in their Abilities to perform their Duty; this whole Reverend Body, who are the established Instructors of the Nation in Christianity and Moral Virtues, and are the only Persons concerned; should be the sole Persons not consulted. Let any Scholar shew the like Precedent in *Christendom* for twelve hundred Years past. An Act of Parliament for setling or selling an Estate in a private Family, is never passed until all Parties give Consent. But in the present Case the whole Body of the *Clergy* is, as themselves apprehend, determined to utter Ruin, without once expecting or asking their Opinion; and this by a Scheme contrived only by one Part of the Convocation, while the other Part which hath been chosen in the usual Forms, wants only the regal Permission to assemble, and consult about the Affairs of the Church, as their Predecessors have always done in former Ages; where it is presumed, the *Lower House* hath a Power of proposing Canons, and a negative Voice, as well as the Upper. And, *God* forbid (say these Objectors) that there should be a real separate Interest between the *Bishops* and *Clergy*, any more than there is between a Man and his Wife, a King and his People, or *Christ* and his Church.

I⟨T⟩ seems there is a Provision in the Bill, that no Parish shall be cut into Scraps, without the Consent of several Persons who can be no Sufferers in the Matter; but I cannot find that the *Clergy* lay much Weight on this Caution; because they argue, that the very Persons from whom these Bills took their Rise, will have the greatest Share in the Decision.

I DO not, by any Means, conceive the crying Sin of the *Clergy* in this Kingdom, to be that of *Non-Residence*; I am sure, it is many Degrees less so here than in *England*; unless the Possession of Pluralities may pass under that Name; and if this be a Fault, it is well known to whom it must be imputed: I believe, upon a fair Inquiry (and I hear an Inquiry is to be made) they will appear to be most pardonably Few; especially, considering how many Parishes have not an Inch of *Glebe*; and how difficult it is upon any reasonable Terms, to find a Place of Habitation. And, therefore, GOD knows, whether, my *Lords the Bishops* will be soon able to convince the *Clergy*, or those who have any Regard for that venerable Body, that the chief Motive in their *Lordships* Minds, by procuring these Bills, was to prevent the Sin of *Non-Residence*, while the universal Opinion of almost every *Clergyman* in the Kingdom, without Distinction of Party, taking in even those who are not likely to be Sufferers, stands directly against them.

I⟨F⟩ some Livings in the *North* may be justly thought too large a Compass of Land, which makes it inconvenient for the remotest Inhabitants to attend the Service of the Church, which in some Instances may be true; no reasonable *Clergyman* would oppose a proper Remedy by particular Acts of Parliament.

THUS for Instance, the *Deanery of Down*, a Country *Deanery*, I think, without a Cathedral, depending wholly upor an Union of Parishes joined together, in a Time when the Land lay waste and thinly inhabited; since those Circumstances are so prodigiously changed for the Better, may properly be lessened, leaving a decent Competency to the *Dean*, and placing *Rectories* in the remaining Churches, which are now served only by stipendary *Curates*.

THE Case may be probably the same in other Parts: And such a Proceeding discreetly managed would be truly for the Good of the Church.

FOR, it is to be observed, that Dean and Chapter Lands, which in *England* were all seized under the Fanatick Usurpation, are Things unknown in *Ireland*, having been long ravished from the Church, by a Succession of Confusions; and Tythes applied in their Stead, to support that Ecclesiastical Dignity.

THE late * *Arch-Bishop of Dublin* had a very different Way of encouraging the *Clergy* of his Diocese to Residence: When a Lease had ran out seven Years or more, he stipulated with the Tenant to resign up twenty or thirty Acres to the Minister of the Parish where it lay convenient, without lessening his former Rent; and with no great Abatement of the Fine; and this he did in the Parts near *Dublin*, where Land is at the highest Rates, leaving a small Chiefry for the Minister to pay, hardly a sixth Part of the Value: I doubt not, that almost every *Bishop* in the Kingdom may do the same generous Act with less Damage to their Sees, than his late *Grace of Dublin*; much of whose Lands were out in Fee Farms, or Leases for Lives; and I am sorry that the good Example of such a *Prelate* hath not been followed.

BUT a great Majority of the *Clergy*'s Friends cannot hitherto reconcile themselves to this Project; which they call a *levelling Principle*, that must inevitably root out the Seeds of all honest Emulation, the legal Parent of the greatest Virtues, and most

* *The Right Reverend Dr.* William King.

generous Actions among Men; but in the general Opinion (for I do not pretend to offer my own) will never more have room to exert it self in the Breast of any *Clergyman* whom this Kingdom shall produce.

BUT, whether the Consequences of these Bills may, by the Virtues and Frailties of future *Bishops*, sent over hither to rule the Church, terminate in Good and Evil, I shall not presume to determine, since *God* can work the *Former* out of the *Latter*. However, one Thing I can venture to assert; that from the earliest Ages of Christianity to the Minute I am now Writing, there never was a Precedent of such a Proceeding, much less to be feared, hoped, or apprehended from such Hands in any Christian Country; and so it may pass for more than a *Phœnix*; because it hath risen without any Assistance from the *Ashes* of its *Sire*.

THE Appearance of so many *Dissenters* at the Hearing of this Cause, is what, I am told, hath not been charged to the Account of their Prudence or Moderation; because that Action hath been censured as a Mark of *Triumph* and Insult before the *Victory* is compleat; since neither of these Bills hath yet passed the *House of Commons*, and some are pleased to think it not impossible that they may be rejected. Neither do I hear, that there is an enacting Clause in either of the Bills to apply any Part of the divided or sub-divided Tythes, towards encreasing the Stipends of the *Sectaries*. So, that these Gentlemen seem to be gratified like him, who, after having been kicked down Stairs, took Comfort when he saw his Friend kicked down after him.

I HAVE heard many more Objections against several Particulars of both these Bills; but they are of so high a Nature, and carry such dreadful *Innuendoes*, that I dare not mention them, resolving to give no Offence, because I well know how obnoxious I have long been (although I conceive without any Fault of my own) to the Zeal and Principles of those, who place all Difference in Opinion, concerning publick Matters, to the Score of *Disaffection*; whereof I am at least as innocent as the loudest of my *Detractors*.

Dublin, February 24,
    1731-2.

A Proposal for an Act of Parliament to pay off the Debt of the Nation, &c.

A

PROPOSAL

FOR AN

Act of PARLIAMENT,

To pay off the

D E B T

OF THE

N A T I O N,

Without taxing the SUBJECT, by
which the Number of landed Gentry, and substantial Farmers will be considerably encreased, and
no one Person will be the poorer, or contribute
one Farthing to the Charge.

By A——— P———, Esq;

D U B L I N:

Printed in the Year M,DCC,XXXII.

A

PROPOSAL

FOR AN

ACT of PARLIAMENT to pay off the DEBT of the Nation, without taxing the Subject, by which the Number of landed Gentry, and substantial Farmers will be considerably encreased, and no Person will be the poorer, or contribute one Farthing to the Charge.

Written in the Year 1732.

THE Debts contracted some Years past, for the Service and Safety of the Nation, are grown so great, that under our present distressed Condition, by the Want of Trade, the great Remittances to pay *Absentees*, Regiments serving abroad, and many other Drains of Money, well enough known and felt; the Kingdom seems altogether unable to discharge them by the common Methods of Payment: And either a *Pole* or *Land Tax*, would be too odious to think of, especially the latter; because the Lands which have been let for these Ten or Dozen Years past, were raised so high, that the Owners can, at present, hardly receive any Rent at all. For, it is the usual Practice of an *Irish* Tenant, rather than want Land, to offer more for a Farm than he knows he can be ever able to pay; and in that Case he grows desperate, and pays nothing at all. So that a *Land Tax*, upon a rackt Estate, would be a Burthen wholly insupportable.

THE Question will then be, how these national Debts

can be paid; and how I can make good the several Particulars of my Proposal; which I shall now lay open to the Publick.

THE Revenues of their Graces and Lordships, the Archbishops and Bishops of this Kingdom, (excluding the Fines) do amount by a moderate Computation, to 36,800 *l. per Ann.* I mean the Rents which the Bishops receive from their Tenants. But the real Value of those Lands, at a full Rent, taking the several Sees one with another, is reckoned to be, at least, three Fourths more; so that multiplying 36,800 *l.* by 4, the full Rent of all the Bishops Lands, will amount to 147200 *l. per Ann.* from which subtracting the present Rent received by their Lordships, that is 36,800 *l.* the Profits of the Lands received by the first and second Tenants (who both have great Bargains) will rise to the Sum of 110400 *l. per Ann.* which Lands, if they were to be sold at Twenty-two Years Purchase, would raise a Sum of 2,428,800 *l.* reserving to the Bishops their present Rents, only excluding Fines.

OF this Sum I propose, that out of the one Half which amounts to 1,214,400 *l.* so much be applied, as will entirely discharge the Debts of the Nation; and the Remainder laid up in the Treasury, to supply Contingencies, as well as to discharge some of our heavy Taxes, until the Kingdom shall be in a better Condition.

BUT, whereas the present Set of Bishops would be great Losers by this Scheme, for want of their Fines; which would be hard Treatment to such *religious*, *loyal*, and *deserving* Personages; I have therefore set a-part the other Half, to supply that Defect; which it will more than sufficiently do.

A BISHOP's Lease for the full Term, is reckoned to be worth Eleven Years Purchase; but if we take the Bishops round, I suppose there may be four Years of each Lease elapsed; and many of the Bishops being well stricken in Years, I cannot think their Lives round to be worth more than seven Years Purchase; so that the Purchasers may very well afford Fifteen Years Purchase for the Reversion; especially by one great additional Advantage, which I shall soon mention.

THIS Sum of 2,428,800 *l.* must likewise be sunk very considerably; because the Lands are to be sold only at Fifteen

Years Purchase, and this lessens the Sum to about 1,656,000 *l.* of which I propose Twelve Hundred Thousand Pounds, to be applied partly for the Payment of the national Debt, and partly as a Fund for future Exigencies; and the remaining 456,000 *l.* I propose as a Fund for paying the present Set of Bishops their Fines; which it will abundantly do, and a great Part remain as an Addition to the publick Stock.

ALTHOUGH the Bishops round do not, in Reality, receive three Fines a Piece, which take up 21 Years, yet I allow it to be so; but then, I will suppose them to take but one Year's Rent, in Recompence of giving them so large a Term of Life; and thus multiplying 36800 *l.* by 3, the Product will be only 110400 *l.* so that above three Fourths will remain, to be applied to publick Use.

IF I have made wrong Computations, I hope to be excused, as a Stranger to the Kingdom; which I never saw till I was called to an Employment, and yet where I intend to pass the Rest of my Days; but I took Care to get the best Information I could, and from the most proper Persons; however, the Mistakes I may have been guilty of, will very little affect the Main of my Proposal; although they should cause a Difference of one Hundred Thousand Pounds, more or less.

THESE Fines are only to be paid to the Bishop, during his Incumbency in the same See: If he change it for a better, the Purchasers of the vacant See Lands, are to come immediately into Possession of the See he hath left; and both the Bishop who is removed, and he who comes into his Place, are to have no more Fines; for the removed Bishop will find his Account by a larger Revenue; and the other See will find Candidates enough. For the Law Maxim will here have Place: *Caveat Emptor.* I mean the Persons who succeed, may chuse whether they will accept or no.

As to the Purchasers, they will probably be Tenants to the See, who are already in Possession, and can afford to give more than any other Bidders.

I WILL further explain myself. If a Person already a Bishop, be removed into a richer See, he must be content with the bare Revenues, without any Fines; and so must he who comes into a

R

Bishoprick vacant by Death: And this will bring the Matter sooner to bear; which, if the Crown shall think fit to countenance, will soon change the present Set of Bishops, and consequently encourage Purchasers of their Lands. For Example: If a Primate should die, and the Gradation be wisely made, almost the whole Set of Bishops might be changed in a Month, each to his great Advantage, although no Fines were to be got; and thereby save a great Part of that Sum, which I have appropriated towards supplying the Deficiency of Fines.

I HAVE valued the Bishops Lands two Years Purchase, above the usual computed Rate; because those Lands will have a Sanction from the King and Council in *England*, and be confirmed by an Act of Parliament here: Besides, it is well known, that higher Prices are given every Day for worse Lands, at the remotest Distances, and at Rack Rents, which I take to be occasioned by Want of Trade: When there are few Borrowers, and the little Money in private Hands lying dead, there is no other way to dispose of it, but in buying of Land; which consequently makes the Owners hold it so high.

BESIDES paying the Nation's Debts, the Sale of these Lands would have many other good Effects upon the Nation. It will considerably increase the Number of Gentry, where the Bishops Tenants are not able or willing to purchase; for the Lands will afford an Hundred Gentlemen a good Revenue to each. Several Persons from *England*, will probably be glad to come over hither, and be the Buyers, rather than give Thirty Years Purchase at home, under the Loads of Taxes for the Publick and the Poor, as well as Repairs; by which Means, much Money may be brought among us; and probably some of the Purchasers themselves, may be content to live cheap in a worse Country, rather than be at the Charge of Exchange and Agencies; and perhaps of *Non-solvencies* in Absence, if they lett their Lands too high.

THIS Proposal will also multiply Farmers, when the Purchasers will have Lands in their own Power, to give long and easy Leases to industrious Husbandmen.

I HAVE allowed some Bishopricks, of equal Income, to be of more or less Value to the Purchaser, according as they are circumstanced. For Instance: The Lands of the Primacy, and some other Sees, are lett so low, that they hardly pay a fifth Penny of the real Value to the Bishop, and there the Fines are the greater. On the contrary, the Sees of *Meath* and *Clonfert*, consisting, as I am told, much of Tythes, those Tythes are annually lett to the Tenants, without any Fines. So the See of *Dublin* is said to have many Fee-Farms, which pay no Fines; and some Leases for Lives, which pay very little, and not so soon nor so duly.

I CANNOT but be confident, that their Graces my Lords the Arch-bishops, and my Lords the Bishops, will heartily join in this Proposal, out of Gratitude to his late and present Majesty, the best of Kings, who have bestowed on them such high and opulent Stations; as well as in Pity to this Country, which is now become their own; whereby they will be instrumental towards paying the Nation's Debts, without impoverishing themselves; enrich an Hundred Gentlemen, as well as free them from Dependance; and thus remove that Envy which is apt to fall upon their Graces and Lordships, from considerable Persons; whose Birth and Fortunes, rather qualify them to be Lords of Mannors, than servile Dependents upon Churchmen, however dignified or distinguished.

IF I do not flatter my self, there could not be any Law more popular than this. For the immediate Tenants to Bishops, being some of them Persons of Quality, and good Estates; and more of them grown up to be Gentlemen by the Profits of these very Leases, under a Succession of Bishops; think it a Disgrace to be Subject both to Rents and Fines, at the Pleasure of their Landlords. Then, the Bulk of the Tenants, especially the *Dissenters*, who are our *true loyal* Protestant Brethren, look upon it, both as an unnatural and iniquitous Thing, that Bishops should be Owners of Land at all; (wherein I beg to differ from them) being a Point so contrary to the Practice of the Apostles, whose Successors they are deemed to be, and who, although they were contented that Land should be sold, for the common Use of the Brethren; yet would not buy it themselves; but had it laid at their Feet, to be distributed to poor Proselytes.

I WILL add one Word more; that by such a wholesome Law, all the Oppressions felt by under Tenants of Church Leases, which are now laid on by the Bishops; would entirely be prevented, by their Graces and Lordships consenting to have their Lands sold for Payment of the Nation's Debts; reserving only the present Rent for their own plentiful and honourable Support.

I BEG Leave to add one Particular; that, when Heads of a Bill (as I find the Style runs in this Kingdom) shall be brought in for forming this Proposal into a Law; I should humbly offer, that there might be a Power given to every Bishop, (except those who reside in *Dublin*) for applying one Hundred Acres of profitable Land, that lies nearest to his Palace, as a Demesne for the Conveniency of his Family.

I KNOW very well, that this Scheme hath been much talked of for some Time past, and is in the Thoughts of many Patriots; neither was it properly mine, although I fell readily into it, when it was first communicated to me.

ALTHOUGH I am almost a perfect Stranger in this Kingdom; yet since I have accepted an Employment here, of some Consequence as well as Profit; I cannot but think my self in Duty bound to consult the Interest of a People, among whom I have been so well received. And if I can be any way instrumental, towards contributing to reduce this excellent Proposal into a Law; which, being not in the least injurious to *England*, will, I am confident, meet with no Opposition from that Side; my sincere Endeavours to serve this Church and Kingdom, will be well rewarded.

An Examination of Certain Abuses, &c.

A N

EXAMINATION

OF CERTAIN

Abuses, Corruptions,

A N D

ENORMITIES

IN THE

City of *DUBLIN.*

Dublin: Printed in the Year 1732.

EXAMINATION

OF

*Certain Abuses, Corruptions, and Enormities, in the
City of* Dublin

Written in the Year 1732.

NOTHING is held more commendable in all great
Cities, especially the Metropolis of a Kingdom, than
what the *French* call the *Police*: By which Word is
meant the Government thereof, to prevent the many Disorders
occasioned by great Numbers of People and Carriages,
especially through narrow Streets. In this Government our
famous City of *Dublin* is said to be very defective; and universally complained of. Many wholesome Laws have been
enacted to correct those Abuses, but are ill executed; and
many more are wanting; which I hope the united Wisdom of
the Nation (whereof so many good Effects have already
appeared this Session) will soon take into their profound
Consideration.

As I have been always watchful over the Good of mine
own Country; and particularly for that of our renowned City;
where, (*absit invidia*) I had the Honour to draw my first
Breath; I cannot have a Minute's Ease or Patience to forbear
enumerating some of the greatest Enormities, Abuses, and
Corruptions spread almost through every Part of *Dublin*; and
proposing such Remedies, as, I hope, the Legislature will
approve of.

THE narrow Compass to which I have confined my self
in this Paper, will allow me only to touch the most important

Defects; and such as I think, seem to require the most speedy Redress.

AND first: Perhaps there was never known a wiser Institution than that of allowing certain Persons of both Sexes, in large and populous Cities, to cry through the Streets many Necessaries of Life: It would be endless to recount the Conveniences which our City enjoys by this useful Invention; and particularly Strangers, forced hither by Business, who reside here but a short time: For, these having usually but little Money, and being wholly ignorant of the Town, might at an easy Price purchase a tolerable Dinner, if the several Criers would pronounce the Names of the Goods they have to sell, in any tolerable Language. And therefore until our Law-makers shall think it proper to interpose so far as to make those Traders pronounce their Words in such Terms, that a plain Christian Hearer may comprehend what is cryed; I would advise all new Comers to look out at their Garret Windows, and there see whether the Thing that is cryed be *Tripes*, or *Flummery*, *Buttermilk*, or *Cowheels*. For, as Things are now managed, how is it possible for an honest Countryman, just arrived, to find out what is meant, for instance, by the following Words, with which his Ears are constantly stunned twice a Day, *Muggs, Juggs, and Porringers, up in the Garret, and down in the Cellar*. I say, how is it possible for any Stranger to understand that this Jargon is meant as an Invitation to buy a Farthing's Worth of Milk for his Breakfast or Supper, unless his Curiosity draws him to the Window, or until his Landlady shall inform him? I produce this only as one Instance, among a Hundred much worse; I mean where the Words make a Sound wholly inarticulate, which give so much Disturbance, and so little Information.

THE Affirmation solemnly made in the Cry of *Herrings*, is directly against all Truth and Probability; *Herrings alive, alive here*: The very Proverb will convince us of this; for what is more frequent in ordinary Speech, than to say of some Neighbour for whom the Passing-Bell rings, that *he is dead as a Herring*. And, pray how is it possible, that a *Herring*, which, as *Philosophers* observe, cannot live longer than One

Minute, Three Seconds and a half out of Water, should bear
a Voyage in open Boats from *Howth* to *Dublin*, be tossed into
twenty Hands, and preserve its Life in Sieves for several
Hours? Nay, we have Witnesses ready to produce, that many
Thousands of these Herrings, so impudently asserted to be
alive, have been a Day and a Night upon dry land. But this
is not the worst. What can we think of those impious
Wretches, who dare in the Face of the Sun, vouch the very
same Affirmative of their *Salmon*; and cry, *Salmon alive, alive*;
whereas, if you call the Woman who cryes it, she is not ashamed
to turn back her Mantle, and shew you this individual Salmon
cut into a dozen Pieces. I have given good Advice to these
infamous Disgracers of their Sex and Calling, without the
least Appearance of Remorse; and fully against the Conviction
of their own Consciences. I have mentioned this Grievance to
several of our Parish Ministers; but all in vain: So that it must
continue until the Government shall think fit to interpose.

T H E R E is another *Cry*, which, from the strictest Observation I can make, appears to be very modern, and it is that of
* *Sweet-hearts*; and is plainly intended for a Reflection upon the
Female Sex; as if there were at present so great a Dearth of
Lovers, that the Women instead of receiving Presents from
Men, were now forced to offer Money, to purchase *Sweet-
hearts*. Neither am I sure, that this *Cry* doth not glance at
some Disaffection against the Government; insinuating, that
while so many of our Troops are engaged in foreign Service;
amd such a great Number of our gallant Officers constantly
reside in *England*; the Ladies are forced to take up with *Parsons*
and *Attornies*: But this is a most unjust Reflection; as may
soon be proved by any Person who frequents the *Castle*, our
public Walks, our Balls and Assemblies; where the Crowds of
†*Toupees* were never known to swarm as they do at present.

T H E R E is a *Cry* peculiar to this City, which I do not
remember to have been used in *London*; or at least, not in the
same Terms that it hath been practised by both Parties, during

---

* *A Sort of Sugar-Cakes in the Shape of Hearts.*
    † *A new Name for a modern Periwig, and for its owner; now in Fashion, Dec. 1,*
1733.

each of their Power; but, very unjustly by the *Tories*. While these were at the Helm, they grew daily more and more impatient to put all true *Whigs* and *Hanoverians* out of Employments. To effect which, they hired certain ordinary Fellows, with large Baskets on their Shoulders, to call aloud at every House, *Dirt to carry out*; giving that Denomination to our whole Party; as if they would signify, that the Kingdom could never be *cleansed*, until we were *swept* from the Earth like *Rubbish*. But, since that happy Turn of Times, when we were so *miraculously* preserved by just an *Inch*, from *Popery*, *Slavery*, *Massacre*, and the *Pretender*; I must own it Prudence in us, still to go on with the same *Cry*; which hath ever since been so effectually observed, that the true *political Dirt* is wholly removed, and thrown on its proper Dunghills, there to corrupt and be no more heard of.

BUT, to proceed to other Enormities: Every Person who walks the Streets, must needs observe the immense Number of human Excrements at the Doors and Steps of waste Houses, and at the Sides of every dead Wall; for which the disaffected Party hath assigned a very false and malicious Cause. They would have it that these Heaps were laid there privately by *British Fundaments*, to make the World believe, that our *Irish* Vulgar do daily eat and drink; and consequently, that the Clamour of Poverty among us, must be false; proceeding only from *Jacobites* and *Papists*. They would confirm this, by pretending to observe, that a *British Anus* being more narrowly perforated than one of our own Country; and many of these Excrements, upon a strict View appearing Copple-crowned, with a Point like a Cone or Pyramid, are easily distinguished from the *Hibernian*, which lie much flatter, and with less Continuity. I communicated this Conjecture to an eminent Physician, who is well versed in such profound Speculations; and at my Request was pleased to make Trial with each of his Fingers, by thrusting them into the *Anus* of several Persons of both Nations; and professed he could find no such Difference between them as those ill-disposed People alledge. On the contrary, he assured me, that much the greater Number of narrow Cavities were of *Hibernian* Origin. This I only mention to shew how ready the *Jacobites* are to lay hold of any Handle to express their Malice against the Government. I had almost forgot to add, that my Friend the Physician could, by smelling each Finger, distinguish the *Hibernian* Excrement from the *British*; and was not above twice mistaken in an Hundred Experiments; upon which he intends very soon to publish a learned Dissertation.

THERE is a Diversion in this City, which usually begins among the *Butchers*; but is often continued by a Succession of other People, through many Streets. It is called the COS-SING *of a Dog*: And I may justly number it among our Corruptions. The Ceremony is thus: A strange Dog happens to pass through a Flesh-Market: Whereupon an expert *Butcher* immediately cries in a loud Voice, and the proper Tone, *Coss*, *Coss*, several Times: The same Word is repeated by the People. The Dog, who perfectly understands the Term of Art, and consequently the Danger he is in, immediately flies. The People, and even his own *Brother Animals* pursue: The Pursuit and Cry attend him perhaps half a Mile; he is well worried in his Flight; and sometimes hardly escapes. This, our Ill-wishers of the *Jacobite* Kind, are pleased to call a *Persecution*; and affirm, that it always falls upon *Dogs* of the *Tory* Principle. But, we can well defend our selves, by justly alledging, that, when they were uppermost, they treated our *Dogs* full as inhumanly: As to my own Part, who have in former Times often attended these *Processions*; although I can very well distinguish between a *Whig* and a *Tory Dog*; yet I never carried my Resentments very far upon a *Party Principle*, except it were against certain malicious *Dogs*, who most discovered their Enmity against us in the *worst of Times*. And, I remember too well, that in the wicked Ministry of the Earl of *Oxford*, a large Mastiff of our Party being unmercifully *cossed*; ran, without Thinking, between my Legs, as I was coming up *Fishamble-street*; and, as I am of low Stature, with very short Legs, bore me riding backwards down the Hill, for above Two Hundred Yards: And, although I made use of his Tail for a Bridle, holding it fast with both my Hands, and clung my Legs as close to his Sides as I could; yet we both came down together into the Middle of the Kennel; where after rowling three or four Times over each other, I got up with much ado, amidst the Shouts and Huzza's of a Thousand malicious *Jacobites:* I cannot, indeed, but gratefully acknowledge, that for this and many other *Services* and *Sufferings*, I have been since more than over-paid.

THIS Adventure, may, perhaps, have put me out of Love with the Diversion of *Cossing*; which I confess myself an Enemy too; unless we could always be sure of distinguishing *Tory Dogs*; whereof great Numbers have since been so prudent, as entirely to change their Principles; and are now justly esteemed the best *Worriers* of their former Friends.

I AM assured, and partly know, that all the Chimney-Sweeper Boys, where Members of Parliament chiefly lodge, are hired by *our Enemies* to sculk in the Tops of Chimneys, with their Heads no higher than will just permit them to look round; and at the usual Hours when Members are going to the House, if they see a Coach stand near the Lodging of any *loyal* Member; they call *Coach, Coach*, as loud as they can bawl, just at the Instant when the Footman begins to give the same Call. And this is chiefly done on those Days, when any Point of Importance is to be debated. This Practice may be of very dangerous Consequence. For, these Boys are all hired by Enemies to the Government: And thus, by the Absence of a few Members for a few Minutes, a Question may be carried against the *true Interest* of the Kingdom; and, very probably, not without an Eye towards the *Pretender*.

I HAVE not observed the Wit and Fancy of this Town, so much employed in any one Article as that of contriving Variety of Signs to hang over Houses, where *Punch* is to be sold. The Bowl is represented full of *Punch*; the Ladle stands erect in the middle; supported sometimes by one, and sometimes by two Animals, whose Feet rest upon the Edge of the Bowl. These Animals are sometimes one black *Lion*, and sometimes a Couple; sometimes a single *Eagle*, and sometimes a spread One; and we often meet a *Crow, a Swan*, a *Bear*, or a *Cock*, in the same Posture.

NOW, I cannot find how any of these Animals, either

separate, or in Conjunction, are, properly speaking, fit Emblems or Embellishments, to advance the Sale of *Punch*. Besides, it is agreed among *Naturalists*, that no Brute can endure the Taste of strong Liquor; except where he hath been used to it from his Infancy: And, consequently, it is against all the Rules of *Hieroglyph*, to assign those Animals as Patrons, or Protectors of *Punch*. For, in that Case, we ought to suppose that the Host keeps always ready the real Bird, or Beast, whereof the Picture hangs over his Door, to entertain his Guests; which, however, to my Knowledge, is not true in Fact: Not one of those Birds being a proper Companion for a *Christian*, as to aiding and assisting in making the *Punch*. For, as they are drawn upon the Sign, they are much more likely to mute, or shed their Feathers into the Liquor. Then, as to the *Bear*, he is too terrible, awkward, and slovenly a Companion to converse with; neither are any of them all *handy* enough to fill Liquor to the Company: I do, therefore, vehemently suspect a *Plot* intended against the Government, by these Devices. For, although the *Spread-Eagle* be the Arms of *Germany*, upon which Account it may possibly be a lawful *Protestant* Sign; yet I, who am very suspicious of fair Outsides, in a Matter which so nearly concerns our Welfare, cannot but call to Mind, that the *Pretender*'s Wife is said to be of *German* Birth: And that many *Popish* Princes, in so vast an Extent of Land, are reported to excel both at making and drinking *Punch*. Besides, it is plain, that the *Spread-Eagle* exhibits to us the perfect Figure of a *Cross*; which is a Badge of *Popery*. Then, as to the *Cock*, he is well known to represent the *French* Nation, our old and dangerous Enemy. The *Swan*, who must of Necessity cover the entire Bowl with his Wings, can be no other than the *Spaniard*; who endeavours to engross all the Treasures of the *Indies* to himself. The *Lion* is indeed the common Emblem of Royal Power, as well as the Arms of *England*: But to paint him black, is perfect *Jacobitism*; and a manifest Type of those who *blacken* the Actions of the best Princes. It is not easy to distinguish whether that other Fowl painted over the *Punch-Bowl*, be a *Crow* or *Raven*? It is true, they have both been held ominous Birds: But I rather take it to be the former; because it is the Disposition of a *Crow*, to pick out the Eyes of other Creatures; and often even of *Christians*, after they are dead; and is therefore drawn here, with a Design to put the *Jacobites* in Mind of their old Practice; first to lull us a-sleep, (which is an Emblem of Death) and then to blind our Eyes, that we may not see their dangerous Practices against the State.

To speak my private Opinion; the least offensive Picture in the whole Sett, seems to be the *Bear*; because he represents *Ursa Major*, or the *Great Bear*, who presides over the *North*; where the *Reformation* first began; and which, next to *Britain*, (including *Scotland* and the *North of Ireland*) is the great Protector of the *true Protestant* Religion. But, however, in those Signs where I observe the *Bear* to be *chained*, I cannot help surmising a *Jacobite* Contrivance; by which, these Traytors hint an earnest Desire of using all *true Whigs*, as their Predecessors did the primitive Christians: I mean, to represent us as *Bears*, and then halloo their *Tory-Dogs* to bait us to Death.

Thus I have given a fair Account of what I dislike, in all the Signs set over those Houses that invite us to *Punch*. I own it was a Matter that did not need explaining; being so very obvious to common Understanding: Yet, I know not how it happens, but methinks there seems a fatal Blindness, to overspread our corporeal Eyes, as well as our intellectual; and I heartily wish, I may be found a false Prophet. For, these are not bare Suspicions, but manifest Demonstrations.

Therefore, away with these *Popish*, *Jacobite*, and idolatrous Gew-gaws. And I heartily wish a Law were enacted, under severe Penalties, against drinking any *Punch* at all: For, nothing is easier, than to prove it a disaffected Liquor. The chief Ingredients, which are *Brandy*, *Oranges*, and *Lemons*, are all sent us from *Popish* Countries; and nothing remains of *Protestant* Growth, but *Sugar* and *Water*. For, as to Biscuit, which formerly was held a necessary Ingredient, and is truly *British*, we find it is entirely rejected.

But I will put the Truth of my Assertion past all Doubt: I mean, that this Liquor is by one important Innovation, grown of ill Example, and dangerous Consequence to the

Publick. It is well known, that, by the true original Institution of making *Punch*, left us by Captain *Ratcliff*, the Sharpness is only occasioned by the Juice of *Lemons*; and so continued until after the happy *Revolution. Oranges*, alas! are a meer Innovation, and, in a manner, *but of Yesterday*. It was the Politicks of *Jacobites* to introduce them gradually: And, to what Intent? The Thing speaks it self. It was cunningly to shew their Virulence against his sacred Majesty King *William, of ever glorious and immortal Memory*. But of late (to shew how fast Disloyalty increaseth) they came from one to two, and then to three *Oranges*; nay, at present, we often find *Punch* made all with *Oranges*; and not one single *Lemon*. For, the *Jacobites*, before the Death of that immortal Prince, had, by a Superstition, formed a private Prayer; that, as they *squeezed* the *Orange*, so might that *Protestant* King be *squeezed* to Death: According to the known *Sorcery* described by *Virgil*; *Limus ut hic durescit, & hæc ut cera liquescit*, &c. And, thus the *Romans*, when they sacrificed an Ox, used this Kind of Prayer: *As I knock down this Ox, so may thou*, O Jupiter, *knock down our Enemies*. In like Manner, after King *William's* Death, whenever a *Jacobite squeezed* an *Orange*, he had a mental Curse upon the *glorious Memory*; and a hearty Wish for Power to *squeeze* all his Majesty's Friends to Death, as he *squeezed* that *Orange*, which bore one of his Titles, as he was Prince of *Orange*. This I do affirm for Truth; many of that Faction having confessed it to me, under an *Oath of Secrecy*; which, however, I thought it my Duty not to keep, when I saw my dear Country in Danger. But, what better can be expected from an *impious* Set of Men, who never scruple to drink CONFUSION to all *true Protestants*, under the Name of *Whigs*? A most unchristian and inhuman Practice; *which, to our great Honour and Comfort, was* never *charged upon us, even by our most malicious Detractors*.

THE Sign of two *Angels*, hovering in the Air, and with their Right Hands supporting a *Crown*, is met with in several Parts of this City; and hath often given me great Offence: For, whether by the Unskilfulness, or dangerous Principles of the Painters, (although I have good Reasons to suspect the latter) those *Angels* are usually drawn with such horrid, or indeed

S

rather diabolical *Countenances*, that they give great Offence to every loyal Eye; and equal Cause of Triumph to the *Jacobites*; being a most infamous Reflection upon our able and excellent Ministry.

I NOW return to that great Enormity of City *Cries*; most of which we have borrowed from *London*. I shall consider them only in a *political* View, as they nearly affect the Peace and Safety of both Kingdoms: And having been originally contrived by wicked *Machiavels*, to bring in *Popery*, *Slavery*, and *arbitrary Power*, by defeating the *Protestant* Succession, and introducing the *Pretender*; ought, in Justice, to be here laid open to the World.

ABOUT two to three Months after the happy *Revolution*, all Persons who possess any Employment or Office, in Church or State, were obliged by an Act of Parliament, to take the Oaths to King *William* and Queen *Mary:* And a great Number of disaffected Persons, refusing to take the said Oaths, from a pretended Scruple of Conscience, but really from a Spirit of *Popery* and Rebellion, they contrived a Plot, to make the swearing to those Princes odious in the Eyes of the People. To this End, they hired certain Women of ill Fame, but loud shrill Voices, under the Pretence of selling Fish, to go through the Streets, with Sieves on their Heads, and cry, *buy my Soul, buy my Soul*; plainly insinuating, that all those who swore to King *William*, were just ready to sell their *Souls* for an Employment. This Cry was revived at the Death of Queen *Anne*, and I hear still continues in *London*, with much Offence to all *true Protestants*; but, to our great Happiness, seems to be almost dropt in *Dublin*.

BUT, because I altogether contemn the Displeasure and Resentment of *High-flyers*, *Tories*, and *Jacobites*, whom I look upon to be *worse even than profest Papists*; I do here declare, that those Evils which I am going to mention, were all brought upon us in the * *worst of Times*, under the late Earl of *Oxford*'s Administration, during the four last Years of Queen *Anne*'s

* *A Cant-Word used by Whigs for the last four Years of Queen* Anne's *Reign, during the Earl of* Oxford's *Ministry; whose Character here is an exact Reverse in every Particular.*

Reign. *That wicked Minister was universally known to be a Papist in his Heart. He was of a most avaricious Nature, and is said to have died worth four Millions, sterl. besides his vast Expences in Building, Statues, Plate, Jewels, and other costly Rarities. He was of a mean obscure Birth, from the very Dregs of the People; and so illiterate, that he could hardly read a Paper at the Council Table. I forbear to touch at his open, prophane, profligate Life; because I desire not to rake into the Ashes of the Dead; and therefore I shall observe this wise Maxim:* De mortuis nil nisi bonum.

THIS flagitious Man, in order to compass his black Designs, employed certain wicked Instruments (which great Statesmen are never without) to adapt several *London* Cries, in such a Manner as would best answer his Ends. And, whereas it was upon good Grounds grievously suspected, that all *Places* at Court were sold to the highest Bidder: Certain Women were employed by his Emissaries, to carry *Fish* in Baskets on their Heads, and bawl through the Streets, *Buy my fresh Places.* I must, indeed, own that other Women used the same Cry, who were innocent of this wicked Design, and really sold their Fish of that Denomination, to get an honest Livelihood: But the rest, who were in the *Secret*, although they carried *Fish* in their Sieves or Baskets, to save Appearances; yet they had likewise a certain Sign, somewhat resembling that of the *Free-Masons*, which the Purchasers of *Places* knew well enough, and were directed by the Women whither they were to resort, and make their Purchase. And, I remember very well, how oddly it lookt, when we observed many Gentlemen finely drest, about the Court-End of the Town, and as far as *York-Buildings*, where the Lord-Treasurer *Oxford* dwelt; calling the Women who cried *Buy my fresh Places*, and talking to them in the Corner of a Street, until they understood each other's Sign. But we never could observe that any Fish was bought.

SOME Years before the Cries last mentioned; the Duke of *Savoy* was reported to have made certain Overtures to the Court of *England*, for admitting his eldest Son, by the Dutchess of *Orleans*'s Daughter, to succeed to the Crown, as next Heir, upon the *Pretender*'s being rejected; and that Son was immediately to turn *Protestant*. It was confidently reported, that great Numbers of People disaffected to the then *Illustrious* but now *Royal* House of *Hanover*, were in those Measures. Whereupon, another Sett of Women were hired by the *Jacobite* Leaders, to cry through the whole Town, *Buy my* Savoys, *dainty* Savoys, *curious* Savoys. But, I cannot directly charge the late Earl of *Oxford* with this *Conspiracy*, because he was not then chief Minister. However, this wicked Cry still continues in *London*, and was brought over hither; where it remains to this Day; and is in my humble Opinion, a very offensive Sound to every true Protestant, who is old enough to remember those *dangerous* Times.

During the Ministry of that corrupt and *Jacobite* Earl abovementioned, the secret pernicious Design of those in Power, was to sell *Flanders* to *France:* The Consequence of which, must have been the infallible Ruin of the *States-General*, and would have opened the Way for *France* to obtain that universal Monarchy, they have so long aimed at; to which the *British* Dominions must next, after *Holland*, have been compelled to submit. Whereby the *Protestant* Religion would be rooted out of the World.

A Design of this vast Importance, after long Consultation among the *Jacobite* Grandees, with the Earl of *Oxford* at their Head; was at last determined to be carried on by the same Method with the former: It was therefore again put in Practice; but the Conduct of it was chiefly left to chosen Men, whose Voices were louder and stronger than those of the other Sex. And upon this Occasion, was first instituted in *London*, that famous Cry of Flounders. But the Cryers were particularly directed to pronounce the Word *Flaunders*, and not *Flounders*. For, the Country, which we now by Corruption call *Flanders*, is in its true Orthography spelt *Flaunders*, as may be obvious to all who read old *English* Books. I say, from hence begun that thundering Cry, which hath ever since stunned the Ears of all *London*, made so many Children fall into Fits, and Women miscarry; *Come buy my fresh* Flaunders, *curious* Flaunders, *charming* Flaunders, *alive, alive, ho*; which last Words can with no Propriety of Speech, be applied to Fish manifestly dead, (as I observed before in *Herrings* and *Salmon*) but very justly to ten Provinces, containing many Millions of living *Christians*. But the Application is still closer, when we consider that all the People were to be taken like *Fishes* in a Net; and, by Assistance of the *Pope*, who sets up to be the *universal Fisher of Men*, the whole innocent Nation was, according to our common Expression, to be *laid as flat as a* Flounder.

I REMEMBER, my self, a particular Cryer of *Flounders* in *London*, who arrived at so much Fame for the Loudness of his Voice, as to have the Honour of being mentioned, upon that Account, in a Comedy. He hath disturbed me many a Morning, before he came within Fifty Doors of my Lodging: And although I were not, in those Days, so fully apprized of the Designs which our common Enemy had then in Agitation; yet, I know not how, by a secret Impulse, young as I was, I could not forbear conceiving a strong Dislike against the Fellow; and often said to my self, this Cry seems to be forged in the *Jesuites* School: *Alas, poor* England! *I am grievously mistaken, if there be not some* Popish *Plot at the Bottom*. I communicated my Thoughts to an intimate Friend, who reproached me with being too visionary in my Speculations. But it proved afterwards, that I conjectured right. And I have since reflected, that if the wicked Faction could have procured only a Thousand Men, of as strong Lungs as the Fellow I mentioned, none can tell how terrible the Consequences might have been, not only to these two Kingdoms, but over all *Europe*, by selling *Flanders* to *France*. And yet these Cries continue unpunished, both in *London* and *Dublin*; although, I confess, not with equal Vehemency or Loudness; because the Reason for contriving this desperate Plot, is, to our great Felicity, wholly ceased.

IT is well known, that the Majority of the *British* House of Commons, in the last Years of Queen *Anne*'s Reign, were in their Hearts directly opposite to the Earl of *Oxford*'s pernicious Measures; which put him under the Necessity of bribing them with Sallaries. Whereupon he had again Recourse to his old Politicks. And accordingly, his Emissaries were very busy in employing certain artful Women, of no good Life or

Conversation, (as it was fully proved before Justice * *Peyton*) to cry that Vegetable commonly called *Sollary*, through the Town. These Women differed from the common Cryers of that Herb, by some private Mark which I could never learn; but the Matter was notorious enough, and sufficiently talked of; and about the same Period was the Cry of *Sollary* brought over into this Kingdom. But since there is not, at this present, the least Occasion to suspect the Loyalty of our Cryers upon that Article, I am content that it may still be tolerated.

I SHALL mention but one Cry more, which hath any Reference to Politicks; but is, indeed, of all others, the most insolent, as well as treasonable, under our present happy Establishment. I mean that of *Turnups*; not of *Turnips*, according to the best Orthography, but absolutely *Turnups*. Although this Cry be of an older Date than some of the preceding Enormities; for it began soon after the Revolution; yet was it never known to arrive at so great an Height, as during the Earl of *Oxford*'s Power. Some People, (whom I take to be private Enemies) are indeed, as ready as my self to profess their Disapprobation of this Cry, on Pretence that it began by the Contrivance of certain old Procuresses, who kept Houses of ill Fame, where lewd Women met to draw young Men into Vice. And this they pretend to prove by some Words in the Cry; because, after the Cryer had bawled out *Turnups, ho, buy my dainty Turnups*, he would sometimes add the two following Verses.

> *Turn up the Mistress, and turn up the Maid,*
> *And turn up the Daughter, and be not afraid.*

THIS, say some political Sophists, plainly shews, that there can be nothing further meant in so infamous a Cry, than an Invitation to Lewdness; which, indeed, ought to be severely punished in all well regulated Governments; yet cannot be fairly interpreted as a Crime of State. But, I hope, we are not so weak and blind to be deluded at this Time of Day, with such poor Evasions. I could, if it were proper, demonstrate the very Time when those two Verses were composed, and

---

* *A famous Whig Justice in those Times.*

name the Author, who was no other than the famous Mr. *Swan*, so well known for his Talent at Quibbling; and was as virulent a *Jacobite* as any in *England*. Neither could he deny the Fact, when he was taxed for it in my Presence, by Sir *Harry Dutton-Colt*, and Colonel *Davenport*, at the *Smyrna* Coffee-House, on the 10th of *June*, 1701. Thus it appears to a Demonstration, that those Verses were only a Blind to conceal the most dangerous Designs of the Party; who from the first Years after the happy Revolution, used a Cant-way of talking in their Clubs, after this Manner: *We hope to see the Cards shuffled once more, and another King* TURNUP *Trump:* And, *when shall we meet over a Dish of* TURNUPS? The same Term of Art was used in their Plots against the Government, and in their treasonable Letters writ in Cyphers, and decyphered by the famous Dr. *Wallis*, as you may read in the Tryals of those Times. This I thought fit to set forth at large, and in so clear a Light; because the *Scotch* and *French* Authors have given a very different Account of the Word TURNUP; but whether out of Ignorance or Partiality, I shall not decree; because, I am sure the Reader is convinced by my Discovery. It is to be observed, that this Cry was sung in a particular Manner, by Fellows in Disguise, to give Notice where those Traytors were to meet, in order to concert their villainous Designs.

I HAVE no more to add upon this Article, than an humble Proposal, that those who cry this Root at present in our Streets of *Dublin*, may be compelled by the Justices of the Peace, to pronounce *Turnip*, and not *Turnup*; for, I am afraid, we have still too many Snakes in our Bosom; and it would be well if their Cellars were sometimes searched, when the Owners least expect it; for I am not out of Fear, that *latet anguis in Herba*.

THUS, we are zealous in Matters of small Moment, while we neglect those of the highest Importance. I have already made it manifest, that all these Cries were contrived in the *worst of Times*, under the Ministry of that desperate Statesman, *Robert*, late Earl of *Oxford*; and for that very Reason, ought to be rejected with Horror, as begun in the Reign of *Jacobites*, and may well be numbered among the Rags of *Popery* and *Treason:* Or if it be thought proper, that these Cries must continue, surely they ought to be only trusted in the Hands of *true Protestants* who have given Security to the Government.

(Final paragraph first added in the London edition for Roberts, 1732)

HAVING already spoken of many Abuses relating to Sign-Posts; I cannot here omit one more, because it plainly relates to Politics; and is, perhaps, of more dangerous Consequence than any of the City Cries, because it directly tends to destroy the Succession. It is the Sign of his present Majesty King *George* the Second, to be met with in many Streets; and yet, I happen to be not only the first, but the only Discoverer of this audacious Instance of *Jacobitism*. And, I am confident, that, if the Justices of the Peace, would please to make a strict Inspection, they might find in all such Houses, before which those Signs are hung up, in the manner I have observed, that the Landlords were malignant Papists, or, which is worse, notorious *Jacobites*. Whoever views those Signs, may read over his Majesty's head the following Letters and Cyphers, *G.R.II.*, which plainly signifies *George*, King the Second; and not King *George* the Second, or *George* the Second King; but laying the Point after the letter *G.* by which the Owner of the House manifestly shews, that he renounces his Allegiance to King *George* the Second; and allows him to be only the second King, In-uendo, that the Pretender is the first King; and looking upon King *George* to be only a Kind of second King, or Vice-roy, till the Pretender shall come over and seize the Kingdom. I appeal to all Mankind, whether this be a strained or forced Interpretation of the Inscription, as it now stands in almost every Street; whether any Decypherer would make the least Doubt or Hesitation, to explain it as I have done; whether any other Protestant Country would ensure so publick an Instance of Treason in the Capital City, from such vulgar Conspirators; and, lastly, whether *Papists* and *Jacobites* of great Fortunes and Quality, may not probably stand behind the Curtain in this dangerous, open, and avowed Design against the Government. But I have perform'd my Duty, and leave the reforming these Abuses to the Wisdom, the Vigilance, the Loyalty, and Activity of my Superiors.

The humble Petition of the Footmen in and about the City of Dublin

Houſe of COMMONS, &c.

The humble PETITION of the Footmen *in and about the City of DUBLIN.*

Written in the Year 1732.

HUMBLY SHEWETH,

THAT your *Petitioners* are a great and numerous *Society*, endowed with several Privileges, Time out of Mind. THAT certain *lewd, idle,* and *disorderly* Persons, for several Months past, as it is notoriously known, have been daily seen in the publick Walks of this City, habited sometimes in *Green Coats,* and sometimes *laced,* with long *Oaken Cudgels* in their Hands, and without Swords; in hopes to procure Favour, by that Advantage, with a great Number of Ladies who frequent those Walks; pretending and giving themselves out to be true genuine *Irish Footmen.* Whereas they can be proved to be no better than common *Toupees*; as a judicious Eye may soon discover, by their *awkward, clumsy, ungenteel* Gait, and Behaviour; by their Unskilfulness in Dress, even with the Advantage of wearing our Habits; by their ill-favoured Countenances; with an Air of *Impudence* and *Dullness* peculiar to the rest of their Brethren: Who have not yet arrived at that transcendent Pitch of Assurance. Although, it may be justly apprehended, that they will do so in time, if these *Counterfeits* shall happen to succeed in their evil Design, of passing for *real Footmen*, thereby to render themselves more amiable to the Ladies.

Your *Petitioners* do further alledge; that many of the said *Counterfeits*, upon a strict Examination, have been found in the very Act of *strutting, staring, swearing, swaggering*, in a Manner that plainly shewed their best Endeavours to imitate us. Wherein, although they did not succeed; yet by their ignorant and ungainly Way of copying our Graces, the utmost Indignity was endeavoured to be cast upon our whole Profession.

Your *Petitioners* do therefore make it their humble Request, that this *Honourable House* (to many of whom your *Petitioners* are nearly *allied*) will please to take this Grievance into your most serious Consideration: Humbly submitting, whether it would not be proper, that certain *Officers* might, at the Publick Charge, be employed to search for, and discover all such *Counterfeit Footmen*, and carry them before the next *Justice* of Peace; by whose Warrant, upon the first Conviction, they should be stripped of their *Coats* and *Oaken* Ornaments, and be set two Hours in the Stocks. Upon the second Conviction, besides stripping, be set six Hours in the Stocks, with a Paper pinned on their Breast, signifying their Crime, in large Capital Letters, and in the following Words. *A. B.* commonly called *A. B.* Esq; a *Toupee*, and a notorious *Impostor*, who presumed to personate a *true Irish Footman*.

And for any further Offence, the said *Toupee* shall be committed to *Bridewell*, whipped three Times, forced to hard Labour for a Month, and not to be set at Liberty, till he shall have given sufficient Security for his good Behaviour.

Your *Honours* will please to observe, with what Lenity we propose to treat these enormous Offenders, who have already brought such a Scandal on our *Honourable Calling*, that several well-meaning People have mistaken them to be of our *Fraternity*; in Diminution to that Credit and Dignity wherewith we have supported our Station, as we always did, in the *worst of Times*. And we further beg Leave to remark, that this was manifestly done with a *seditious* Design, to render

us less capable of serving the _Publick_ in any great Employments, as several of our _Fraternity_, as well as our _Ancestors_
have done.

WE do therefore, humbly implore your _Honours_ to give
necessary Orders for our Relief, in this present Exigency,
and your _Petitioners_ (as in Duty bound) shall ever pray, _&c._

Dublin,
  1732.

The Advantages
Proposed by Repealing the
Sacramental Test

THE
ADVANTAGES
PROPOS'D BY
REPEALING

Swift Vol. VI. P. 261

THE
SACRAMENTAL TEST,
IMPARTIALLY
CONSIDERED.

DUBLIN:

Printed by GEORGE FAULKNER, in *Essex street*, opposite to the *Bridge*, MDCCXXXII.

T

ADVANTAGES

Proposed by Repealing the

SACRAMENTAL TEST,

Impartially Considered

Written in the Year 1732.

WHOEVER writes impartially upon this Subject, must do it not only as a meer secular Man; but as one who is altogether indifferent to any particular System of Christianity. And, I think, in whatever Country that Religion predominates, there is one certain Form of Worship and Ceremony, which is looked upon as the Established; and consequently only the Priests of that particular Form, are maintained at the publick Charge; and all Civil Employments are bestowed among those who comply (at least outwardly) with the same Establishment.

THIS Method is strictly observed, even by our Neighbours the *Dutch*, who are confessed to allow the fullest Liberty to Conscience, of any Christian State; and yet are never known to admit any persons into Civil Offices, who do not conform to the legal Worship. As to their Military Men, they are indeed not so scrupulous; being, by the Nature of their Government, under a Necessity of hiring foreign Troops of whatever Religious Denomination, upon every great Emergency; and maintaining no small Number in Time of Peace.

THIS Caution therefore of making one Established Faith, seems to be universal, and founded upon the strongest Reasons; the mistaken, or affected Zeal of Obstinacy, and Enthusiasm, having produced such a Number of horrible destructive Events, throughout all *Christendom*. For, whoever begins to think the National Worship is wrong, in any important Article of Practice or Belief; will, if he be serious, naturally have a Zeal to make as many Proselytes as he can: And a Nation may possibly have an Hundred different Sects with their Leaders: every one of which, hath an equal Right to plead, that they must *obey God rather than Man*, must *cry aloud and spare not*; must *lift up their Voice like a Trumpet*.

THIS was the very Case of *England*, during the Fanatick Times. And against all this, there seems to be no Defence, but that of supporting one established Form of Doctrine and Discipline; leaving the rest to a bare Liberty of Conscience; but without any Maintenance or Encouragement from the Publick.

WHEREVER this National Religion grows so corrupt, or is thought to do so by a very great Majority of landed People, joined to the governing Party, whether Prince or Senate, or both; it ought to be changed; provided the Work might be done without Blood or Confusion. Yet, whenever such a Change shall be made, some other Establishment must succeed, although for the worse; allowing all Deviations that would break the Union, to be only tollerated. In this Sense, those who affirm that every Law, which is contrary to the Law of God, is void in its self, seem to be mistaken. For, many Laws in *Popish* Kingdoms and States; many more among the *Turks*; and perhaps not a few in other Countries, are directly against the Divine Laws; and yet, God knows, are very far from being void in the executive Part.

THUS, for Instance: If the three Estates of Parliament in *England* (whereof the Lords Spiritual, who represent the *Church*, are one) should agree, and obtain the Royal Assent to abolish Episcopacy; together with the Liturgy, and the whole Frame of the *English* Church, as *burthensome, dangerous, and contrary to Holy Scripture*; and that *Presbytery, Anabaptism, Quakerism, Independency, Muggletonianism, Brownism, Familism*, or any other subdivided Sect among us, should be established in its Place; without Question, all peaceable Subjects ought passively to submit; and the predominant Sect must become the Religion established; the Publick maintaining no other Teachers, not admitting any Persons of a different religious Profession, into Civil Offices; at least, if their Intention be to preserve the Nation in Peace.

SUPPOSING then, that the present System of Religion were abolished; and *Presbytery*, which I find stands the fairest; with its Synods and Classes, and all its Forms and Ceremonies, essential or circumstantial, were erected into the National Worship: Their Teachers, and no others, could have any legal Claim, to be supported at the publick Charge, whether by Stipends or Tythes; and only the rest of the same Faith to be capable of Civil Employments.

IF there be any true Reasoning in what I have laid down; it should seem, that the Project now in Agitation for repealing the *Test Act*, and yet leaving the Name of an Establishment to the present National Church, is altogether inconsistent; and may admit of Consequences, which those, who are the most indifferent to any Religion at all, are possibly not aware of.

I PRESUME, whenever the *Test* shall be repealed, which obliges all Men, who enter into Office under the Crown, to receive the Sacrament according to the Rites of the Church of *Ireland*; the Way to Employments will immediately be left open to all *Dissenters*, (except *Papists*) whose Consciences can suffer them to take the common Oaths, in such Cases prescribed; after which, they are qualified to fill any Lay-Station in this Kingdom, from that of Chief Governor, to an Excise-Man.

THUS, of the three Judges on each Bench, the first may be a *Presbyterian*, the second a *Free-will Baptist*, and the third a *Churchman*; the *Lord Chancellor* may be an *Independant*; the Revenues may be managed by seven Commissioners of as many different Sects; and the like of all other Employments. Not to mention the strong Probability, that the Lawfulness of taking Oaths may be *revealed* to the Quakers; who then will stand upon as good a Foot for Preferment, as any other loyal Subject. It is obvious to imagine, under such a motly Administration of Affairs, what a clashing there will be of Interests and Inclinations; what Pullings and Hawlings backwards and forwards; what a Zeal and Byass in each Religionist, to advance his own Tribe, and depress the others. For, I suppose, nothing will be readier granted, than that how indifferent soever most Men are in Faith and Morals; yet, whether out of Artifice, natural Complexion, or Love of Contradiction, none are more obstinate in maintaining their own Opinions, and worrying all who differ from them, than those who publickly shew the least Sense, either of Religion, or common Honesty.

As to the latter, Bishop *Burnet* tells us, that the *Presbyterians*, in the Fanatick Times, professed themselves to be above Morality; which, as we find in some of their Writings, was numbered among the *beggarly Elements:* And accordingly, at this Day, no Scruples of Conscience, with regard to Conformity, are in any Trade or Calling, inconsistent with the greatest Fraud, Oppression, Perjury, or any other Vice.

THIS brings to my Memory a Passage in *Montaigne*, of a common Prostitute; who, in the storming of a Town, when a Soldier came up to her Chamber, and offered Violence to her Chastity, rather chose to venture her Neck, by leaping out of the Window, than suffer a Rape; yet still continued her Trade of Lewdness, while she had any Customers left.

I CONFESS, that, in my private Judgment, an unlimited Permission of all Sects whatsoever (except *Papists*) to enjoy Employments, would be less pernicious to the Publick, than a fair Struggle between two Contenders; because, in the former Case, such a Jumble of Principles, might possibly have the Effect of contrary Poysons mingled together; which a strong Constitution might perhaps be able for some Time to survive.

BUT, however, I shall take the other, and more probable Supposition, that this Battle for Employments, is to be fought only between the *Presbyterians*, and those of the Church *yet* established. I shall not enter into the Merits of either Side, by examining which of the two is the better spiritual Oeconomy, or which is most suited to our Civil Constitution. But the Question turns upon this Point: When the *Presbyterians* shall have got their Share of Employments, (which must be one full half, or else they cannot look upon themselves as fairly dealt with) I ask, whether they ought not by their own Principles, and by the strictest Rules of Conscience, to use the utmost of their Skill, Power, and Influence, in order to reduce the whole Kingdom to an Uniformity in Religion, both as to Doctrine and Discipline, most agreeable to the Word of God. Wherein, if they can succeed without Blood (as under the present Disposition of Things it is very possible they may) it is to be hoped they will at last be satisfied: Only I would warn them of a few Difficulties. The first is; for compromising among themselves, that important Controversy about the *Old Light* and the *New*; which otherwise may, after this Establishment, split them as wide as *Papist* and *Protestant*, *Whig* and *Tory*, or *Churchman* and *Dissenter*; and consequently the Work will be to begin again. For in Religious Quarrels, it is of little Moment how few or small the Differences are; especially when the Dispute is only about Power. Thus the jealous *Presbyterians* of the *North*, are more alienated from the established Clergy, than from the *Romish* Priests; taxing the former with idolatrous Worship, as disguised *Papists, Ceremony Mongers*, and many other Terms of Art; and this for a very powerful Reason; because the Clergy stand in their Way, which the *Popish* Priests do not. Thus I am assured, that the Quarrel between *Old* and *New Light-Men*, is managed with more Rage and Rancour, than any other Dispute of the highest Importance; and this, because it serves to lessen or increase their several Congregations, from whom they receive their Contributions.

ANOTHER Difficulty, which may embarrass the *Presbyterians* after their Establishment, will be how to adjust their Claim of the *Kirk*'s Independency on the Civil Power, with the Constitution of this Monarchy; a Point so delicate, that it hath often filled the Heads of great Patriots with dangerous Notions of the Church Clergy, without the least Ground of Suspicion.

As to the *Presbyterians* allowing Liberty of Conscience to those of Episcopal Principles, when their own *Kirk* shall be predominant; their Writers are so universally agreed in the Negative, as well as their Practice during *Oliver*'s Reign; that I believe no reasonable Churchman, (who must then be a *Dissenter*) will expect it.

I SHALL here take Notice, that in the Division of Employments among the *Presbyterians*, after this approaching Repeal of the *Test-Act*; supposing them, in proper Time, to have an equal Share, I compute the Odds will be three or four to one on their Side, in any further Scheme they may have towards making their Religion National. For I reckon, all those Gentlemen sent over from *England*, whatever Religion they profess, or have been educated in, to be of that Party: Since it is no Mark of Prudence, for any Persons to oppose the Current of a Nation, where they are in some Sort only Sojourners; unless they *have it in Direction*.

IF there be any Maxim in Politicks, not to be controuled, it must be the following. That those whose private Interest is united with the Interest of their Country; supposing them to be of equal Understanding with the rest of their Neighbours, will heartily wish, that the Nation should thrive. Out of these are indubitably excepted all Persons who are sent from another Kingdom, to be employed in Places of Profit or Power; because they can possibly bear no Affection to the Place where they sojourn, even for Life; their sole Business being to advance themselves, by following the Advice of their *Principals*. I except likewise, those Persons who are taken into Offices, although Natives of the Land; because they are greater Gainers while they keep their Offices, than they could possibly be by mending the miserable Condition of their Country.

I EXCEPT, Thirdly, all Hopers, who, by ballancing Accounts with themselves, turn the Scale on the same Side; because the strong Expectation of a good certain Salary, will outweigh the Loss by bad Rents, received out of Lands in moneyless Times.

IF my Lords, the Bishops, who, I hear, are now employed in a Scheme for regulating the Conduct and Maintenance of the inferior Clergy; shall, in their Wisdom and Piety, and Love of the Church, consent to this Repeal of the *Test*; I have not the least Doubt, that the whole Reverend Body will chearfully submit to their Spiritual Fathers; of whose paternal Tenderness for their Welfare, they have already found so many *amazing* Instances.

I AM not, therefore, under the least Concern about the Clergy on this Account. They will (*for some Time*) be no great Sufferers by this Repeal; because I cannot recollect, among all our Sects, any one that gives Latitude enough to take the Oaths required at an Institution, to a Church-living; and until that Bar shall be removed, the present Episcopal Clergy are safe for two Years. Although it may be thought somewhat unequal, that in the *Northern* Parts, where there may be three *Dissenters* to one *Churchman*, the whole Revenue should be engrossed by Him who hath so small a Part of the Cure.

IT is true, indeed, that this Disadvantage, which the *Dissenters* at present lye under, of a Disability to receive Church-Preferments, will be easily remedied by the Repeal of the *Test*. For the *Dissenting* Teachers are under no Incapacity of accepting Civil and Military Employments; wherein they agree perfectly with the *Popish* Clergy; among whom, great Cardinals and Prelates have been Commanders of Armies, chief Ministers, Knights of many Orders, Ambassadors, Secretaries of State, and in most high Offices under the Crown; although they assert the *indelible Character*, which no Sectaries among us did ever assume. But that many, both *Presbyterians* and *Independants*, Commanders as well as private Soldiers were professed Preachers in the Time of their Dominion, is allowed by all. *Cromwell* himself was a Preacher; and hath left us one of his Sermons in Print, exactly in the same Style and Manner with those of our modern *Presbyterian* Teachers: So was Colonel *Howard*, Sir *George Downing*, and several others whose Names are on Record. I can, therefore, see no Reason why a painful *Presbyterian* Teacher, as soon as the *Test* shall be repealed, may not be priviledged to hold, along with his Spiritual Office and Stipend, a Commission in the Army, or the Civil List in *Commendam:* For, as I take it, the Church of *England* is the only Body of Christians, which, in Effect, disqualifies those, who are employed to preach its Doctrine, from sharing in the Civil Power, further than as Senators: Yet this was a Priviledge begun in Times of *Popery*, many Hundred Years before the *Reformation*; and woven with the very Institution of our limited Monarchy.

THERE is indeed another Method, whereby the Stipends of dissenting Teachers may be raised, and the Farmer much relieved; if it should be thought proper to reward a People so deserving, and so loyal by their Principles. Every Bishop, upon the Vacancy of a Church-living, can sequester the Profits for the Use of the next Incumbent. Upon a Lapse of half a Year, the Donation falls to the Archbishop, and after a full Year to the Crown during Pleasure. Therefore, it would be no Hardship for any Clergyman *alive*, if, in those Parts of *Ireland*, where the Number of Sectaries much exceeds that of the Conformists, the Profits, when sequestered, might be applied to the Support of the dissenting Teacher, who hath so many Souls to take Care of: Whereby the poor Tenants would be much relieved in these hard Times, and in a better Condition to pay their Rents.

BUT there is another Difficulty in this Matter, against which a Remedy doth not so readily occur. For, supposing the Test-Act repealed, and the Dissenters in Consequence fully qualified for all secular Employments; the Question may still be put, whether those of *Ireland* will be often the Persons on whom they shall be bestowed; because it is imagined, there may be another *Seminary* in View, *more numerous* and *more needy*, as well as *more meriting*, and more easily contented with such low Offices; which some nearer Neighbours hardly think it worth stirring from their Chimney-sides to obtain. And, I am told, it is the common practice of those who are skilled in the Management of Bees; that when they see a foreign Swarm, at some Distance, approaching with an Intention to plunder their Hives; these Artists have a Trick to divert them into some neighbouring Apiary, there to make what Havock they please. This I should not have hinted, if I had not known it already to have gotten Ground in many suspecting Heads: For it is the peculiar Talent of this Nation, to see Dangers afar off: To all which, I can only say, that our native *Presbyterians* must, by Pains and

Industry, raise such a Fund of *Merit*, as will answer to a Birth six Degrees more to the *North*. If they cannot arrive at this Perfection, as several of the established Church have compassed by indefatigable Pains; I do not well see, how their Affairs will much mend by repealing the *Test:* For, to be qualified by Law to accept an Employment; and yet to be disqualified in Fact, as it will much increase the Mortification, so it will withdraw the Pity of many among their Wellwishers; and utterly deprive them of that *Merit* they have so long made, of being a loyal *true Protestant* People, persecuted only for Religion.

If this happen to be their Case, they must wait Maturity of Time; until they can by prudent, gentle Steps, make their Faith become the Religion Established in the Nation; after which, I do not in the least doubt, that they will take the most effectual Methods, to secure their Power against those who must then be *Dissenters* in their Turn; whereof, if we may form a future Opinion from present Times, and the Disposition of *Dissenters*, who love to make a *thorow Reformation*; the Number and Qualities will be very inconsiderable.

Thus I have, with the utmost Sincerity, after long thinking, given my Judgment upon this arduous Affair; but with the utmost Deference, and Submission to publick Wisdom and Power.

Queries Relating to the
Sacramental TEST

QUERIES

Relating to the

Sacramental TEST

Written in the Year 1732

Query

WHETHER Hatred and Violence between Parties in a State be not more inflamed by different Views of Interest, than by the greater or lesser Differences between them, either in Religion or Government?

Whether it be any Part of the Question at this Time, which of the two Religions is worse, *Popery*, or *Fanaticism*: or not rather, which of the two, (having both the same good Will) is in the hopefullest Condition to ruin the Church?

WHETHER the Sectaries, whenever they come to prevail, will not ruin the Church as infallibly and effectually as the *Papists*?

WHETHER the prevailing Sectaries could allow Liberty of Conscience to *Dissenters*, without belying all their former Practice, and almost all their former Writings?

WHETHER many hundred thousand *Scotch* Presbyterians, are not full as virulent against the Episcopal Church, as they are against the *Papists*; or, as they would have us think, the *Papists* are against them?

WHETHER the *Dutch*, who are most distinguished for allowing Liberty of Conscience, do ever admit any Persons, who profess a different Scheme of Worship from their own, into Civil Employments; although, they *may* be forced by the Nature of their Government, to receive mercenary Troops of all Religions?

WHETHER the *Dissenters* ever pretended until of late Years, to desire more than a bare Toleration?

WHETHER, if it be true, what a sorry Pamphleteer asserts, who lately writ for repealing the *Test*, that the *Dissenters* in this Kingdom are equally numerous with the Churchmen: It would not be a necessary Point of Prudence, by all proper and lawful Means to prevent their further Increase?

THE great Argument given by those whom they call *low* Churchmen, to justify the large Tolerations allowed to *Dissenters*, hath been; that by such Indulgences, the Rancour of those Sectaries would gradually wear off, many of them would come over to us, and their Parties in a little Time crumble to nothing.

Query. If what the above Pamphleteer asserts, that the Sectaries, are in equal Numbers with Conformists, it doth not clearly follow, that those repeated Tolerations, have operated directly contrary to what those *low* Church Politicians pretended to foresee and expect?

WHETHER any Clergyman, however dignified or distinguished, if he thinks his own Profession most agreeable to Holy Scriptures, and the primitive Church, can really wish in his Heart, that all Sectaries should be upon an equal Foot with the Churchmen, in the Point of Civil Power and Employments?

WHETHER Episcopacy, which is held by the Church to be a Divine and Apostolical Institution, be not a fundamental Point of Religion, particularly in that essential one of conferring Holy Orders?

WHETHER, by necessary Consequences, the several Expedients among the Sectaries to constitute their Teachers, are not absolutely null and void?

WHETHER the Sectaries will ever agree to accept Ordination only from Bishops?

WHETHER the Bishops and Clergy will be content to give up Episcopacy, as a Point indifferent, without which the Church can well subsist?

WHETHER that great Tenderness towards Sectaries, which now so much prevails, be chiefly owing to the Fears of *Popery*, or to that Spirit of Atheism, Deism, Scepticism, and universal Immorality, which all good Men so much lament?

GRANTING *Popery* to have many more Errors in Religion than any one Branch of the Sectaries; let us examine the Actions of both, as they have each affected the Peace of these Kingdoms, with Allowance for the short Time which the Sectaries had to act in, who are, in a Manner *but of Yesterday.* The *Papists* in the Time of King *James* the IId. used all Endeavours to establish their Superstition; wherein they failed, by the united Power of *English* Church Protestants, with the Prince of *Orange*'s Assistance. But it cannot be asserted, that these bigotted *Papists* had the least Design to depose or murder their King, much less to abolish kingly Government; nor was it their Interest or Inclination to attempt either.

ON the other Side, the *Puritans*, who had almost from the Beginning of Queen *Elizabeth*'s Reign, been a perpetual Thorn in the Church's Side, joining with the *Scotch* Enthusiasts, in the Time of King *Charles* the First, were the principal Cause of the *Irish Rebellion* and *Massacre*, by distressing that Prince, and making it impossible for him to send over timely Succours. And, after that pious Prince had satisfied his Parliament in every single Point to be complained of; the same Sectaries by poisoning the Minds and Affections of the People, with the most false and wicked Representations of their King, were able in the Compass of a few Years to embroil the three Nations in a bloody Rebellion, at the Expence of many thousand Lives; to turn the kingly Power into Anarchy; to murder their Prince in the Face of the World, and (in their own Style) to destroy the Church *Root and Branch.*

THE Account therefore stands thus. The *Papists* aimed at one pernicious Act, which was to destroy the *Protestant* Religion; wherein, by God's Mercy, and the Assistance of our Glorious King *William*, they absolutely failed. The *Sectaries* attempted the three most infernal Actions, that could possibly enter into the Hearts of Men, forsaken by God; which were, the Murder of a most pious King, the Destruction of the

U

Monarchy, and the Extirpation of the Church; and succeeded in them all.

UPON which, I put the following Queries, Whether any of those Sectaries have ever yet in a solemn publick Manner, renounced any one of those Principles upon which their Predecessors then acted?

WHETHER, considering the cruel Persecutions of the Episcopal Church, during the Course of that horrid Rebellion and the Consequences of it, until the happy *Restoration*; is it not manifest, that the persecuting Spirit lyes so equally divided between the *Papists* and the Sectaries, that a Feather would turn the Balance on either Side?

AND, therefore, lastly, Whether any Person of common Understanding, who professeth himself a Member of the Church established, although, perhaps, with little inward Regard to any Religion (which is too often the Case) if he loves the Peace and Welfare of his Country; can, after cool Thinking, rejoyce to see a Power placed again in the Hands of so restless, so ambitious, and so merciless a Faction, to act over all the same Parts a second Time?

WHETHER the Candor of that Expression, so frequent of late in Sermons and Pamphlets, of the *Strength and Number of the* Papists *in* Ireland, can be justified? For as to their Number, however great, it is always magnified in Proportion to the Zeal, or Politicks, of the Speaker and Writer; but it is a gross Imposition upon common Reason, to terrify us with their Strength. For *Popery*, under the Circumstances it lies in this Kingdom; although it be offensive, and inconvenient enough, from the Consequences it hath to encrease the Rapine, Sloth and Ignorance, as well as Poverty of the Natives; is not properly dangerous in that Sense, as some would have us take it; because it is universally hated by every Party of a different religious Profession. It is the Contempt of the Wise: The best Topick for Clamours of designing Men: But the real Terror only of Fools. The landed *Popish* Interest in *England*, far exceeds that among us, even in Proportion to the Wealth and Extent of each Kingdom. The little that remains here, is daily dropping into *Protestant* Hands, by Purchase or Descent;

and that affected Complaint of counterfeit Converts, will fall with the Cause of it in half a Generation; unless it be raised or kept alive, as a continual Fund of Merit and Eloquence. The *Papists* are wholly disarmed. They have neither Courage, Leaders, Money, or Inclinations to rebel. They want every Advantage which they formerly possessed, to follow that Trade; and wherein, even with those Advantages, they always miscarried. They appear very easy, and satisfied under that Connivance which they enjoyed during the whole last Reign; nor ever scrupled to reproach another Party, under which they pretend to have suffered so much Severity.

Upon these Considerations I must confess to have suspended much of my Pity towards the great Dreaders of *Popery*; many of whom appear to be hail, strong, active young Men; who, as I am told, eat, drink, and sleep heartily; and are very chearful (as they have exceeding good Reason) upon all other Subjects. However, I cannot too much commend the generous Concern, which our Neighbours and others, who come from the same Neighbourhood, are so kind to express for us upon this Account; although the former be further removed from the Dangers of *Popery*, by Twenty Leagues of Salt-Water: But this, I fear, is a Digression.

When an artificial Report was raised here many Years ago, of an intended Invasion by the *Pretender*, (which blew over after it had done its Office) the *Dissenters* argued in their Talk, and in their Pamphlets, after this Manner, applying themselves to those of the Church. Gentlemen, if the *Pretender* had landed, as the Law now stands, we durst not assist you; and therefore, unless you take off the *Test*, whenever you shall happen to be invaded in earnest, if we are desired to take up Arms in your Defence, our Answer shall be, Pray Gentlemen fight your own Battles, we will lie by quietly; conquer your Enemy by your selves, if you can; we will not do your Drudgery. This Way of Reasoning I have heard from several of their Chiefs and Abettors, in an Hundred Conversations; and have read it in Twenty Pamphlets: And, I am confident, it will be offered again, if the Project should fail to take off the *Test*.

Upon which Piece of Oratory and Reasoning I form the

following Query. Whether, in Case of an Invasion from the *Pretender* (which is not quite so probable as from the Grand *Seignior*) the *Dissenters* can, with Prudence and Safety, offer the same Plea; except they shall have made a previous Stipulation with the Invaders? And, Whether the full Freedom of their Religion and Trade, their Lives, Properties, Wives and Children, are not, and have not always been reckoned sufficient Motives for repelling Invasions; especially in our Sectaries, who call themselves the *truest Protestants*, by Virtue of their pretended or real Fierceness against *Popery*?

WHETHER omitting or neglecting to celebrate the Day of the Martyrdom of the blessed King *Charles* the First, enjoined by Act of Parliament, can be justly reckoned a particular and distinguishing Mark of good Affection to the present Government?

WHETHER in those Churches where the said Day is observed, it will fully answer the Intent of the said Act; if the Preacher shall commend, excuse, palliate, or extenuate the Murder of that Royal Martyr; and lay the Guilt of that horrid Rebellion, with all its Consequences, the following Usurpations, the intire Destruction of the Church, the cruel and continual Persecutions of those who could be discovered to profess its Doctrines, with the ensuing *Babel* of Fanaticism; to the Account of that blessed King; who, by granting the Petition of Right, and passing every Bill that could be asked for the Security of the Subject, had, by the Confession even of those wicked Men, before the War began, left them nothing more to demand?

WHETHER such a Preacher as I have named, (whereof there have been more than *one*, not many Years past, even in the Presence of Viceroys) who takes that Course as a Means for Promotion; may not be thought to step a little out of the common Road, in a Monarchy where the Descendants of that most blessed Martyr have reigned to this Day?

I GROUND the Reason of making these Queries, on the Title of the Act; to which I refer the Reader.

The *Presbyterians* Plea
of Merit, &c.

THE
Presbyterians PLEA
OF
MERIT;

In Order to take off the

TEST,

Impartially Examined.

DUBLIN:

Printed and fold by GEORGE FAULKNER, in
Essex-street, opposite to the *Bridge*, 1733.

THE

Presbyterians PLEA

OF

MERIT, &c.

WE have been told in the common News-Papers, that all Attempts are to be made this Sessions by the *Presbyterians*, and their Abettors, for taking off the Test; as a Kind of preparatory Step, to make it go down smoother in *England*. For, if once *their Light would so shine*, the *Papists*, delighted with the Blaze, would all come in, and dance about it. This I take to be a prudent Method; like that of a discreet Physician, who first gives a new Medicine to a *Dog*, before he prescribes it to a human Creature.

THE *Presbyterians* have, ever since the Revolution, directed their learned Casuists to employ their Pens on this Subject; by shewing the Merits and Pretensions upon which they claim this *Justice*; as founded upon the Services they did towards the Restoration of King *Charles* the Second; and at the *Revolution*, under the Prince of *Orange*. Which Pleas I take to be the most singular, in their Kind, that ever were offered in the Face of the Sun, against the most glaring Light of Truth, and against a Continuation of Publick Facts, known to all *Europe* for twenty Years together. I shall, therefore, impartially examine the Merits and Conduct of the *Presbyterians*, upon those two great Events; and the Pretensions to Favour, which they challenge upon them.

SOON after the Reformation of the Church in *England*, under *Edward* the Sixth, upon Queen *Mary*'s succeeding to the Crown, who restored *Popery*; many *Protestants* fled out of *England*, to escape the Persecution raised against the Church, as her Brother had left it established. Some of these Exiles went to *Geneva*; which City had received the Doctrine of *Calvin*, and rejected the Government of Bishops; with many other Refinements. These *English* Exiles readily embraced the *Geneva* System; and having added further Improvements of their own, upon Queen *Mary*'s Death, returned to *England*; where they preached up their new Opinions; inveighing bitterly against *Episcopacy*, and all Rites and Ceremonies, however innocent and ancient in the Church: Building upon this Foundation; to run as far as possible from *Popery*, even in the most minute and indifferent Circumstances: This Faction, under the Name of *Puritan*, became very turbulent, during the whole Reign of Queen *Elizabeth*, and were always discouraged by that wise Queen, as well as by her two Successors. However, their Numbers, as well as their Insolence and Perverseness, so far increased, that soon after the Death of King *James* the First, many Instances of their Petulancy and Scurrility, are to be seen in their Pamphlets, written for some Years after; which was a Trade they began in the Days of Queen *Elizabeth:* Particularly with great Rancour against the Bishops, the Habits, and the Ceremonies: Such were those scurrilous Libels under the Title of *Martin Mar-Prelate*, and several others. And, although the Earl of *Clarendon* tells us, until the Year 1640, (as I remember) the Kingdom was in a State of perfect Peace and Happiness, without the least Appearance of Thought or Design, towards making any Alterations in Religion or Government; yet I have found, by often rumaging for old Books in *Little Britain* and *Duck-lane*, a great Number of Pamphlets printed from the Year 1630 to 1640, full of as bold and impious railing Expressions against the lawful Power of the Crown, and the Order of Bishops, as ever were uttered during the Rebellion, or the whole subsequent Tyranny of that Fanatick Anarchy. However, I find it manifest, that *Puritanism* did not erect it self into a new separate Species of Religion, till some Time after the Rebellion began. For, in the latter Times of King *James* the First, and the former Part of his Son, there were several *Puritan* Bishops, and many *Puritan* private Clergymen; while People went, as their Inclinations led them, to hear Preachers of each Party in the Parish Churches. For, the *Puritan* Clergy had received Episcopal Orders as well as the rest. But, soon after the Rebellion broke out, the Term *Puritan* gradually dropt, and that of *Presbyterian* succeeded; which Sect was, in two or three Years, established in all its Forms, by what they call an Ordinance of the Lords and Commons, without consulting the King, who was then at War against his Rebels. And, from this Period, the Church continued under Persecution until Monarchy was restored in the Year 1660.

IN a Year or two after, we began to hear of a new Party risen, and growing in the Parliament, as well as the Army; under the Name of *Independent:* It spread, indeed, somewhat more in the latter; but not equal with the *Presbyterians*, either in Weight or Number, until some Time before the King was murdered.

WHEN the King, who was then a Prisoner in the Isle of *Wight*, had made his last Concessions for a Peace to the Commissioners of the Parliament, who attended him there; upon their Return to *London*, they reported his Majesty's Answer in the House. Whereupon, a Number of moderate Members, who, as *Ludlow* says, had secured their own Terms with that Prince, managed with so much Art, as to obtain a Majority, in a thin House, for passing a Vote, that *the King's Concessions were a Ground for a future Settlement.* But the great Officers of the Army, joining with the discontented Members, came to a Resolution, of excluding all those who had consented to that Vote; which they executed in a military Way. *Ireton* told *Fairfax* the General, a rigid *Presbyterian*, of this Resolution; who thereupon issued his Orders for drawing out the Army the next Morning, and placing Guards in *Westminster Hall*, the *Court of Requests*, and the *Lobby*; who, in Obedience to the General, in Conjunction with those Members who had opposed the Vote, would let no Member enter the House, except those of their own Party. Upon which, the Question for bringing the King to Justice, was immediately put and carried, without Opposition, that I can find. Then, an Order was made for his Tryal: the Time and Place appointed; the

Judges named; of whom *Fairfax* himself was one; although by the Advice, or Threats of his Wife, he declined sitting among them. However, by fresh Orders under his own Hand, which I have seen in Print, he appointed Guards to attend the Judges at the Tryal, and to keep the City in Quiet; as he did likewise to prevent any Opposition from the People, upon the Day of Execution.

FROM what I have already deduced, it appears manifest, that the Differences between those two Sects, *Presbyterian* and *Independent*, did not then amount to half so much as what there is between a *Whig* and *Tory* at present among us. The Design of utterly extirpating Monarchy and Episcopacy, was equally the same in both; evidently the Consequence of the very same Principles, upon which the *Presbyterians* alone began, continued, and would have ended in the same Events; if towards the Conclusion they had not been bearded by that new Party, with whom they could not agree about dividing the Spoil. However, they held a good Share of Civil and Military Employments during the whole Time of the Usurpation; whose Names, and Actions, and Preferments, are frequent in the Accounts of those Times. For, I make no Doubt, that all the prudent *Presbyterians* complied in proper Seasons, falling in with the Stream; and thereby got that Share in Employments, which many of them held to the Restoration; and, perhaps, too many of them after. In the same Manner, we find our wisest *Tories*, in both Kingdoms, upon the Change of Hands and Measures at the Queen's Death, have endeavoured for several Years, by due Compliances, to recover the Time they had lost by a temporary Obstinacy; wherein they have well succeeded, according to their Degrees of Merit. Of whose Names I could here make honourable mention, if I did not fear it might offend their Modesty.

As to what is alledged, that some of the *Presbyterians* declared openly against the King's Murder; I allow it to be true. But, from what Motives? No other can possibly be assigned than perfect Spight, Rage, and Envy, to find themselves wormed out of all Power, by a new infant Spawn of *Independants*, sprung from their own Bowels. It is true, the

Differences in religious Tenets between them, are very few and trifling; the chief Quarrel, as far as I remember, relating to Congregational and National Assemblies. But, wherever Interest or Power think fit to interfere, it little imports what Principles the opposite Parties think fit to charge upon each other: For, we see, at this Day, that the *Tories* are more hated by the whole Set of zealous *Whigs*, than the very *Papists* themselves; and, in Effect, as much unqualified for the smallest Office: Although, both these Parties assert themselves to be of the same Religion, in all its Branches of Doctrine and Discipline; and profess the same Loyalty to the same *Protestant* King, and his Heirs.

IF the Reader would know what became of this *Independant* Party, upon whom all the Mischief is charged by their *Presbyterian* Brethren; he may please to observe, that during the whole Usurpation, they contended by Degrees with their Parent Sect, and, as I have already said, shared in Employments; and gradually, after the Restoration, mingled with the Mass of *Presbyterians*; lying ever since undistinguished in the Herd of *Dissenters*.

THE *Presbyterian* Merit is of as little Weight, when they alledge themselves instrumental towards the King's Restoration. The Kingdom grew tired with those ridiculous Models of Government: First, by a House of Lords and Commons, without a King; then without Bishops; afterwards by a Rump and Lords Temporal; then by a Rump alone: Next, by a single Person for Life, in Conjunction with a Council: By Agitators: By Major-Generals: By a new Kind of Representatives from the three Kingdoms: By the Keepers of the Liberties of *England*; with other Schemes that have slipt out of my Memory. *Cromwell* was dead; his Son *Richard*, a weak, ignorant Wretch, who gave up his Monarchy much in the same Manner with the two usurping Kings of *Brentford*. The People, harassed with Taxes, and other Oppressions; the King's Party, then called the *Cavaliers*, began to recover their Spirits. The few Nobility scattered through the Kingdom, who lived in a most retired Manner, observing the Confusion of Things, could no longer endure to be ridden by Bakers, Coblers,

Brewers, and the like, at the Head of Armies; and plundering every where like *French* Dragoons: The *Rump* Assembly grew despicable to those who had raised them. The City of *London*, exhausted by almost twenty Years contributing to their own Ruin, declared against them. The *Rump*, after many Deaths and Resurrections, was, in the most contemptuous Manner, kick't out, and burnt in Effigy. The excluded Members were let in: A free Parliament called in as legal a Manner as the Times would allow; and the King restored.

THE second Claim of *Presbyterian* Merit, is founded upon their Services against the dangerous Designs of King *James* the Second; while that Prince was using all his Endeavours to introduce *Popery*, which he openly professed upon his coming to the Crown: To this they add, their eminent Services at the Revolution, under the Prince of *Orange*.

NOW, the *Quantum* of *Presbyterian* Merit, during the four Years Reign of that weak, bigotted, and ill-advised Prince, as well as at the Time of the Revolution, will easily be computed, by a Recourse to a great Number of Histories, Pamphlets, and public Papers, printed in those Times, and some afterwards; beside the Verbal Testimonies of many Persons yet alive, who are old enough to have known and observed the *Dissenters* Conduct in that critical Period.

IT is agreed, that upon King *Charles* the Second's Death, soon after his Successor had publickly owned himself a *Roman Catholick*; he began with his first Caresses to the Church Party; from whom having received very cold discouraging Answers; he applied to the *Presbyterian* Leaders and Teachers; being advised by his Priests and *Popish* Courtiers, that the safest Method towards introducing his own Religion, would be by taking off the *Sacramental Test*, and giving a full Liberty of Conscience to all Religions, (I suppose that professed Christianity.) It seems, that the *Presbyterians*, in the latter Years of King *Charles* the Second, upon Account of certain Plots, (allowed by Bishop *Burnet* to be genuine) had been, for a short Time, forbid to hold their Conventicles. Whereupon, these charitable Christians, out of perfect Resentment against the Church, received the gracious Offers of King *James* with

the strongest Professions of Loyalty, and highest Acknow-
ledgments for his Favour. I have seen several of their
Addresses, full of Thanks and Praises, with bitter Insinuations
of what they had suffered; putting themselves and the *Papists*
upon the same Foot; as Fellow-Sufferers for Conscience;
and with the Style of, *Our Brethren the Roman Catholicks*. About
this Time began the Project of *Closetting*, (which hath since
been practised many Times, with more Art and Success)
where the principal Gentlemen of the Kingdom were privately
catechised by his Majesty, to know whether, if a new Parliament were called, they would agree to pass an Act for repealing
the *Sacramental Test*, and establishing a general Liberty of
Conscience. But he received so little Encouragement, that,
despairing of Success, he had Recourse to his dispensing
Power, which the Judges had determined to be Part of his
Prerogative. By Colour of this Determination, he preferred
several *Presbyterians*, and many *Papists*, to Civil and Military
Employments. While the King was thus busied, it is well
known that Monsieur *Fagel*, the *Dutch* Envoy in *London*,
delivered the Opinion of the Prince and Princess of *Orange*,
concerning the Repeal of the *Test*; whereof the King had sent
an Account to their Highnesses, to know how far they
approved of it. The Substance of their Answer, as reported by
Fagel, was this, *That their Highnesses thought very well of a
Liberty of Conscience; but by no Means of giving Employments to any
other Persons than those who were of the National Church*. This
Opinion was confirmed by several Reasons: I cannot be more
particular, not having the Paper by me, although it hath
been printed in many Accounts of those Times. And thus
much every moderate Churchman would perhaps submit to:
But to trust any Part of the Civil Power in the Hands of those
whose Interest, Inclination, Conscience, and former Practices
have been wholly turned to introduce a different System of
Religion and Government, hath very few Examples in any
Christian State; nor any at all in *Holland*, the great Patroness of
Universal Toleration.

Upon the first Intelligence King *James* received of an
intended Invasion by the Prince of *Orange*; among great

Numbers of *Papists*, to increase his Troops, he gave Commissions to several *Presbyterians*; some of whom had been Officers under the *Rump*; and particularly he placed one *Richards*, a noted *Presbyterian*, at the Head of a Regiment, who had been Governor of *Wexford* in *Cromwell*'s Time, and is often mentioned by *Ludlow* in his Memoirs. This Regiment was raised in *England* against the Prince of *Orange:* The Colonel made his Son a Captain, whom I knew, and was as zealous a *Presbyterian* as his Father. However, at the Time of the Prince's Landing, the Father easily foreseeing how Things would go, went over, like many others, to the Prince, who continued him in his Regiment; but coming over a Year or two after, to assist in raising the Siege of *Derry*, he behaved himself so like either a Coward or a Traytor, that his Regiment was taken from him.

I WILL now consider the Conduct of the Church-Party during the whole Reign of that unfortunate King. They were so unanimous against promising to pass an Act for repealing the Test, and establishing a general Liberty of Conscience; that the King durst not trust a Parliament; but encouraged by the Professions of Loyalty given him by his *Presbyterian* Friends, went on with his dispensing Power.

THE Church-Clergy at that Time are allowed to have written the best Collection of Tracts against *Popery* that ever appeared in *England*; which are to this Day in the highest Esteem. But, upon the strictest Enquiry, I could never hear of above one or two Papers published by the *Presbyterians* at that Time upon the same Subject. Seven great Prelates (he of *Canterbury* among the rest) were sent to the Tower, for presenting a Petition, wherein they desired to be excused in not obeying an illegal Command from the King. The Bishop of *London*, Dr. *Compton*, was summoned to answer before the Commissioners for Ecclesiastical Affairs, for not suspending Dr. *Sharp* (afterwards Archbishop of *York*) by the King's Command. If the *Presbyterians* expressed the same Zeal upon any Occasion, the Instances of it are not as I can find, left upon Record, or transmitted by Tradition. The Proceedings against *Magdalen College* in *Oxford*, for refusing to comply with the

King's Mandate for admitting a professed *Papist* upon their
Foundation, are a standing Proof of the Courage and Firmness
in Religion shewn by that learned Society, to the Ruin of their
Fortunes. The *Presbyterians* know very well, that I could
produce many more Instances of the same Kind. But these
are enough in so short a Paper as I intend at present.

IT is indeed very true, that after King *William* was settled
on the *English* Throne, the *Presbyterians* began to appear,
and offer their Credentials, and demand Favour: And, the new
King having been originally bred a *Calvinist*, was desirous
enough to make them easy (if that would do it) by a legal
Toleration; although in his Heart he never bore much Affection
to that Sect; nor designed to favour them further than as it
stood with the present Scheme of Politicks: As I have long
since been assured by the greatest Men of Whig-Principles at
that Time in *England*.

IT is likewise true, nor will be denied; that when the King
was possessed of the *English* Crown; and the Remainder of
the Quarrel was left to be decided in this Kingdom; the
Presbyterian wisely chose to join with the *Protestant* Army,
rather than with that of King *James* their old Friend, whose
Affairs were then in a Manner desperate. They were wise
enough to know, that this Kingdom, divided against it self,
could never prevail against the united Power of *England*.
They fought *pro aris & focis*; for their Estates and Religion;
which latter will never suffer so much by the Church of
England, as by that of *Rome*, where they are counted Hereticks
as well as we: And consequently they had no other Game to
play. But, what Merit they can build upon having joined with
a *Protestant* Army, under a King they acknowledged, to defend
their own Liberties and Properties against a *Popish* Enemy
under an abdicated King; is, I confess, to me absolutely
inconceivable; and, I believe, will equally be so for ever, to
any reasonable Man.

WHEN these Sectaries were several Years ago making the
same Attempt for abolishing the Test, many groundless
Reports were industriously and seasonably spread of an
Invasion threatned by the *Pretender*, on the North of *Ireland*.

At which Time the *Presbyterians* in their Pamphlets argued in a menacing Manner, that if the *Pretender* should invade those Parts of the Kingdom, where the Numbers and Estates of the Dissenters chiefly lay; they would sit still, and *let us fight our own Battles*; since they were to reap no Advantage, which ever Side should be Victors. If this were the Course they intended to take in such a Case; I desire to know, how they could contrive safely to stand Neuters, otherwise than by a Compact with the *Pretender* and his Army, to support their Neutrality, and protect them against the Forces of the Crown? This is a necessary Supposition; because they must else have inevitably been a Prey to both. However, by this frank Declaration, they sufficiently shewed their good Will; and confirmed the common Charge laid at their Door; that a *Scottish* or Northern *Presbyterian* hates our Episcopal Established Church, more than *Popery* it self. And, the Reason for this Hatred is natural enough, because it is the Church alone, that stands in the Way between them, and Power; which *Popery* doth not.

Upon this Occasion I am in some doubt, whether the political Spreaders of those chimerical Invasions, made a judicious Choice in fixing the Northern Parts of *Ireland* for that romantick Enterprize. Nor, can I well understand the Wisdom of the *Presbyterians* in countenancing and confirming those Reports. Because, it seemed to cast a most infamous Reflection upon the Loyalty and religious Principles of their whole Body: For, if there had been any Truth in the Matter, the Consequence must have been allowed, that the *Pretender* counted upon more Assistance from his Father's Friends the *Presbyterians*, by chusing to land in those very Parts, where their Number, Wealth, and Power most prevailed; rather than among those of his own Religion. And therefore, in Charity to this Sect, I rather incline to believe, that those Reports of an Invasion were formed and spread by the Race of small Politicians, in order to do a seasonable Jobb.

As to *Popery* in general, which for a thousand Years past hath been introducing and multiplying Corruptions both in Doctrine and Discipline; I look upon it to be the most absurd

System of Christianity professed by any Nation. But I cannot apprehend this Kingdom to be in much Danger from it. The Estates of Papists are very few; crumbling into small Parcels, and daily diminishing. Their common People are sunk in Poverty, Ignorance, and Cowardice; and of as little Consequence as Women and Children. Their Nobility and Gentry are at least by one half ruined, banished, or converted: They all soundly feel the Smart of what they suffered in the last *Irish* War: Some of them are already retired into foreign Countries; others, as I am told, intend to follow them; and the rest, I believe, to a Man, who still possess any Lands, are absolutely determined never to hazard them again for the Sake of establishing their Superstition. If it hath been thought fit, as some observe, to abate of the Laws Rigour against *Popery* in this Kingdom, I am confident it was done for very wise Reasons, considering the Situation of Affairs abroad at different Times, and the Interest of the *Protestant* Religion in general. And, as I do not find the least Fault in this Proceeding; so I do not conceive why a sunk discarded Party, who neither expect nor desire any Thing more than a quiet Life, should, under the Names of *High-flyers*, *Jacobites*, and many other vile Appellations, be charged so often in Print, and at common Tables, with endeavouring to introduce *Popery* and the *Pretender*; while the *Papists* abhor them above all other Men, on Account of Severities against their Priests in her late Majesty's Reign; when the *now disbanded Reprobate Party* was in Power. This I was convinced of some Years ago by a long Journey into the Southern Parts; where I had the Curiosity to send for many Priests of the Parishes I passed through, and to my great Satisfaction found them every where abounding in Professions of Loyalty to the late King *George*; for which they gave me the Reasons abovementioned; at the same Time complaining bitterly of the Hardships they suffered under the QUEEN's *last Ministry*.

I RETURN from this Digression to the modest Demands of the *Presbyterians* for a Repeal of the *Sacramental Test*, as a Reward for their Merits at the *Restoration*, and the *Revolution*; which Merits I have fairly represented as well as my Memory

x

would allow me. If I have committed any Mistakes, they must be of little Moment. The Facts and principal Circumstances are what I have obtained and digested, from reading the Histories of those Times, written by each Party; and many Thousands have done the same as well as I, who I am sure have in their Minds drawn the same Conclusions.

THIS is the Faction, and these the Men who are now resuming their Applications, and giving in their Bills of Merit to both Kingdoms upon two Points, which of all others, they have the least Pretensions to offer. I have collected the Facts with all possible Impartiality, from the current Histories of those Times; and have shewn, although very briefly, the gradual Proceedings of those Sectaries under the Denominations of *Puritans*, *Presbyterians*, and *Independants*, for about the Space of an hundred and eighty Years, from the beginning of Queen *Elizabeth*, to this present Time. But, notwithstanding all that can be said, these very Schismaticks, (for such they are in Temporals as well as Spirituals) are now again expecting, solliciting, and demanding, (not without insinuated Threats, according to their Custom) that the Parliament should fix them upon an equal Foot with the Church Established. I would fain know to what Branch of the Legislature they can have the Forehead to apply. Not to my Lords the Bishops; who must have often read, how the Predecessors of this very Faction, acting upon the same Principles, drove the whole Bench out of the House; who were then, and hitherto continue one of the three Estates. Not to the Temporal Peers, the second of the three Estates; who immediately after those rebellious Fanaticks had murdered their King, voted a House of Lords to be useless and dangerous, and would let them sit no longer, otherwise than when elected as Commoners: Not to the House of Commons; who must have heard, that in those Fanatick Times the *Presbyterian* and *Independant* Commanders in the Army, by military Power, expelled all the moderate Men out of the House, and left a *Rump* to govern the Nation. Lastly, not to the Crown, which those very *Saints* destined *to Rule the Earth*, trampled under their Feet, and then in cold Blood murdered the Blessed Wearer.

But, the Session now approaching, and a Clan of Dissenting Teachers come up to Town from their Northern Head Quarters, accompanied by many of their Elders and Agents, and supported by a general Contribution, to sollicit their Establishment, with a Capacity of holding all Military as well as Civil Employments; I think it high Time, that this Paper should see the Light. However, I cannot conclude without freely confessing, that if the *Presbyterians* should obtain their Ends, I could not be sorry to find them mistaken in the Point which they have most at Heart by the Repeal of the *Test*; I mean the Benefit of Employments. For, after all, what Assurance can a *Scottish* Northern Dissenter, born on *Irish* Ground, have, that he shall be treated with as much Favour as a *TRUE SCOT* born beyond the *Tweed.*

I am ready enough to believe that all I have said will avail but little. I have the common Excuse of other Men, when I think my self bound by all religious and civil Ties, to discharge my Conscience, and to warn my Countrymen upon this important Occasion. It is true, the Advocates for this Scheme promise a new World, after this blessed Work shall be compleated; that all Animosity and Faction must immediately drop: That, the only Distinction in this Kingdom will then be of *Papist* and *Protestant.* For, as to *Whig* and *Tory*, *High Church* and *Low Church*, *Jacobite* and *Hanoverian*, *Court* and *Country Party*, *English* and *Irish* Interest, *Dissenters* and *Conformists*, *New Light* and *Old Light*, *Anabaptist* and *Independant*, *Quaker* and *Muggletonian*; they will all meet and jumble together into a perfect Harmony, at the Sessions and Assizes, on the Bench, and in the Revenues; and upon the Whole, in all Civil and Military Trust, not excepting the great Councils of the Nation. For, it is wisely argued thus: That, a Kingdom being no more than a larger Knot of Friends met together, it is against the Rules of good Manners to shut any Person out of the Company, except the *Papists*; who profess themselves of another Club.

I am at a Loss to know what Arts the *Presbyterian* Sect intends to use, in convincing the World of their Loyalty to kingly Government; which long before the Prevalence, or even the Birth of their *Independant* Rivals, as soon as the King's Forces were overcome, declared their Principles to be against Monarchy, as well as Episcopacy and the House of Lords, even until the King was restored: At which Event, although they were forced to submit to the present Power, yet I have not heard that they did ever, to this Day, renounce any one Principle by which their Predecessors then acted; yet this they have been challenged to do, or at least to shew that others have done it for them, by a certain * Doctor, who, as I am told, hath much employed his Pen in the like Disputes. I own, they will be ready enough to insinuate themselves into any Government: But, if they mean to be honest and upright, they will and must endeavour by all Means, which they shall think lawful, to introduce and establish their own Scheme of Religion, as nearest approaching to the Word of GOD, by casting out all superstitious Ceremonies, Ecclesiastical Titles, Habits, Distinctions, and Superiorities, as Rags of *Popery*; in order to a *thorough Reformation*; and, as in Charity bound, to promote the Salvation of their Countrymen: Wishing with St. *Paul*, *That the whole Kingdom were as they are*. But, what Assurance will they please to give, that when their Sect shall become the National Established Worship, they will treat Us DISSENTERS as we have treated them. Was this their Course of Proceeding during the Dominion of the *Saints*? Were not all the Remainders of the Episcopal Church, in those Days, especially the Clergy, under a Persecution for above a dozen Years equal to that of the Primitive Christians under Heathen Emperors? That this Proceeding was suitable to their Principles, is known enough; for many of their Preachers then writ Books expressly against allowing any Liberty of Conscience, in a Religion different from their own; producing many Arguments to prove that Opinion; and among the rest, one frequently insisted on; that, allowing such a Liberty would be to *establish Iniquity by a Law:* † Many of these Writings

* The late Dr. TISDEL, who died June, 1736.
† See many hundred Quotations to prove this, in the Treatise called *Scotch Presbyterian. Eloquence*.

are yet to be seen; and, I hear, have been quoted by the Doctor above mentioned.

As to their great Objection of prostituting that holy Institution, the blessed Sacrament, by Way of a Test, before Admittance into any Employment; I ask, whether they would not be content to receive it *after their own Manner*, for the Office of a Judge, for that of a Commissioner in the Revenue, for a Regiment of Horse, or to be a Lord Justice. I believe they would scruple it as little, as a long Grace before and after Dinner; which they can say without *bending a Knee*. For, as I have been told, their Manner of taking Bread and Wine in their Conventicles, is performed with little more Solemnity than at their common Meals. And, therefore, since they look upon our Practice in receiving the Elements, to be idolatrous; they neither can, nor ought, in Conscience, to allow us that Liberty, otherwise than by Connivance; and a bare Toleration, like what is permitted to the *Papists*. *But, lest we should offend them,* I am ready to change this Test for another; although, I am afraid, that sanctified Reason is, by no Means, the Point where the Difficulty pinches; and only offered by pretended Churchmen, as if they could be content with our believing, that the Impiety and Prophanation of making the Sacrament a Test, were the only Objection. I therefore propose, that before the present Law be repealed, another may be enacted; that no Man shall receive any Employment, before he swears himself to be a true Member of the Church of *Ireland*, in Doctrine and Discipline, *&c.* And, that he will never frequent, or communicate with any other Form of Worship. It shall likewise be further enacted, that whoever offends, *&c.* shall be fined five hundred Pounds, imprisoned for a Year and a Day, and rendered incapable of all publick Trust for ever. Otherwise, I do insist, that those pious, indulgent, external Professors of our National Religion, shall either give up that fallacious hypocritical Reason for taking off the Test; or freely confess, that they desire to have a Gate wide open for every Sect, without any Test at all, except that of swearing Loyalty to the King; Which however, considering their

Principles, with regard to Monarchy yet unrenounced, might, if they would please to look deep enough into their own Hearts, prove a more bitter Test, than any other that the Law hath yet invented.

FOR, from the first Time that these Sectaries appeared in the World, it hath been always found, by their whole Proceeding, that they professed an utter Hatred to kingly Government. I can recollect, at present, three Civil Establishments, where *Calvinists*, and some other Reformers who rejected *Episcopacy*, possess the supreme Power; and, these are all Republicks; I mean, *Holland*, *Geneva*, and the reformed *Swiss* Cantons. I do not say this in Diminution, or Disgrace to Commonwealths; wherein, I confess, I have much altered many Opinions under which I was educated, having been led by some Observation, long Experience, and a thorough Detestation for the Corruptions of Mankind: Insomuch, that I am now justly liable to the Censure of *Hobbs*, who complains, that the Youth of *England* imbibe ill Opinions, from reading the Histories of ancient *Greece* and *Rome*, those renowned Scenes of Liberty and every Virtue.

BUT, as to Monarchs, who must be supposed well to study and understand their own Interest; they will best consider, whether those People, who in all their Actions, Preachings, and Writings, have openly declared themselves against Regal Power, are to be safely placed in an equal Degree of Favour and Trust, with those who have been always found the true and only Friends to the *English* Establishment. From which Consideration, I could have added one more Article to my new Test, if I had thought it worth my Time.

I HAVE been assured by some Persons who were present, that several of these Dissenting Teachers, upon their first Arrival hither to sollicit the Repeal of the Test, were pleased to express their Gratitude, by publickly drinking the Healths of certain eminent Patrons, whom they pretend to have found among us; if this be true, and that the Test must be delivered up by the very *Superiors appointed to defend it*; the Affair is already, in Effect, at an End. What *secret* Reasons those Patrons may have given for such a Return of brotherly Love, I shall not inquire: *For, O my Soul come not thou into their* Secret, *unto their* Assembly *mine Honour be not thou united. For in their Anger they slew a Man, and in their Self-will they digged down a Wall. Cursed be their Anger, for it was fierce, and their Wrath, for it was cruel; I will divide them in* Jacob, *and scatter them in* Israel.

Reasons humbly offered to the Parliament of *Ireland*

REASONS

HUMBLY OFFERED TO THE

PARLIAMENT of *IRELAND*,

FOR REPEALING THE

SACRAMENTAL TEST,

IN FAVOUR OF THE

C A T H O L I C K S,

OTHERWISE CALLED

R O M A N C A T H O L I C K S,

AND,

By their ILL-WILLERS, PAPISTS,

DRAWN

Partly from ARGUMENTS as they are
C A T H O L I C K S,

AND

Partly from ARGUMENTS common to them with
their Brethren the DISSENTERS.

WRITTEN in the Year 1733

ADVERTISEMENT.

IN the Years 1732, and 1733, an Attempt was made for repealing the Test Act in *Ireland*, introductory of a like Attempt in *England*. The various Arguments for it were answered in every Shape; but no Way more effectually than by examining what Pretence the *Presbyterians* had to share in all the Privileges of Government, either from their own Principles and Behaviour, or compared with those of other Sectaries. Under the former Head they were fully silenced by our Author, in *The Presbyterians Plea of Merit impartially examined*. They are now put in the Ballance with *Papists*, whom, although they have sometimes styled their Brethren in Adversity, yet, when placed in Competition, they will hate as Brethren likewise. But let them here dispute the Preference, and then put in their Claim to be Part of the Establishment.

R E A S O N S

HUMBLY OFFERED TO THE

PARLIAMENT of *IRELAND*

FOR REPEALING THE

SACRAMENTAL TEST, *&c.*

IT is well known, that the first Conquerors of this Kingdom
were *English Catholicks*, Subjects to *English Catholick* Kings,
from whom, by their Valour and Success, they obtained
large Portions of Land given them as a Reward for their many
Victories over the *Irish:* To which Merit our *Brethren* the
Dissenters of any Denomination whatsoever, have not the least
Pretensions.

It is confessed, that the Posterity of those first victorious
Catholicks were often forced to rise in their own Defence,
against new Colonies from *England*, who treated them like
mere native *Irish*, with innumerable Oppressions; depriving
them of their Lands, and driving them by Force of Arms into
the most desolate Parts of the Kingdom; until in the next
Generation, the Children of these Tyrants were used in the
same Manner by the new *English* Adventurers, which Practice
continued for many Centuries. But it is agreed on all Hands,
that no Insurrections were ever made, except after great
Oppressions by fresh Invaders: Whereas all the Rebellions of
Puritans, *Presbyterians*, *Independents*, and other Sectaries, constantly began before any Provocations were given, except
that they were not suffered to change the Government in
Church and State, and seize both into their own Hands; which,
however, at last they did, with the Murder of their King,
and of many thousands of his best Subjects.

The *Catholicks* were always Defenders of Monarchy, as constituted in these Kingdoms; whereas our *Brethren* the *Dissenters* were always Republicans both in Principle and Practice.

It is well known, that all the *Catholicks* of these Kingdoms, both Priests and Laity, are true *Whigs* in the best and most proper Sense of the Word; bearing as well in their Hearts, as in their outward Profession, an entire Loyalty to the Royal House of *Hanover*, in the Person and Posterity of *George* II. against the Pretender, and all his Adherents: To which they think themselves bound in Gratitude as well as Conscience, by the Lenity wherewith they have been treated since the Death of Queen *Anne*, so different from what they suffered in the four last Years of that Princess, during the Administration of that *wicked* Minister, the Earl of *Oxford*.

The *Catholicks* of this Kingdom humbly hope, that they have at least as fair a Title as any of their *Brother* Dissenters, to the Appellation of *Protestants*. They have always *protested* against the selling, dethroning, or murdering their Kings; against the Usurpations and Avarice of the *Court* of *Rome*; against *Deism*, *Atheism*, *Socinianism*, *Quakerism*, *Muggletonianism*, *Fanaticism*, *Brownism*, as well as against all *Jews*, *Turks*, *Infidels*, and *Hereticks*. Whereas the Title of *Protestants*, assumed by the whole Herd of Dissenters, (except ourselves) dependeth entirely upon their *protesting against Archbishops*, *Bishops, Deans, and Chapters, with their Revenues; and the whole Hierarchy*; which are the very Expressions used in *The Solemn League and Covenant*, where the Word *Popery* is only mentioned *ad invidiam*; because the *Catholicks* agree with the episcopal Church in those Fundamentals.

Although the *Catholicks* cannot deny, that in the great Rebellion against King *Charles* I. more Soldiers of their Religion were in the Parliament Army, than in his Majesty's Troops; and that many Jesuits and Friars went about, in the Disguise of *Presbyterian* and *Independent* Ministers, to preach up Rebellion, as the best Historians of those Times inform us; yet the Bulk of *Catholicks* in both Kingdoms preserved their Loyalty entire.

The *Catholicks* have some Reason to think it a little hard, when their Enemies will not please to distinguish between the Rebellious Riot committed by that brutal Ruffian, Sir *Phelim O Neal*, with his tumultuous Crew of Rabble; and the Forces raised afterwards by the *Catholick* Lords and Gentlemen of the *English* Pale, in Defence of the King, after the *English* Rebellion began. It is well known, that his Majesty's Affairs were in great Distraction some Time before, by an Invasion of the *Covenanting, Scottish, Kirk Rebels*, and by the base Terms the King was forced to accept, that they might be kept in Quiet, at a Juncture when he was every Hour threatned at Home by that Fanatick Party, which soon after set all in a Flame. And, if the *Catholick* Army in *Ireland* fought for their King against the Forces sent out by the Parliament, then in actual Rebellion against him, what Person of loyal Principles can be so partial to deny, that they did their Duty, by joining with the Marquis of *Ormond*, and other Commanders, who bore their Commissions from the King? For which, great Numbers of them lost their Lives, and forfeited their Estates; a great Part of the latter being now possessed by many Descendants from those very Men who had drawn their Swords in the Service of that rebellious Parliament which cut off his Head, and destroyed Monarchy. And what is more amazing, although the same Persons, when the *Irish* were intirely subdued, continued in Power under the *Rump*; were chief Confidents, and faithful Subjects to *Cromwell*, yet being wise enough to foresee a *Restoration*, they seized the Forts and Castles here, out of the Hands of their *old Brethren in Rebellion*, for the Service of the King; just saving the Tide, and putting in a Stock of Merit, sufficient not only to preserve the Lands which the *Catholicks* lost by their Loyalty; but likewise to preserve their Civil and Military Employments, or be higher advanced.

Those Insurrections wherewith the *Catholicks* are charged, from the Beginning of the Seventeenth Century to the great *English* Rebellion, were occasioned by many Oppressions they lay under. They had no Intention to introduce a *new* Religion, but to enjoy the Liberty of preserving the *old*; the very same which their Ancestors professed from the Time that

Christianity was first introduced into this Island, which was by *Catholicks*; but whether mingled with Corruptions, as some pretend, doth not belong to the Question. They had no Design to change the Government; they never attempted to fight against, to imprison, to betray, to sell, to bring to a Tryal, or to murder their King. The Schismaticks acted by a Spirit directly contrary; they united in a *Solemn League and Covenant*, to alter the whole System of Spiritual Government, established in all Christian Nations, and of Apostolick Institution; concluding the Tragedy with the Murder of the King in cold Blood, and upon mature Deliberation; at the same Time changing the Monarchy into a Commonwealth.

The *Catholicks* of *Ireland*, in the great Rebellion, lost their Estates for fighting in Defence of their King. The Schismaticks, who cut off the Father's Head, forced the Son to fly for his Life, and overturned the whole ancient Frame of Government, Religious and Civil; obtained Grants of those very Estates which the *Catholicks* lost in Defence of the ancient Constitution, many of which Estates are at this Day possessed by the Posterity of those Schismaticks: And thus they gained by the *Rebellion*, what the *Catholicks* lost by their *Loyalty*.

We allow the *Catholicks* to be *Brethren* of the Dissenters; some People, indeed, (which we cannot allow) would have them to be our Children, because *we* both dissent from the Church established, and both agree in abolishing this persecuting Sacramental Test; by which *negative Discouragement* we are both rendered incapable of Civil and Military Employments. However, we cannot but wonder at the bold Familiarity of these Schismaticks, in calling the Members of the National Church their *Brethren* and *Fellow-Protestants*. It is true, that all these Sects (except the *Catholicks*) are *Brethren* to each other in Faction, Ignorance, Iniquity, Perverseness, Pride, and (if we except the *Quakers*) in Rebellion. But, how the Churchmen can be styled their *Fellow Protestants*, we cannot comprehend. Because, when the whole *Babel* of Sectaries joined against the Church, the King, and the Nobility, for twenty Years, in a MATCH AT FOOT-BALL; where the Proverb expressly tells us, that *All are* FELLOWS; while the three Kingdoms were tossed to and fro, the Churches, and Cities, and Royal Palaces, shattered to Pieces, by their *Balls*, their *Buffets*, and their *Kicks*; the Victors would allow no more FELLOWS AT FOOT-BALL; but murdered, sequestered, plundered, deprived, banished to the Plantations, or enslaved all their Opposers who had *lost the Game*.

It is said the World is governed by *Opinion*; and Politicians assure us, that all Power is founded thereupon. Wherefore, as all human Creatures are fond to Distraction of their own Opinions; and so much the more, as those Opinions are absurd, ridiculous, or of little Moment; it must follow, that they are equally fond of Power. But no Opinions are maintained with so much Obstinacy as those in Religion, especially by such Zealots who never bore the least Regard to Religion, Conscience, Honour, Justice, Truth, Mercy, or common Morality, farther than in outward Appearance; under the Mask of Hypocrisy, to promote their diabolical Designs. And, therefore, Bishop *Burnet*, one of their Oracles, tells us honestly, that the *Saints* of those Fanatick Times, pronounced themselves above Morality, which they reckoned among *beggarly Elements*; but the Meaning of those two last Words thus applied, we confess to be above our Understanding.

Among those Kingdoms and States which first embraced the Reformation, *England* appeareth to have received it in the most regular Way; where it was introduced in a peaceable Manner, by the supreme Power of a King, and the three Estates in Parliament; to which, as the highest legislative Authority, all Subjects are bound passively to submit. Neither was there much Blood shed on so great a Change of Religion. But a considerable Number of Lords, and other Persons of Quality through the Kingdom still continued in their old Faith, and were, notwithstanding their Difference in Religion, employed in Offices Civil as well as Military, more or less in every Reign, until the Test Act in the Time of King *Charles* II. However, from the Time of the Reformation, the Number of *Catholicks* gradually and considerably lessened: So that in the Reign of King *Charles* I. *England* became, in a great Degree, a Protestant Kingdom, without taking the Sectaries into the

Y

Number; the Legality whereof, with respect to human Laws, the *Catholicks* never disputed: But the *Puritans*, and other Schismaticks, without the least Pretence to any such Authority, by an open Rebellion, destroyed that legal Reformation, as we observed before, murdered their King, and changed the Monarchy into a Republick. It is therefore not to be wondered at, if the *Catholicks*, in such a *Babel* of Religions, chose to adhere to their own Faith left them by their Ancestors, rather than seek for a better among a Rabble of hypocritical, rebellious, deluding Knaves, or deluded Enthusiasts.

We repeat once more, that if a national Religion be changed, by the supreme Legislative Power, we cannot dispute the human Legality of such a Change. But we humbly conceive, that if any considerable Party of Men, which differs from an Establishment, either old or new, can deserve Liberty of Conscience, it ought to consist of those, who, for want of Conviction, or of a right Understanding the Merits of each Cause, conceive themselves bound in Conscience to adhere to the Religion of their Ancestors; because they are of all others least likely to be Authors of Innovations, either in Church or State.

On the other Side: If the Reformation of Religion be founded upon Rebellion against the King, without whose Consent, by the Nature of our Constitution, no Law can pass: If this Reformation be introduced by only one of the three Estates, I mean the Commons, and not by one half even of those Commons, and this by the Assistance of a Rebel Army: Again, if this Reformation were carried on by the Exclusion of Nobles, both Lay and Spiritual, (who constitute the two other Parts of the three Estates) by the Murder of their King, and by abolishing the whole System of Government; the *Catholicks* cannot see why the Successors of those Schismaticks, who are universally accused by all Parties except themselves, and a few infamous Abettors, for still retaining the same Principles in Religion and Government, under which their Predecessors acted, should pretend to a better Share of Civil or Military Trust, Profit and Power, than the *Catholicks*, who, during all that Period of twenty Years, were continually persecuted with

the utmost Severity, merely on account of their Loyalty
and constant Adherence to Kingly Power.

We now come to those Arguments for repealing the
Sacramental Test, which equally affect the *Catholicks*, and their
Brethren the Dissenters.

First, We agree with our Fellow-Dissenters; that * *Persecution, merely for Conscience Sake, is against the Genius of the Gospel.*
And so likewise is *any Law for depriving Men of their natural and
civil Rights which they claim as Men.* We are also ready enough
to allow, that *the smallest negative Discouragements for Uniformity's Sake are so many Persecutions.* Because, it cannot be
denied, that the Scratch of a Pin is in some Degree a real
Wound, as much as a Stab through the Heart. In like Manner,
an Incapacity by Law for any Man to be made a Judge, a
Colonel, or Justice of the Peace, *merely on a Point of Conscience, is
a negative Discouragement*, and consequently a real Persecution:
For, in this Case, the Author of the Pamphlet quoted in the
† Margin, puts a very pertinent and powerful Question: That,
*If God be the sole Lord of the Conscience, why should the Rights of
Conscience be subject to human Jurisdiction?* Now to apply this
to the *Catholicks*: The Belief of Transubstantiation *is a Matter
purely of Religion and Conscience, which doth not affect the political
Interest of Society as such. Therefore, Why should the Rights of
Conscience, whereof* GOD *is the sole Lord, be subject to human
Jurisdiction?* And why should GOD be deprived of this Right
over a *Catholick's* Conscience any more than over that of any
other Dissenter?

And whereas another Author among our Brethren the
Dissenters, hath very justly complained, that by this persecuting Test Act, great Numbers of *true Protestants* have been
forced to leave the Kingdom, and fly to the Plantations, rather
than stay here BRANDED with an Incapacity for Civil and
Military Employments; we do affirm, that the *Catholicks* can
bring many more Instances of the same Kind; some thousands
of their Religion having been forced, by the Sacramental Test,
to retire into other Countries, rather than live here under the

* *Vide* Reasons for the Repeal of the Sacramental Test.
† Idem.

Incapacity of wearing Swords, sitting in Parliament, and getting that Share of Power and Profit which belongs to them as *Fellow Christians*, whereof they are deprived *merely upon Account of Conscience, which would not allow them to take the Sacrament after the Manner prescribed in the Liturgy.* Hence it clearly follows, in the Words of the same * Author, That, *if we* Catholicks *are uncapable of Employments, we are punished for our Dissent,* that is, *for our Conscience, which wholly turns upon political Considerations.*

The *Catholicks* are willing to acknowledge the King's Supremacy, whenever their Brethren the Dissenters shall please to shew them an Example.

Further, the *Catholicks*, whenever their Religion shall come to be the national established Faith, are willing to undergo the same *Test* offered by the Author already quoted. His Words are these: *To end this Debate, by putting it upon a Foot, which, I hope, will appear to every impartial Person a fair and equitable one; we* Catholicks *propose, with Submission to the proper Judges, that effectual Security be taken against Persecution, by obliging all who are admitted into Places of Power and Trust, whatever their religious Profession be, in the most solemn manner, to disclaim persecuting Principles.* It is hoped the Publick will take Notice of these Words, *Whatever their religious Profession be;* which plainly includes the *Catholicks;* and for which we return Thanks to *our Dissenting Brethren.*

And, whereas it is objected by those of the established Church, that, if the Schismaticks and Fanaticks were once put into a Capacity of professing Civil and Military Employments; they would never be at Ease, until they had raised their own Way of Worship into the National Religion, through all his Majesty's Dominions, equal with the *true orthodox Scottish Kirk;* which, when they had once brought to pass, they would no more allow Liberty of Conscience to Episcopal Dissenters, than they did in the Time of the great *English* Rebellion, in the succeeding Fanatick Anarchy, until the King was restored. There is another very learned schismatical † Pamphleteer,

---

* See Reasons against the Test.
† Vindication of the Protestant Dissenters.

who, in Answer to a malignant Libel, called, *The Presbyterians Plea of Merit, &c.* clearly wipes off this Aspersion; by assuring all Episcopal Protestants of the present Church, upon his own Word, and to his own Knowledge, that our Brethren the Dissenters will never offer at such an Attempt. In like Manner, the *Catholicks*, when legally required, will openly declare, *upon their Words and Honours*, that as soon as their *negative Discouragements* and their *Persecutions* shall be removed by repealing the Sacramental Test, they will leave it entirely to the Merits of the Cause, whether the Kingdom shall think fit to make their Faith the established Religion, or not.

And again, Whereas our *Presbyterian* Brethren, in many of their Pamphlets, take much Offence, that the great Rebellion in *England*, the Murder of the King, with the entire Change of Religion and Government, are perpetually objected against them both in and out of Season, by our common Enemy, the present Conformists: We do declare, in the Defence of our said Brethren, that the Reproach aforesaid is *an old worn-out thread-bare Cant*, which they always disdained to answer: And I very well remember, that, having once told a certain Conformist, how much I wondered to hear him and his Tribe, dwelling perpetually on so beaten a Subject; he was pleased to divert the Discourse with a foolish Story, which I cannot forbear telling to his Disgrace. He said, there was a Clergyman in *Yorkshire*, who, for fifteen Years together, preached every *Sunday* against Drunkenness: Whereat, the Parishioners being much offended, complained to the Archbishop; who, having sent for the Clergyman, and severely reprimanded him, the Minister had no better an Answer, than by confessing the Fact; adding, that all the Parish were Drunkards; that he desired to reclaim them from one Vice, before he would begin upon another; and, since they still continued to be as great Drunkards as before, he resolved to go on, except his Grace would please to forbid him.

We are very sensible, how heavy an Accusation lyeth upon the *Catholicks* of *Ireland*; that some Years before King *Charles* II. was restored, when theirs and the King's Forces were entirely reduced, and the Kingdom declared by the Rump to be settled;

after all his Majesty's Generals were forced to fly to *France*, or other Countries, the Heads of the said *Catholicks*, who remained here in an enslaved Condition, joined to send an Invitation to the Duke of *Lorrain*; engaging, upon his appearing here with his Forces, to deliver up the whole Island to his Power, and declare him their Sovereign; which, after the Restoration, was proved against them by Dean *Boyle*, since Primate, who produced the very original Instrument at the Board. The *Catholicks* freely acknowledge the Fact to be true; and, at the same Time, appeal to all the World, whether a wiser, a better, a more honourable, or a more justifiable Project could have been thought of. They were then reduced to Slavery and Beggary by the *English* Rebels, many thousands of them murdered, the rest deprived of their Estates, and driven to live on a small Pittance in the Wilds of *Connaught*; at a Time, when either the *Rump* or *Cromwell* absolutely governed the three Kingdoms. And the Question will turn upon this, Whether the *Catholicks*, deprived of all their Possessions, governed with a Rod of Iron, and in utter Despair of ever seeing the Monarchy restored, for the Preservation of which they had suffered so much, were to be blamed for calling in a foreign Prince of their own Religion, who had a considerable Army to support them; rather than submit to so infamous an Usurper as *Cromwell*, or such a bloody and ignominious Conventicle as the *Rump*. And I have often heard, not only our Friends the Dissenters, but even our common Enemy the Conformists, who are conversant in the History of those Times, freely confess, that considering the miserable Situation the *Irish* were then in, they could not have thought of a braver or more virtuous Attempt; by which they might have been Instruments of restoring the lawful Monarch, at least to the Recovery of *England* and *Scotland*, from those Betrayers, and Sellers, and Murderers of his Royal Father.

To conclude, Whereas the last quoted Author complains, very heavily and frequently, of a BRAND that lyes upon them; it is a great Mistake; for the first original BRAND hath long been taken off. Only, we confess, *the* Scar will probably remain and be visible for ever to those who know the Principles by which they acted, until those Principles shall be openly renounced; else it must continue to all Generations, like the Mark set upon *Cain*, which some Authors say descended to all his Posterity; or, like the *Roman* nose, and *Austrian* Lip, or like the long Bag of Flesh hanging down from the Gills of the People in *Piedmont*. But, as for any *Brands* fixed on Schismaticks for several Years past, they have all been made with *cold Iron*; like Thieves, who, by the BENEFIT OF THE CLERGY, are condemned to be only burned in the Hand; but escape the Pain and the Mark, by being in *Fee* with the JAYLOR. Which Advantage the Schismatical Teachers will never want, who, as we are assured, and of which there is a *very fresh Instance*, have the Souls, and Bodies, and Purses of their People an hundred Times more at their Mercy, than the *Catholick* Priests could ever pretend to.

Therefore, upon the Whole, the *Catholicks* do humbly petition (*without the least Insinuation of Threatening*) that upon this *favourable* Juncture their Incapacity for Civil and Military Employments may be wholly taken off, for the very same Reasons (besides others more cogent) that are now offered by their *Brethren* the *Dissenters*.

And your Petitioners, as in Duty bound, shall ever pray, &c.

Dublin, Nov.
    1733.

Some Few Thoughts Concerning the Repeal of the Test

THOUGHTS

The REPEAL OF THE TEST

THOSE of either side who have written upon this subject of the Test, in making or answering objections, seem to fail by not pressing sufficiently the chief point upon which the controversy turns. The arguments used by those who write for the church are very good in their kind, but will have little force under the present corruptions of mankind, because the authors treat this subject *tanquam in republica Platonis, et non in fœce Romuli*.

It must be confessed, that, considering how few employments of any consequence fall to the share of those English who are born in this kingdom, and those few very dearly purchased, at the expence of conscience, liberty, and all regard for the public good, they are not worth contending for: And, if nothing but profit were in the case, it would hardly cost me one sigh when I should see those few scraps thrown among every species of Fanaticks, to scuffle for among themselves.

And this will infallibly be the case, after repealing the Test. For, every subdivision of sect will, with equal justice, pretend to have a share; and, as it is usual with sharers, will never think they have enough, while any pretender is left unprovided. I shall not except the Quakers; because, when the passage is once let open for all sects to partake in public emoluments, it is very probable the lawfulness of taking oaths, and wearing carnal weapons, may be revealed to the brotherhood; which thought, I confess, was first put into my head by one of the shrewdest Quakers in this kingdom.*

* Undoubtedly the Quaker hinted at by Dr. Swift was the late Mr. Rooke; a man who had a very good taste for wit, had real abundance of history, and was, perhaps, the most learned Quaker, one of them, in the world. To the best of my recollection, he was the author of a good humorous pastoral in the Quaker-style.

APPENDIXES

THE

MEMORIAL

Of the Poor INHABITANTS, TRADESMEN, and LABOURERS of the *Kingdom* of *IRELAND*.

Most Humbly sheweth,

THAT last Year, 1727, there was a very great Scarcity of Bread Corn That the Grainerys were exhausted; and were it not for the Supplys from Great-Britain, many of the Poor would have perished for want of Bread, which was so Dear in most Places, that Multitudes have sunk themselves so far in Debt for the support of their Familys, that they are now reduced to Beggary.

A Famine among the Poor, has often been the Occasion of Pestilential and contagious Distempers, whereby the Rich have become sharers in the general Calamity, as it happened of late in some of the Danish and Swedish Dominions, and other Places.

When Provisions fail, Trade and Industry ceases, Lands become waste; thus Landlords and Rich Men may soon be on the Level with the Poor Tennants and Cottiers.

People in Extremity often Robb, Plunder and Steal, rather than Starve; so that few will Escape it's dismal Effects.

Many were forced last Year to fall too soon upon their early Corn and Potatoes; and it is certain, that by the Wetness of the Season, heavy Rains, and other Accidents, a great part of the last Year's Crop of Corn was so hungary and Weak, that there is more than a third Part wanting of the usual Product as in other Years; and it is fear'd, that encouraging Tillage for the time to come, will not relieve the present Necessities of the Poor; and that the Merchants will not of themselves Import in due time, such Quantities of Grain, as may be Sufficient.

That the Price of Corn is risen so high in Great-Britain, that there is no hopes of Relief from thence as formerly; and we will need many more, than was last Year imported.

There is a good Premium offered for Exportation of Corn out of Great-Britain, and there is something allowed to that Purpose in this Kingdom, in favour of Tillage, when Corn is very Cheap.

Surely, there is as much Reason for this Nation to give a Premium for its Importation for a few Months, now in the time of Scarcity, until the Danger of a Famine be over: It is good to provide in Time, considering that the Winds do not always serve to bring in our Ships when there is Occasion for them.

It is certain, that the Price of Corn, is now Risen higher, than ever it was known to be, so early in the Year; especially, in many of the Country Villages, which increases the fears and Crys of the Poor; who cannot gain by their Labour, what will feed them and their Familys.

There is plenty of Corn in our Plantations abroad, and in some of our neighbouring Countries; so that if a Premium of about two Shillings per Barrel of Wheat, &c, and some ease in the Duty was allowed in due Time, it would encourage Merchants and others to turn themselves that way; Ten thousand Pounds, which is no heavy Sum upon a whole Nation under such Circumstances, would by good Management be sufficient to encourage the Importation of One hundred thousand Barrels, which destributed by prudent Managers into the Ports nearest to the Places where there is the greatest Necessity, under proper Restrictions, would (under God) be a means to prevent the great Danger that threatens Us; then the Rich Farmers, the Ingrosers, and such as keep up their Grain, hearing of a Supply from abroad, would find it convenient to be selling off their Stores at the current Price, so the Markets would in a great Measure be kept down; Perhaps a lesser Premium per Barrel would be Sufficient, then more Corn (if needfull) may be imported.

To raise a Fund for this charitable Use, if a further Tax was laid upon Tea, Coffee, Sugar, Spices, Wine, foreign Cloaths, and other foreign Things, as are chiefly for the use of the Great and Wealthy, or on any Thing whatsoever, whereby the Money would be advanced on this pressing Occasion. That it may be considered how strange and suprizing it would be in foreign Parts to hear that the Poor was Starving in a rich Country, where such immence Sums were daily laid out on several Occasions, where there was timely warning, even to a Demonstration of the approaching Danger.

And there are presidents of Money being rais'd to prevent eminent Dangers. These and all other Things are most humbly submitted to the great Care and Wisdom of those in Power and Trust in this Nation.

May it therefore please you to consider this Case, and as you find proper, to recommend to his Excellency, the Lord Lieutenant and Council, and to the Right Honourable the Lords and Commons in Parliament.

F I N [I] S.

HINTS FOR
INTELLIGENCER PAPERS &c.

The following Hints *are printed from Swift's autograph drafts (Rylands Eng. Mss. 659) as far as it is possible to reproduce words, which are sometimes abbreviated, sometimes crossed out or blotted. Italics indicate that these words or phrases have been struck through with a pen: see illustration facing p.* 131.

Beau's dresses

Clergy preaching. bad Engl- &c

Universal knavery of all handicrafts,
Shopkeepers, and in the Country of all farmers
Cottagers, &c. Scotch worse than Irish, but worst when partake of both nations

Building, and praise of Pearce.

Improvemts, penal clause, as to time &c for improvemt. & preservation of trees & their kinds — abuse Squires on this head.

Knavery the effect of poverty and oppression: they steal or cheat, as the quickest way to live, when industry is not encouraged: therefore they do not stand on credit on yr buying anothr time. Sacrifice your custom for cheating you half a Crown.

That great rogue (?) Bedgers.

   what I did; and how the weavers acted.

Peter Walters —

HINTS:
EDUCATION OF LADYES

No great matter for the bulk of women since the men are as foolish & ignorant.

Begin. A person of Quality a little absolute, a man of tast and letters who well knew how to support his opinions, which were generally right, fell into one, which I thought he held in a sense not sufficiently limited, although he had many old proverbs and maxims on his side, which carry the authority of ages with them that women shoud only regard their Children and family &c.

My practise of advising Ldys to read, and what; and my way of instructing young Misses.

I used to stay a month or two in the Country desolate, the Neighbourhood scarce and not very inviting.

A Companion for life to a man of Sense especially without Employmt and violent lover of the Country, should have a reasonable companion, who could distinguish a man of sense &c. and relish good conversation without being talkative, positive or assuming.

It would make the women love home better, and able to teach their daughters.

The Lady was a considerable heiress used too fondly, lives in Town, had that kind of Education which is calld the best. learning Italian, French, musick and singing, all which she forgot &c. fell into play, visits, assemblies &c.

No French Romances, and few plays for young Ladyes.

How hard for a woman to live solitary and not read; A generall inspection into family affairs right; but not to be a House-keeper &c. any more than an Architect should have his hands in mortar.

I have often thanked God that custom has made it detestable otherwise. otherwise they have a good plea to keep a Gallant rather than marry. I mean a great heiress, who when she is marryed can call nothing her own, & may want common necessaryes, by the churlishness of a husband &c. therefore I was never a (*sic*) against what they call pin-money. nor see the reason why people should not part when all agreemt. is desperate.

Women I own do often want balast &c. but it is often through ignorance or half knoledge.

A shame that not one in a million can properly be said to read or write, or understand.

MAXIMS EXAMIND

Dearness of things necessary for Life

Lowness of Interest

High purchase of Land

Buildings added to the Metropolis

People the Riches of a Nation

Tax upon Luxury

   Res nolunt diu male administrari

Parlmt not minding any thing printed; tis but a Pamphlt

Folly of those who argue from Engld, Irld. &c

Who would write in Bedlam, that Society is a good thing:
Tis otherwise there, they would burn the house

Accidental and unpresidented impediments

So if a Legislator should form a Scheam for the
Governmt of Bedlam and upon the Principle that man being
a sociable Creature, they ought to go into Councils &c

Parlmt not minding Pamphlets, made me write this when all
was over, that they may judge from effects.

Nothing will do but wearing our own growth &c

I have talked & writ a little on this subject before

  Nevr love our Country . . . .
I write this on purpose when it is too late
Because there is no arguing with them

Who would live in Ireld, without a great balance
The(y) can live saving in Engld yet honorable, nor
need invite as here, & have many dishes

August Assembly

Lost all Idea of Liberty

Of those vermin writers too low too answer, yet lye so
horridly of more Clergy in London from Ireld and that if
Linnen Scarves hurt Engd we should not wear them since
they are not hired. like Rats in a bag

These singularityes of Governmt have turned the very heads
of the people made them think themselves not upon the par
(*or* foot) with others of their own Species, & a Spirit of
Servitude

I own that in Scotld & some Times in Italy, Interest is low,
& land dear. . but worse trade

Bad seasons a trifle where are they not?

Not (*get th*) redress their grievances before they pass their
money bills In Ireld We cannot pretend to that &c

Leeson's way of buying
houses

Not so among us till we can sell them as the Africans do.

Nations encourage marriage

The Engl contempt for absentees

I speak not this from any regard to their persons

If they had stayd, an assembly of great severeness might have
prevented some fatal events. I know their contempt well,
these 30 years past &c

Encouragin marriage as all wise nations did, is an appendix
to the Maxim of people the riches of **a** Nation; we ought to
discourage it. The wretches we see with children

THE

CRAFTSMAN

No. 227.   SATURDAY, *Nov.* 7, 1730.

THE following Article, which hath lately appeared in the News-papers, deserves our immediate Consideration, *viz.*

'THEY write from *Dublin*, that one Officer from every 'Regiment in the *French Service* is arrived there, in order to 'raise Recruits for their respective Corps; which is not to be 'done in a *clandestine Manner* as formerly, when several Persons 'suffer'd *Death* for it, but *publickly*. These Gentlemen are to 'disperse Themselves into the several Counties, where They 'have the *best Interest*; and a *Field-Officer* is to reside constantly 'at *Dublin* to hear all Complaints, which may be made by any 'of the Recruits against their Officers; and also to prepare 'for sending them off.—Count *Broglio* hath been solliciting an 'Order, to this Purpose, these two Years.'

WHEN I first read this Account in the publick Prints, I look'd upon it as a common Piece of *false Intelligence*, and was in full Expectation of seeing it contradicted in the next Day's Papers, according to frequent Custom; but having since heard it confidently affirm'd to be true, (though I can hardly yet believe it; especially, as to *every Part*) the Duty, which I owe my *Country*, and my Zeal for the *present Establishment* oblige me to take some Notice of an Affair, which I apprehend to be of very great Importance to *both*.

IT will be necessary, in the first Place, to give the Reader a short Account of the Nature of *these Troops*, as They are now establish'd in *France*.

THEY consist, as We have been inform'd, of one Regiment of *Horse*, and five Regiments of *Foot*, all *doubly* or *trebly officer'd*; so that They are, of Themselves, a very considerable Body of Men.

But their *Number* is the least Point to be consider'd in this Affair. There are other Circumstances, which render *these Troops* infinitely more formidable to *Great Britain*. They are not only all *Roman-Catholicks*, but the most dangerous of that Communion; with respect to Us. I mean, *Roman-Catholick Subjects of our own Dominions*; many of whom have been oblig'd to fly their native Country, on Account of *Rebellions* or *Conspiracies*, in which They have been engag'd; and all of them devoted by Inclination, by Interest, by Conscience, by every Motive human and divine, to the Service of the *Pretender*, in Opposition to the *Protestant Succession in his Majesty's Royal Family*.

To This We may add, that They are generally esteem'd the best Forces in the *French Service*; that They have always behav'd themselves as such in the late Wars; and are commanded by *Officers* of approv'd Courage, as well as great Skill and Experience in military Affairs.

It is said likewise, that the *Serjeants, Corporals*, and *private Men* are so well season'd to Danger, and expert in their Duty, that, by a gradual Promotion, They could furnish *Officers* for a very formidable Army, in Case of any sudden Invasion or Insurrection.

In the next Place, it will not be improper to examine this Affair with Regard to our *Laws*.

It is made *Felony*, by Act of Parliament in *Ireland*, for any Subject of that Kingdom to inlist Himself, or to inlist others, in the Service of any *foreign State*; and it is well known that Multitudes of poor Wretches have suffer'd *Death* upon that Account.

We know it may be said, that a Power is reserv'd to his Majesty, by a Clause in *that Act*, to dispense with it, by granting any *foreign Prince* a Licence to raise Forces in his Dominions, and indemnifying his Subjects from the Penalties of the *Law*.

Though it is far from my Intention to dispute any of his Majesty's *legal Prerogatives*, or to call the Wisdom of the *Legislature* in Question; yet I must take the Liberty to observe that *such Powers* have been sometimes granted out of Complaisance to the *Crown*, that the Prince's Hands may not be absolutely ty'd up, and in full Confidence that they will never be exerted but for the Benefit of *this Nation*, or possibly of some *Protestant Ally*, upon great Emergencies of State. The Exercise of the *Prerogative*, in these Cases, is therefore meerly a *prudential Part*, which is left to the Discretion of the *Prince* and his *Ministers*, who ought always to be supposed the best Judges of these Affairs; and therefore how ridiculous would it be to send to the *Attorney General* for his Opinion in such a Case, who can be a competent Judge of nothing but the *Legality* of it, and whether the Affair be *actionable* or not; but *Ministers* ought to regulate their Conduct, in these Respects, according to the Situation of Affairs, and the Exigencies of Government.

I MUST therefore beg Leave to consider the present Subject, of the *Irish Forces*, in this Light.

IT will not be deny'd, I presume, that a Licence to recruit *Roman-Catholick* Regiments of *English* Subjects, in *Foreign Service*, and in the Interest of a *Pretender* to the Crown, (which is *Death* by the *Law*, without his Majesty's Permission) is a Favour of a very extraordinary Nature, and ought to be attended with some extraordinary Circumstances.—I confess that I can see no such extraordinary Circumstances at present; unless it should be said that *this Favour* was granted, in order to engage our *good Allies* in the Demolition of *Dunkirk*; but I hope they have more Generosity than to insist upon such hard Terms for the effectual Performance of That, which They are oblig'd by *Treaty* to do. I am sure, such Conditions seem unreasonable on *our Part*, after We have made them so many other Concessions; particularly with Relation to the *Flag* and *Santa Lucia*; which I think are sufficient to make Them comply with all our Demands, without expecting any farther Favours, and even Superogations of Friendship.

PERHAPS, my *Adversaries* (if They have any Conceit) may take an Opportunity of ridiculing me for writing in this Strain; but as it sometimes serves their Turn to make me a *great Man*, and to argue against me as such, I will for once suppose myself so; and, methinks, if I had the Honour of being but half an Hour in that Station, I could reason against such an Order, for the Good of my King and my Country, in the following Manner.

1. *These Troops* have always been made Use of, whenever there hath been any Attempt in Favour of the *Pretender*; and indeed, they are, upon many Accounts, the fittest for this Purpose. They are our Fellow-Subjects; they speak our Language; are acquainted with our Manners; and do not raise that Aversion in the People, which they naturally conceive against *other foreign Troops*, who understand neither.—I am afraid I may add, that they are kept up, for *this Purpose*, in *intire Regiments*, without suffering them to be mix'd with the Troops of any *other Nation*. It is well known, at, least, that they supply'd the late King *James* with a Nursery of Soldiers, who were always ready for his Service, whenever any Opportunity offer'd itself for his Restoration; and that, at this Time, the *Pretender* is always the Bait made Use of by their Officers, to raise Recruits. They never mention the King of *France* or the King of *Spain*, upon these Occasions, but list the poor Wretches under an Assurance that they are enter'd into the Service of Him, whom They call their *natural* and *rightful* King.—I will not suspect the present Fidelity of *France*, and their Cordiality to the *Protestant Establishment*; yet methinks We might easily excuse our selves from furnishing them with *Instruments* which They may employ against us, whenever *Ambition*, or *Reason of State* shall dissolve their present Engagements, and induce them to espouse the Cause of the *Pretender* again.

2. I⊤ is very probable that his *Catholick Majesty* (who hath likewise several Regiments, of *this Kind*, in his Service) will expect the same Favour of recruiting them in *Ireland*; and that He may, in Case of Refusal, make it a Pretence, at any Time, for quarrelling with us, interrupting our Commerce, and disturbing us again in the Possession of *Gibraltar*; and here it is proper just to take Notice that *these Troops* did his *Catholick Majesty* the most eminent Service in the last Siege of that important Place.—He may complain, perhaps, of our Partiality to *France*, and alledge that we do not treat *Spain*, in the same

Manner We expect to be treated by them, as *one of the most
favour'd Nations*.

3. THE Kingdom of *Ireland* seems, at this Time, in a very
ill Condition to admit of any such Draughts out of her
Dominions. She hath been already so much exhausted by the
voluntary Transportation of Multitudes of her Inhabitants,
(who have been prevailed upon, by the Calamities of their
own Country, to seek their Bread in other Parts of the World)
that the Interposition of *Parliament* was found necessary to
put a Stop to it; and shall We suffer any *Foreign Power* to drain
her still farther under such Circumstances; especially in *this
Manner*, and for *this Purpose*?—I do not hear that *this Licence* is
confin'd to any particular Number of Men. It is confess'd,
I think, that They want above *Two Thousand Men* to compleat
their Corps; and who knows but They may design to raise a
great many more than they care to own; or even to form some
new Regiments of these Troops? But supposing They are confin'd to a *certain Number* of Recruits, and that *Ireland* were in a
Capacity to spare them; it is well known how easily such
Limitations are evaded, and how difficult it is to know when
People conform exactly to the Terms of their Commission.
This was sufficiently explained in the late, famous Controversy
concerning Mr. *Wood*'s Patent for supplying *Ireland* with a
particular Sum of *Copper Halfpence*; and the Arguments upon
that Subject may be apply'd to *This*, with some Allowances for
the Difference between the two Cases.—It may, perhaps, be
said likewise that all the Vigilance of the Ministry hath been
hitherto found ineffectual to prevent the *French* from *clandestinely* recruiting these Regiments with *Irish Catholicks*; and
therefore that We may as well allow Them to do it *openly*; nay,
that it is our Interest to let them purge *Ireland* of her *Popish*
Inhabitants as much as they please; but I deny this for several
Reasons, which I shall mention presently; and if it were really
the Case, that the *French* can at any time recruit these Troops
clandestinely, I cannot see any Reason why they should sollicit
an Order so pressingly, for *two Years* together, to do it *openly*,
unless they have some *other Design*. Ought not even this
Consideration to put us, at least, a little upon our Guard,

and is it not a tacit Confession, that *these Troops* are thought to be of more Importance to *Them* than *We* ought to wish.— Besides, are We to licence and authorize a *mischievous Practice* because we cannot *totally prevent* it? Every Body justly applauded his Majesty's singular Firmness and Resolution in supporting the Rights of his *German Subjects*, when an Attempt was made to seduce some of them into the King of *Prussia*'s Service, though perhaps it is impossible to prevent that Practice intirely. We all remember that the inlisting a *Miller*'s *Son*, and a few other, ordinary Peasants, occasion'd such a Misunderstanding between the two Crowns, as proceeded almost to a Rupture. Nor was the Zeal of the *English Parliament* backward on this Occasion; but, on this Consideration, amongst others, resolv'd to keep up a Body of 12,000 *Hessian* Troops in our Pay, which have already cost us above a *Million* of Money. I am confident, therefore, that the same paternal Care will always influence his Majesty to guard and protect his *British Subjects* in the same Manner; and if any Measure should be taken, which favours too much of the *French Interest*, and seems of dangerous Consequence to the Interest of *his Family*, the World can impute it to nothing, but the deceitful Representations of *Those*, who lye under such particular Obligations to the Court of *France*, that they can refuse them nothing.

4. SUCH a *Licence* seems to give Encouragement to the People of *Ireland* to continue *Roman Catholicks*; since they are sure to meet with a Provision both in the *French* and *Spanish Service*; whereas We always reject them in *our Troops*, and absolutely prohibit our Officers to recruit in *Ireland*. Now, though it may not be safe to trust Them in our Armies; yet certainly We ought not to give the least Encouragement to their entering into *foreign Service*; especially into such compact *Bodies* as *these Regiments*; And here it will not be amiss, to relate a Story much to the Honour of an *English Nobleman*, who hath also one of the largest Estates in *Ireland* of any Man in the Kingdom. When he went to visit the *Invalides* in *France*, a Place in the Nature of our *Chelsea College* here, all the *Irish* Officers and Soldiers of that Hospital drew out in a Body to

do Him particular Honours. We can make no Question that their chief View was to have some *Present* from his Lordship; but though he hath an *Heart* as well disposed to generous Charity as any Man, and a *Purse* well able to answer the Dictates of it; yet out of Regard to his Country, for which he hath likewise the most disinterested Zeal, his Answer to them was only this. 'Gentlemen, I am very sensible of the Honour you 'have done me, and heartily pity your Misfortunes; but as you 'have drawn them upon yourselves, by *serving against your* 'Country*, you must not expect any Relief or Reward from *me*, 'for having suffer'd in a Service, in which I wish you had never 'engag'd.'

5. Is there not some Reason to apprehend that *this Licence* may, at one Time or other, prove a Snare to that Country, and draw many People into their Destruction; for, unless it is made *perpetual*, can it be suppos'd that all the poor, ignorant Wretches in the Kingdom should be appriz'd how long *this Licence* is to be in Force; or when they may list with *Impunity*, and when they may not? Besides, as it may be presum'd that *these Officers* will never go, for the future, upon such Errands, without some *pretended Orders*, when the *real One* is expir'd; so They will find it no difficult Matter to impose such a *Counterfeit* upon illiterate People; who may thus incur the Penalties of the *Law*, without knowing any Thing of the Matter.—Such a Method of providing for Persons, whose Principles render them unserviceable in *our Army*, is indeed a little more charitable than a *late Project* for preventing *Irish Children* from being starv'd, by fatting them up, and selling them to the *Butcher*.

6. I HAVE often heard that *these Troops* have been made use of, in Parliament, as an Argument for keeping up a *standing Army* in *England*; and I think We need not take any Measures to render *that Argument* stronger.—God knows, there are too many Arguments always ready upon *such Occasions*!

I MIGHT insist upon some other Points, which *this Affair* naturally suggests to a considering Mind; particularly the Danger of suffering several *bigotted Irish Papists*, in *foreign Service*, to disperse Themselves into those Counties, where they have the *best Interest*, and to stroll about *Ireland* amongst their Relations and old Acquaintance, of the *same Principles* with Themselves.—Are We sure that They will not make a bad Use of this Liberty, by enquiring into the Strength of their *Party*; by giving them *Hopes*; and taking an Opportunity to concert Measures for the Advantage of their *Cause*? Have We no Reason to apprehend that They may endeavour to raise *Seamen* as well as *Soldiers*, under Colour of *this Order*; or engage great Numbers of their Countrymen to transport Themselves over to the *French Colonies* and *Plantations* in the *West-Indies*, which are already grown formidable to the trading Interest of *Great-Britain* in *those Parts*?

BUT whatever may be the Motives to such an *extraordinary Favour*, or the Consequence of it, I am sure it is the strongest Mark of our Confidence in *France*, and such an one, as, I believe, They would not place in us, upon any Occasion.— I will illustrate This by a parallel Case.

The *French Protestants*, who fled over hither from a Persecution, on Account of Religion, never discover'd any Principles, which are incompatible with the Civil Government of *France*, nor ever set up any *Pretender* to the *present Royal Family* of that Kingdom; and yet, if We should think fit to form any considerable Number of them into *compleat, distinct Regiments*, to be compos'd of *French Protestants* only, and commanded by *French Officers*, without any Incorporation of *British Soldiers*; I fancy it would give our *good Allies* some Umbrage. But I am almost confident that they would never permit us to send over a *Protestant French Officer* from every Regiment, to recruit their respective Corps, by dispersing themselves into those Provinces, where They have the *best Interest*; or suffer a *Field Officer*, in *English* Pay, to reside constantly in *Paris*, and exercise a Sort of *martial Law* in the *Capital* of their Dominions; I say they would hardly suffer This, even though our Ambassador should solicit such an Order, with the utmost Application, for twenty Years together.

AND yet the Case of these *Irish Forces* is much stronger with Respect to Us. They do not differ with us only in Matters of *Religion*; but hold Principles, absolutely destructive of our

Civil Government; and are generally look'd upon abroad as a *standing Army*, kept on Foot to serve the *Pretender* upon any Occasion.

I MUST ask a Question or two, which naturally offer themselves in this Place.

WHAT Power is this *Field Officer* to exercise during his Residence in *Dublin*? Is the *French martial Law* to take Place, if any of these Recruits should happen to repent of what they have done, and think fit to *desert*?

TROOPS are generally *arm'd* as soon as they are listed.— Is *this Rule* to be observ'd in the present Case? If so, another Question occurs.—It hath been found necessary, for the Security of *Ireland*, to restrain all *Roman Catholicks* from wearing or keeping any *Arms* in their Houses. I ask therefore whether the Authority of *this Licence* is to supercede the *Laws of the Land*?—I may go farther.

THE Garrison of *Dublin* seldom consists of above 800 Men, for the Duty of the Place.—Supposing double that Number of *Popish Recruits* should be brought thither, in order to be view'd by their *Field Officer*; will it be said that there is no just Apprehension of Danger? But as these Suggestions may appear to be founded on the Infidelity of *France* (a Case not to be suppos'd at present) I will press them no farther.

I MUST however repeat it, that *this Order* is the fullest Demonstration of the *Confidence* We repose in Them; and I hope They will scorn to make any bad Use of it; but if it were possible to suspect that they could have any Design to play the Knave with us, they could not wish for a better Opportunity to promote it than by such a *Power*, as is now said to be put into their Hands.

I HOPE my Remarks on this *Article of News* will not be construed in a *Jacobite Sense*, even by the most prostitute Scribblers of the present Times; but I must beg Leave to expostulate a little with the Publick on that mean and infamous Practice, which *these Writers* have lately used, in explaining some of my Papers into treasonable Libels; taking an Occasion from hence to appear formally in Defence of the *Throne*, and laying it down, as a Point granted, that there is an actual,

concerted Design, of setting aside the *present Establishment*.—
This is a Practice, which may be of great Service to the *real
Enemies* of the present Government; and every *Jacobite* in the
Kingdom may make Use of it to publish the most *explicit
Invectives* on the King and his Government, under the Pretence
of interpreting the *implicite Design* of other Writings. It is a
Practice, which was never allow'd of till now, and ought
never to be allow'd; for whatever may be the *secret Meaning*
of any Author, *such Explanations* are certainly *Libels*, which
may have a very bad Effect upon weak Minds, and are punish-
able by the *Laws*, without any extraordinary Methods of
Construction.—*These Writers* ought to remember the Case of
Sir *Richard Steele*, who published the *Pretender*'s *Declaration*,
at the Beginning of the late Reign, with an *Answer* annex'd;
and though he did it with a very good Design, yet it was
universally allowed to be contrary to *Law*; and if his Principles
of *Loyalty* had not been very well known, might have involved
him in a severe Prosecution.—I shall make no Reflections
on *Those*, who encourage such *scandalous Explanations*; and
Those, who are hired to do it, are beneath my Notice. Let them
empty all the trite Common-Places of *servile, injudicious
Flattery*, and endeavour to make their Court by such *nauseous,
dishonest Adulation*, as, I am sure, gives the most Offence to
those Persons, to whom it is paid.—Let them throw as much
foul Dirt at *Me* as they please; and charge me with Designs,
which never enter'd into my Thoughts, and cannot justly be
imputed to me from any Part of my Conduct. God knows
my Heart, I am as zealous for the Welfare of the *present Royal
Family* as the most sordid of *these Sycophants*.—I am sensible,
that our Happiness depends on the Security of his *Majesty's
Title*, and the Preservation of the *present Government*, upon *those
Principles*, which established them, at the late *glorious Revolution*;
and which I hope will continue to actuate the Conduct of
Britons to the latest Generations. These have always been *my
Principles*; and whoever will give himself the Trouble of look-
ing over the Course of these Papers, will be convinced that
They have been my Guide; but I am a blunt, plain-dealing, old
Man, who am not afraid to speak the *Truth*; and as I have no

Relish for *Flattery* myself, I scorn to bestow it on others. I have not, however, been sparing of *just Praise*, nor slipt any seasonable Opportunity to distinguish the Royal Virtues of their *present Majesties*.—More than This I cannot do; and more than This, I hope, will not be expected.—Some of my Expressions, perhaps, may have been thought too rough and unpolish'd for the Climate of a *Court*; but they flow'd purely from the Sincerity of my Heart; and the Freedom of my Writings hath proceeded from my Zeal for the Interest of my *King* and my *Country*.

WITH Regard to my *Adversaries*, I will leave every impartial Reader to judge, whether, even in *private Life*, that Man is not most to be depended upon, who being inwardly convinced of the great and good Qualities of his Friend, never loads him with *fulsome Flatteries*, but takes the honest Liberty of warning him against the Measures of *Those*, who are endeavouring to mislead him.—The Case is much stronger in *publick Life*; and a *Crown* is beset with so many Difficulties, that even a Prince of the most *consummate Wisdom* is not always sufficiently guarded against the Dangers, which surround him, from the Stratagems of *artful Ministers*, or the Blunders of *weak Ones*. Both of them may be equally *bad Ministers*, and pursue the *same Methods* of supporting themselves, by flattering him into *Measures*, which tend to his Destruction.

BUT it is Time to draw to a Conclusion; and I can only add, that if I were really engaged in any Design, contrary to the Interest of the *present Establishment*, I should have sate down contented and secretly rejoyced at the *Affair*, which occasioned this Paper, instead of giving myself and the Reader so much Trouble.

C. D.

TEXTUAL NOTES

1. A SHORT VIEW OF THE STATE OF IRELAND.

First printed by S. Harding, Dublin 1727-8. See facsimile of title-page, p. 3. *Another edition:* Printed for and sold by Combra Daniell, Bookseller, opposite the Main Guard. (Perhaps a piracy; of no textual value.) Printed in part in Mist's *Weekly Journal*, April 20, 1728; and reprinted in 1729 with a Preface by Sheridan as *Intelligencer*, no. 15.
Swift's *Works*, Faulkner, 1735, IV, 250-260.

The text is here printed from Faulkner, collated with first Dublin edition (27) and collected edition of *Intelligencer*, London, 1729 (29).

Page	Line	PRESENT TEXT	VARIANTS
5		H.t. from t.p. of 27	A Short View, &c.
	10	paid	payed 27, 29
	12	happen	happens 27, 29
	16	or so 27	and so 29
		cordially . . . obligingly	cordially . . . obligingly 27, 29
6	11	Priviledge	Liberty 27 29
	23	Prince	Princes 27, 29
	24	Administrator	Administrators 27, 29
7	5	the People	a People 27, 29
	5 *f.b.*	of which, however, we are only defective in	(*this line omitted in* 29)
8	2	hath bestowed so liberally on this Kingdom	bestowed us so liberally 27; bestowed on us so liberally 29
	4	*Ireland*	this Kingdom 27, 29
	13	this Privilege	this 27, 29
	19	go on to the 29	go unto the 27, 35
	22	uncontroverted	unconverted 27
		Lord Chief Justice *Whit-shed's*	my L—C—J—W—'s 27, 29
		(*Fn. added in* 35)	
	9 *f.b.*	decide	divide 27
9	9 *f.b.*	Potatoes are	Potatoes in great quantity are 27,29
	4-2 *f.b.*	(N.B. italicized only in 35, perhaps by Swift)	
	b	half the	half of the 27, 29
10	7	*Commissioners*	C——rs 27, 29
	21	those gentlemen	these gentlemen 27, 29
	24	Irony 29 (& C. Daniell)	Journey 27
	26	*Ysland* 29	Island 27
11	3	*magnus* 27, 29	*magna* 35
	6	Rents 27, 29	Rents, 35
	16	themselves	they 27, 29
	5 *f.b.*	who	that 27, 29
12	3	those	these 27, 29
	29	(*omitted*)	FINIS 27

2. AN ANSWER TO A PAPER CALLED A MEMORIAL

First printed by S. Harding, Dublin, 1728. For facsimile of title-page see p. 15.
Reprinted in Mist's *Weekly Journal*, May 11, 1728
Swift's *Works*, Faulkner, 1735, IV, 261–272
　　The text is here printed from Faulkner (35), collated with the original Dublin edition (28).

Page	Line	PRESENT TEXT	VARIANTS
17		(Ht. and date from orig. t.p.)	h.t. An Answer to a Paper, &c. 28
	12	some Schemes	such Schemes 28
	17	too	two 28
	21	were 28	are 35
18	1	are 28	were 35

　　　　N.B.—A curious transposition, but may have been due to an error in proof correction, the first instead of the second 'were' being corrected.

19	10	until	till 28
	13	All which are 28	All which, are 35
	15	*Tan* them	Tann it 28
20	6	District	Distinct 28
	11	particularly	particular 28
	16–17	but ... *Cash* 28	but, ... *Cash*, 35
21	7–8	of computing	if computing 28
	10	happens	happend 28
	12	At least	And at least 28
	13	Husbands	Husband 28
	15	small	few 28
	17	than	then 28
	18	a Sum	Sum 28
	19	on a	one a 28
	22	that	even that 28
	4 f.b.	*Excise*	excuse 28
22	21	Thousands	thousand 28
	29	could	would 28
23	9	*and ye refused;*	*and ye;* 28; *on ye;* 35
	11	*Counsel,*	*Counsels* 28; *Counsels,* 35

　　　　N.B.—I have restored the reading of the A.V. (*Proverbs* i, 20, 24–6) because the 28 reading *and ye* indicates that the following word at the turn of the line had become omitted by mistake; and 35 wrongly corrected to *on ye*, to make sense.
　　　　Also that in 28, i suggest that *s* was inserted instead of a comma, and 35 wrongly prints both.

	18	lately sent out a Paper	sent out a paper some days ago 28
	20–21	of the late Lord Chief Justice *Whitshed*	of a departed J——ge

　　　　N.B.—Italics in this and the last paragraph added in 35, possibly by Swift himself.

	21	Severity; since	Severity. Since 28, 35

Page	Line	Present Text	Variants
	6–5 *f.b.*	*Virtues,* have from the other; and	Virtues, and
24	24	*hunc tu Romane caveto*	*hanc tu Romane eaveto*
	26	if my	of my 28
	28	me the 28	me, the 35

3. The INTELLIGENCER PAPERS.

First printed by S. Harding, Dublin, 1728. See facsimile of title-page, p. 29.
The Intelligencer, London Reprinted, and sold by A. Moor in St. Paul's Church-yard, and the Booksellers of London and Westminster. MDCCXIX. Nos. 1–19. (29)
The Intelligencer. By the Author of a Tale of a Tub. The Second Edition London: Printed for Francis Cogan, at the Middle-Temple-Gate in Fleet-Street, MDCCXXX. Nos. 1–20. (30)

In a letter to Pope, June 2, 1732 (Corr., iv, 307–8) Swift says that he was responsible for nos. 1, 3, 5, 7, 9, 19; and 15 was a reprint of his *Short View of the State of Ireland*, with a preface by Sheridan. Pope printed Nos. 5 and 7 together as 'An Essay on the Fates of Clergymen' and No. 9 as 'An Essay on Modern Education' in *Miscellanies, The Third Volume*, 1732, pp. 206–236 (32).

N.B.—In Swift's own copy, now in Lord Rothschild's Library, these two papers are marked with a ☞ and a few corrections occur in Swift's hand. (S)
Swift's *Works,* Faulkner, 1735, Vol. I, 267 No. 3
                                275 No. 5 and no. 7
                                286 No. 9
              Vol. IV, 399 No. 19

The present edition is printed from this text, except No. 1, which was not included in either of Faulkner's volumes; it is printed from a photostat of the Trinity College copy of the first Dublin edition, and has been collated with 29 and 30. The only variants are literal misprints which have been corrected.

INTELLIGENCER, No. III

Page	Line	Present Text	Variants in 28, 29, 30
32	8	the	this (*all*)
	10	and Manner	and the Manner (*all*)
33	6	succeed	succeeds (*all*)
	7 *f.b.*	that	which (*all*)
	3 *f.b.*	Corruptions	Corruption (*all*)
34	3	the private	personal (*all*)
	24–5	*whom . . . Veneration*	(whom . . . Veneration) (*all*)
	5 *f.b.*	he hath	hath
	2 *f.b.*	Minister* *Fn.* Sir Robert Walpole	M—— (*all*)
35	4	Prime Minister	great M—— (*all*)
	12	the *Courtiers*	Courtiers (*all*)
		be	is (*all*)
	26	Actors represent	Actors more immediately represent (*all*)

Page	Line	Present Text	Variants
	2 *f.b.*	with such a vicious crew, as might	among such a vicious Crew, as would (*all*)
	b.	at such	and at such lewd (*all*)
36	8	*Clergyman,* who comes	Clergy-Man, who goes (*all*)
	11	Prelate	P——te (*all*)
	9 *f.b.*	those	these (*all*)
	8 *f.b.*	which, without enquiring whether it affects the present Age, may possibly be	which, although it doth by no Means affect the present Age, yet might have been (*all*)
	7 *f.b.*	in Times to come	in the former, and may possibly be so in Ages to come (*all*)
	6 *f.b.*	the Occasion	Occasion (*all*)
		those *common Robbers,* 28, 29	to Robbers 30
37	3	that many 28, 29	many 30
	5	frequent . . .	so frequent that (*all*)
	6	a 28	the 29, 30, 35
	7	want 28, 29, 30	have 35

Page	Line	Present Text	Variants in 28, 29, 30, 32
38		NUMBERS V AND VII	An ESSAY ON THE *Fates of Clergymen* 32
			NUMBER V 35 (F. dropped Pope's title, but printed the two papers together.)
		2 *lines of verse*	*Omitted* in 32, 35
	9	People (*all*)	Men 35
		in	and is in (*all*)
	24	the	that (*all*)
	25	meddle	to meddle (*all*)
39	4	farther 29, 30, 32	further 28
	7	or 30	nor 28, 29, 32
	8	Reason	Reason to do so (*all*)
	10	in *Courts* S	in the Courts (*all*)
	22	of great Affairs 28, 29, 32	of Affairs 30
	24	a One 28	an One 29, 30, 32
		occurs; if 29, 30, 32	occurs. For 28
	26	if this be his Fate, when	thus although, (*all*)
	28	Avarice; what 28, 29, 32	Avarice, he is sure to raise the Hatred of the noisy Crowd, who envy him the quiet Enjoyment of himself. What 30
		he 28, 29, 32	such an one 30
	8 *f.b.*	Ladder, and every 28, 29, 32	Ladder, every 30
	7 *f.b.*	Hand ready 28, 29, 32	Hand will be ready 30
	6 *f.b.*	off, when 28, 29, 32	off, as soon as 30
		Top? And in 28, 29, 32	Top? In 30
		(*Fn. only in* 35 *here and elsewhere*)	
40	6	Station	Stations (*all*)
	11	Promotion	Promotions (*all*)

Page	Line	Present Text	Variants in 28, 29, 30, 32
	14	Observations	Regulations (*all*)
	23	Man 28	Men 29, 30, 32, 35
	24	Archbishop 32; *fa.* 35	A.B.C.T. 28, 29, 30
	28	*Summers*	S——rs (*all*)
	8 *f.b.*	Prelate 32	Pr—— 28, 29, 30
	3 *f.b.*	*Yorkshire*	—— Shire (*all*)
41	14	happens 29, 30, 32	happen 28
		usually 28, 29, 32	generally 30
	15	to be 28	to me 29, 30, 32, 35
	22	resty	rusty (*all*)
	24	I will here give 32	In some following Paper, I will give 28, 29, 30
	26–7	this Discretion S	worldly Discretion (*all*) 35
	29	*CORUSODES*	(Number VII *begins here* 28, 29, 30)
	3 *f.b.*	dragling 29, 30, 32	dagling 28
42	8	*perceived* 28	perceive 29, 30, 32, 35
	12	endowed, and 28	endowed, 29, 30, 32, 35
	15	was Waiting 28, 29, 32	was a waiting 30
	17	Ten	fourteen (*all*)
	24	Houses	House (*all*)
	2 *f.b.*	his frequent 28, 29, 32	his own frequent 30
43	12	great Employment S	high Employment (*all*, 35)
44	8	his short 28, 29, 32	in short 30
	10	Opinions;	Opinions. (*all*)
	10–11	Mitre, in which he succeeded S	Mitre (*all*, 35)
	22	Nephews, or . . . be not in 28, 29, 32	Nephews: Or . . . be in 30
	3 *f.b.*	Street	Streets (*all*)
45	2	small Estate	small Fortune (*all*)
	6	by the Men 28	by Men 29, 30, 32, 35
	23–4	*that he . . . before*	that he . . . before (*all*)
	24	the	this (*all*)
	27	this	his (*all*)
	6 *f.b.*	Pounds 32	Pound 28, 29, 30

INTELLIGENCER, No. IX
Reprinted in Mist's *Weekly Journal*, Aug. 10 & 17, 1728

46	2 *f.b.*	*Scandalum*	*Scandulum* 35
47	1	*some* Care	some additional Care (*all*)
	5–8	which relate . . . follow 28, 29, 30	which relate to *England*. 32, 35
	9	Affairs in that Kingdom hath 28, 29, 30	Affairs hath 32, 35
	10	placed in the Hands of *New-men* 28, 29, 30, 32	placed in *New-men* 35
	11	few Exceptions	very few Exceptions (*all*)
	12	or supplied	or supported only (*all*)
	17–18	The Minors having	The Minors have, or had, (*all*)

Page	Line	PRESENT TEXT	VARIANTS
	24–25	highest Employments of State	chief Conduct of publick Affairs (*all*)
	9 *f.b.*	ample fortunes	good Estates (*all*)
	7 *f.b.*	*Clifford, Osborn* 32	*Clifford, Coonuley, Osborn* 28, 29, 30
	b.	last Reign 28, 29, 30	following Reign 32
		was for many Years 32	was understood for many Years to be 28, 29, 30
48	3	Alliance S	Allowance (*all*)
	8–9	so great a Share	so great Share (*all*)
	9,	most important Parts	most competent Parts (*all*)
	16–17	noble and wealthy (*all*)	noble, wealthy 35
	18	Bodies 28, 30	Body 29, 32, 35
	22	Birth; S	Birth. (*all*)
	23	a Deference	an universal Deference (*all*)
	24	in Princes S	on Princes (*all*, 35)
	25, 6	*Ends . . . Means* 32	Ends . . . Means 28, 29, 30
	6 *f.b.*	*modern*	modern (*all*)
	2 *f.b.*	that the publick	that publick (*all*)
49	16–17	was . . . Standard-Pattern 30, 32	were . . . Standard-Pattern 28, 29
	6 *f.b.*	*reconoitring*	reconoutring 28; rencountring 29, 30, 32
50	1	known a few	known many, and some even in this Kingdom 28, 29, 30 known many 32
	23	the Dancing-Master S, 35	Dancing-master (*all*)
	9 *f.b.*	Vices S, 35	Vice (*all*)
	5–4 *f.b.*	and Posture (*all*)	and the Posture 35
	4 *f.b.*	Change (*all*)	Changes 35
51	15	unprecedented 32	unpresidented 28, 29, 30
	18	own 29, 30, 32	one 28
	21–2	Removal to the University	Removal (*all*)
	23	Firmness of a Governor	Firmness of a very worthy Governor (*all*)
52	6	in their	to their (*all*)
	10	who was	that was (*all*)
	15	*Schools* and *Colleges* 28, 29, 30	*School* and *Colleges* 32, 35
	26	out of (*all*)	by 35
	9 *f.b.*	for (*all*)	But 35
	7 *f.b.*	or never 28, 29, 30	or ever 32
	6 *f.b.*	misled S, 35	mild (*all*)
53	16	Course	Cause (*all*)
	3 *f.b.*	enervated 28, 29, 32	enervate 30

INTELLIGENCER No. XIX

54	4–6	N.B. *In the following . . .* Drapier.	(*not in* 28, 29, 30)
	18	until	till 28, 29, 30

Page	Line	PRESENT TEXT	VARIANTS
54	18	to be not 28	not to be 29, 30, 35
	b.	*Pedlary-Ware*, 28, 29, 30	Pedlary-Ware; 35
55	3	Kinds 28, 29, 30	Kind 35
		until	till 28, 29, 30
	5	left us	left among us 28, 29, 30
	18	all thinking	all other thinking 28, 29, 30
		although	though 28, 29, 30
	25–8	Disadvantage. They consider not . . . that half . . . are annually sent	Disadvantage; of . . . of half . . . sent annually 28, 29, 30
	28	with many	and many 28, 29, 30
	29	which keep	excepted for our Sins, which keeps 28; except . . . keep 29, 30
	b.	so urging	too urging 28, 20, 30
56	4	tamely	timely 28, 29, 30
	14	*being made easy upon this Article*	*being easy upon that Article* 28, 29, 30
	7–6 f.b.	although he dare	though he dares 28, 29, 30
	3 f.b.	*Nine Pence in* (Fn. only in 35)	*Nine Pence to* 28, 29, 30
58	5	*Crawley* 29, 30	*Cowley* 28
	17	until	till 28, 29, 30
	27	could never	would never 28, 29, 30
59	6 f.b.	who come 30	who came 28, 29
60	8	Somebody 28, 29, 30	Some body 35
	21	Assaults 28, 29	Insults 30, 35
	27	Misery: The	Misery; so, the 28, 29, 30
	28	have also wisely	have wisely 28, 29, 30
	2 f.b.	discourage 28, 29	discourse 30
61	1	Effect	Effects 28, 29, 30

4. LETTER TO THE ARCHBISHOP OF DUBLIN CONCERNING THE WEAVERS

Autograph MS. in the Forster Collection, Victoria and Albert Museum. Ten leaves written in the right hand column only, with some additions in the left. No title in Swift's hand, but begins 'My Lord'
Endorsed, probably by Deane Swift:

Lettr to the A Bp. Ap. 1729
About Weavers &c.

First printed by Deane Swift in 1765 in the London collected edition *Works*, VIII, pt. i, pp. 177–84.
Reprinted the same year by Faulkner in Dublin: *Works*, XII, pp. 265–274.
The present text is printed from the manuscript, in which Swift's alterations and corrections are noted as follows:

Page	Line	PRESENT TEXT	VARIANTS IN MS.
65	13	Nation	Kingdom *deleted*
	22	clad and erect	*inserted above the line*

Page	Line	Present Text	Variants
	7 _f.b._	Courage	_inserted after_ Property
66	4	force	oblige _deleted_
	7	present evil Condition	evil _inserted before the line_
	11	entitled	called _deleted_
	12	Trad (_This older spelling sometimes used_)	
	21–4	But our Trad . . . exacting	_added in the left margin_
	8 _f.b._	abortive	crude _deleted_
67	1	manufactures	_Omitted_
	5	other Method	order Method
	14	by two	by _inserted above the line_
	9 _f.b._	parts of the Globe	countryes _deleted_
	4 _f.b._	Tea (including Coffee	Coffee and _deleted_
68	8	sum	some
	16	devouring Serpent	devouring _inserted above the line_
	17	but	and _deleted_
	7 _f.b._	selling the very necessaryes of life in our markets	in our markets at home _deleted after_ selling
69	4	their Brethren in	the Clergy of _deleted_
	13	Opinions; and	but instead _deleted after_ Opinions
	24	more.	more, for your Visitation passed without any Overture at all from the Weavers _deleted_
	8 _f.b._	would enter into Bonds	did bind themselves _deleted_
70	1	And if	then _deleted after_ And
	6	it appeared	there _deleted_
	22	such a	this _deleted_
	7 _f.b._	Weavers	weavers, Linnen-weavers _deleted_
	6 _f.b._	notwithstanding all the care of the Governors at that Board, when we had an offer of commerce with the Spaniards (_written in left margin_)	when we had an offer of the whole trade with Spain . . . notwithstanding all the Care taken by the Governors of that Board _deleted_
71	2	that I would (_written in left margin_)	to _deleted_; that I should _inserted above the line_
	5	one	a _deleted_
	6	shall . . . is	should . . . were _deleted_
	14	and China-ware	_inserted above the line_
	21	and receiving from thence and all other Countryes nothing but what is fully manufactured	_written in the left margin, and marked for insertion after_ England
	8 _f.b._	which hath spent	hath _inserted above the line_
	6 _f.b._	lamenting	complaining _deleted_
	5 _f.b._	ill	_inserted over_ bad

5. ANSWER TO SEVERAL LETTERS FROM UNKNOWN PERSONS

Autograph MS. in the Forster Collection, Victoria and Albert Museum. Eight leaves written in the right hand column only. No title, but addressed 'Gentlemen'. Endorsed probably by Deane Swift on the last page as above.
First printed by Deane Swift in *Works*, 4to, Vol. VIII, pt. i., pp. 185-191. It was reprinted in the same year by Faulkner in Dublin: *Works*, Vol. XII, pp. 275-285.

The present text is printed from the manuscript, in which Swift's alterations and corrections are noted as follows:

Page	Line	PRESENT TEXT	VARIANTS
75	14	is not to be had but by (*written in the left margin*)	we cannot expect without *deleted*
	25	in . . . directed	under . . . sent
76	15	in Praise	the *deleted before* Praise
	5 *f.b.*	or the Army	*inserted above the line*
77	4	these Speculations may probably not much (*written in the left margin*)	they do not *deleted*
	8	been able to persuade	prevailed *deleted*
	9	oratory	*following word deleted* ?made
	11	one	*inserted above a deletion*
	14	having	have *deleted*
	23	three	two *deleted*
	b.	any	a *deleted*
78	4	penal Clauses	clauses for *deleted*
	2 *f.b.*	Expedition	*the next ten lines crossed out:* but, there is likewise another temptation which is not of inconsiderable weight, which is their Itch of living in a Country where their Sect is predominant, and where their eyes and Conscience while (? will) not be offended by the Stumbling block of Ceremonyes. habits and Spiritual Titles.
79	16	sufficient	*following word deleted* reasons
	18	become	grow *deleted*
	24	understanding	knowing *deleted*
	5 *f.b.*	of our own wooll	*inserted above the line*
80	18	few	*inserted above the line*
	7 *f.b.*	ever	*inserted above the line*
	3-2 *f.b.*	well-meaning	*inserted above the line*
81	3	differ	differing *deleted*
	5	half	*inserted above the line*

N.B.—It is possible that Swift was copying out this manuscript with his own hand from a 'foul copy', and that some of these insertions and deletions are not really deliberate alterations or later corrections. They are noted, however, because it seems to me more likely that they do indicate—if not the improvements of revision—at least his second thoughts in the process of composition.

6. ANSWER TO SEVERAL LETTERS FROM UNKNOWN HANDS

First printed by Deane Swift in *Works*, London, 1765, 4to. VIII, pt. i, pp. 192–197. (D). Reprinted in Dublin by Faulkner in the same year, *Works*, XII, pp. 287–295. (L).

The present text is taken from Deane Swift. The Dublin edition is an exact reprint of his London edition, with only one or two modifications in spelling and punctuation, and the following variant:

Page	Line	PRESENT TEXT	VARIANT
88	15	enjoined (L)	joined (D)

7. A LETTER ON MR. MACULLA'S PROJECT ABOUT HALF-PENCE

MS. Fragment. Autograph. Two leaves only. Forster Collection. First printed by Faulkner, *Works*, Vol. X, 1759, pp. 328–348; and by Deane Swift in *Works*, London, 1765, Vol. VIII, pt. i, pp. 148–60. The printed versions vary considerably and it is clear, after comparing them with the fragment of MS., that Deane Swift was printing from this autograph MS., which was probably Swift's first draft, and that Faulkner had access to a different, and in some respects, corrected copy. Since Faulkner has introduced certain peculiarities of spelling, capitalization and punctuation, which were certainly not in the manuscript, it seems better when the MS. ceases, to take Deane Swift's as copy-text, and at the same time to introduce into it all the substantive changes and additions which have the authority of the copy used by Faulkner. The title is also taken from Deane Swift.

Page	Line	PRESENT TEXT	VARIANTS
93	H.t.	A Letter on Mr. Maculla's Project about Halfpence and a new one proposed ———————————— 1729	*No title in Swift's hand, but later endorsed:* McCulla's Project— about Halfpence, & a new one proposed 1729 MS. A Letter concerning Mr. Maculla's Project about Copper Notes to pass for Pence and Half-pence; with a Proposal for another Scheme for providing Copper Change in this Kingdom *To the Rev. Dr. Delany* 59
93	12	Character.	*Here follows in the MS. this passage, afterwards marked through with a pen-stroke:* I happened undeed to hear last summer while I was in the Country that he was in some trouble in England., upon which I examined him, when he charged it all upon the malice of an Irish Attorney. However, his shop is well furnished, and he seems —— with goods, and if his report of the Circumstances be true, it was as throurow (*sic*)

Page	Line	PRESENT TEXT	VARIANTS
			a masterpiece of villany as I have heard of. Mr. McCulla
	13	Style, ... But, I	*first draft, afterwards corrected in MS.:* Style of other Projectors with a good appearance of zeal for the publick good, whereon I
	17	pretence Ms, 59	practice 65
	21	the Contriver Ms., 59	himself 65
	23	some poor relief Ms., 65	some relief 59
	25	that work Ms., 65	the work 59
	6 f.b.	when ... his hand	where ... hand
	5 f.b.	witnesses Ms., 65	witness 59
94	2	of the said copper 59	of the sd Copper Ms.; of copper 65
	6	20*l. percent.* 59	a little more than 16 *per cent.* Ms. 65
	6–8	four pence for laying out twenty pence, allowing his copper at fourteen pence, and the coinage at sixpence *per* pound 59	two pence in every shilling Ms. 65
	10	as large a quantity	fifty or sixty thousand (*deleted in MS*) (*end of MS.*)
	13	sure 65	secure 59
	22	fully equalling 59	equalling 65
	8 f.b.	formed 65	framed 59
	7 f.b.	proposal 65	Proposals 59
	6 f.b.	would be 59	will be 65
95	1	lie 59	be 65
	7	the charges 65	all the charges 59
	10	By this computation 65	By computation 59
	17	20 *per cent.* 59	16 *per cent.* 65
		owneth 59	avows 65
	18	50 *per cent.* 59	about 46 *per cent.* 65
	20	shillings 59	shillings *per* pound 65
	22	Ten pence in every two shillings 59	41*l.* 13*s.* 4*d. per cent.* 65
	24	proposal 65	proposals 59
	29	But Macula hath still 30 *per cent.* by the same, if they be returned. 59	(*omitted in* 65)
	2 f.b.	in fineness 59	fineness 65
96	9	20 *per cent.*	16 *per cent.* 65
	12	will, to 65	will, as to 59
		55 *per cent.*	47 *per cent.* 65
	14	50*l.* 59	60*l.* 65
	15	5 *per cent.* 59	(to avoid fractions) be about five and a half *per cent.* 65

Present text:

$$\begin{array}{r} 50 \\ 5 \\ \hline 55 \end{array} \quad 59$$

Variants:

$$\begin{array}{ccc} 41 & 13 & 4 \\ 5 & 10 & 0 \\ \hline 47 & 3 & 4 \end{array} \quad 65$$

Page	Line	PRESENT TEXT	VARIANTS
	6 *f.b.*	Maculla's above a fifth part, part, or 20 *per cent* 59	Mr M'Culla's a fourth part, or 25 *per cent.*
	3 *f.b.*	was milled 59	milled 65
97	6	opportunity 59	an opportunity 65
	10	finest 59	fairest 65
	11–14	Loser: For, the Benefit of defrauding the Crown never accrueth to the Publick, but is wholly turned to the advantage of those whom the Crown employeth: But 59	Loser. But 65
	14	the officers 65	these officers 59
	19	outweigh 59	did much outweigh 65
	25	from his 59	by his 65
	6 *f.b.*	and as 65	as 59
	5 *f.b.*	20 to 8 59	16 to 8 65
	fn.	This Letter etc. 59	(*not in* 65)
98	3	20 *per cent.* gain four thousand pounds 59	16 per cent. gain three thousand three hundred pounds 65
	8	letters 59	letter 65
	30	that sum 59	the sum 65
99	10	They 65	These 59
	23–4	eight thousand 59	eighty thousand 65
	29	happened 59	arrived 65
100	2	the Mint 59	a mint 65
	6	as of the 65	as the 59
	7	as well and 65	well and as 59
	19	8 65	3 59
	20	five years 59	two years 65
	21	farther 65	further 59
	23	and unsolicited 59	unsolicited 65
	6 *f.b.*	20 *per cent.* 59	somewhat more than 16 *per cent.* 65
101	5–6	above one fifth 59	one fourth 65
	8	their coin 59	the coin 65
	12	and so 65	and to 59
	26	instead of 20 59	instead of somewhat more than 16 65
	4 *f.b.*	computation 65	computations 59
102	20	and vigilant 65	vigilant 59
	24	written 65	writ 59
	9 *f.b.*	all but 59	all 65
103	12	still be 59	be 65
	23	it being a matter wholly out of my trade 59	(*omitted*) 65
	b.	672 59	(*omitted*) 65
104	5	The difference is 18 Which is equal 65	The difference 18 The difference is equal 59
	7 *f.b.*	probably 59	possibly 65

8. A MODEST PROPOSAL.

First printed in Dublin, 1729, by S. Harding. See facsimile of title-page, p. 109.
London reprints:

1. A Modest Proposal For Preventing the Children of Poor People From being
   a Burthen to Their Parents or Country, and For Making them Beneficial
   to the Publick. By Dr. Swift. Dublin, Printed by S. Harding: London,
   Re-printed; and sold by J. Roberts in Warwick-lane, and the Pamphlet-
   Shops. M.DCC.XXIX. 8vo. 19 pages.
   Note.—The number of printer's errors suggest that this was set up very
   hurriedly.

2. A Modest Proposal For preventing the Children of Poor People From being
   a Burthen to their Parents or the Country, and for making them Beneficial
   to the Publick. Dublin: Printed: And Reprinted at London, for Weaver
   Bickerton, in Devereux-Court near the Middle-Temple. M.DCC.XXX. 8vo.
   23 pages.
   A second and third edition of this appeared in the same year.

3. Also included in *A Libel On Dr. Delany And a certain Great Lord*, etc. *Dublin*:
   Printed, London: Reprinted for Capt. Gulliver near the Temple, MDCCXXX.
   and in the Second Edition. Printed at Dublin: And Re-printed at London,
   for A. Moore, near St. Paul's MDCCXXX.

4. Also included in *A View of the Present State of Affairs In the Kingdom of
   Ireland: In Three Discourses*. etc. Printed at Dublin: Reprinted at London,
   for Weaver Bickerton, in Devereux-Court, near the Middle-Temple.
   M.DCC.XXX.

5. *Miscellanies*. The Third Volume. 1732, with Swift's corrections.
   Copy in Lord Rothschild's collection.
Works, (Faulkner) 1735, IV, 273–285.

The text follows Faulkner's edition, which contains alterations clearly due
to Swift himself; but it is collated with the earlier editions, and errors in the
course of reprinting have been corrected, as indicated below. Variants are
recorded in the original Dublin edition (29) Bickerton's first edition (30), The
Miscellanies (32), Swift's corrections (S).

Page	Line	PRESENT TEXT	VARIANTS
109	H.t.	from h.t. of 32 Burden or Country Written in the Year 1729	t.p. Burthen 29, 30 or the Country 29, 30
			h.t. A modest Proposal &c. 29, 30

N.B.—In his copy of (32) Swift has drawn a hand pointing to the half-title,
probably to indicate that this paper was to be included; the collations seem to
indicate that Faulkner used 32 as his copy-text.

110	7	*of other Projectors*	*for no Projectors* 32
			*misprint marked by a	in margin* S
	24	in *Ireland*	in this Kingdom 29, 30, 32
	27	Couples 29, 30, 32, 35	couple (emended by Hawkes- worth 1755, and followed by later editors to conform with usage in previous line.)

Page	Line	PRESENT TEXT	VARIANTS
110	9 f.b.	an Hundred 29, 32	One hundred 30
111	3	until they	till they 29, 30
	16–7	or the Kingdom 29, 30	or Kingdom 32, 35
	2 f.b.	in the	of the 29, 30, 32
112	14	*Author	Author 29, 30, 32
		Fn. *Rabelais*	
	7 f.b.	net Profit	neat Profit 29, 30, 32
	6 f.b.	until she produceth	till she produces 29, 30, 32
113	12	County 29, 30	Country 32
	28	how well soever 32	howsoever well 29; however well 30
114	1	*Mandarins* 29, 30	*Mandarines* 35
	6	the *Play-house* 29, 30	a *Play-house* 32, 35
	22	in a fair way of being	happily 29, 30, 32
	3 f.b.	an idolatrous *Episcopal*	an *Episcopal* 29, 30, 32
115	3 f.b.	as it is 29, 30	as is 32
116	4	Tables, and	Tables, which 29, 30, 32
	5	yearling 29, 30	yearly 32, 35
	11	particularly 29, 30	particularly at 32, 35
	19	and it was	and was 29, 30; and 'twas 32
117	5	a Glimpse	some Glimpse 29, 30, 32
	15	too tender 30, 32	two tender 29
	25	a Hundred 32	One hundred 30 an hundred 29
	29	*Sterling* 32	*Sterl.* 29, 30
118	3–4	Inclemencies of Weather 29, 30	the Inclemencies of the Weather 32

9. A PROPOSAL THAT ALL THE LADIES … SHOULD APPEAR CONSTANTLY IN IRISH MANUFACTURES

First printed by Deane Swift in *Works*, London, 1765, 4to. Vol. VIII, pt. i, pp. 170–176, from which the present text is taken.

It was reprinted in Dublin the same year by Faulkner, without any significant variants, in *Works*, XII, pp. 251–261.

10. MAXIMS CONTROLLED IN IRELAND

Autograph draft of hints, consisting of two small leaves, John Rylands Eng. MSS. 659 (11). Though this contains only some Maxims and a few odd sentences, it is important as proving the tract to be Swift's, and an interesting sample of the very first step in its composition. (See Appendix B.)

First printed by Deane Swift in *Works*, London, 1765, 4to. Vol. VIII, pt. i, pp. 136–142, [L] and reprinted by Faulkner in *Works*, XII, 217–226 [F]. The text is printed from the London 4to. edition.

Page	Line	PRESENT TEXT	VARIANTS
134	12	gentlemen's F	gentlemens L
136	10, 11	that	that … that L, F
	27–8	such a pernicious F	such pernicious a L

11. ADVERTISEMENT AGAINST LORD ALLEN

First printed by John Nichols in his edition of Swift's *Works*, 1801, xiii, 471, from which the present text is taken. I have been unable to find any newspaper in which this advertisement was published; and it is possible that Swift did not carry out his intention to make this protest at the time.

12. THE SUBSTANCE OF WHAT WAS SAID BY THE DEAN

First printed by Deane Swift in *Works*, London, 1765, 4to. Vol. VIII, pt. i, pp. 198–201 and reprinted in Dublin by Faulkner, *Works*, XII, 297–302.

The mistake in the footnote by Deane Swift is corrected by Faulkner; the printer referred to in the text was, of course, Edward Waters, not Harding, but Faulkner is himself mistaken in the following note; the 'Noble Person' was not Carteret but the Duke of Grafton, who was then Lord Lieutenant.

13. A VINDICATION OF HIS EXCELLENCY LORD CARTERET

First printed in Dublin by Faulkner, in April, 1730. See facsimile of title-page, p. 150 (D).

Though this edition is described on the t.p. as a reprint of a London edition, there can be little doubt that it was in fact printed from a copy of Swift's manuscript, and carefully arranged to be published in Dublin immediately after the Parliamentary session was over. See above, p. xxvii. It is unlikely that Swift had anything to do with Warner's edition, or with a 'Second edition' advertised by Curll in 1732, among the books listed at the end of his reprints of Swift's *City Cries* and *A Soldier and a Scholar*. Pilkington sent a copy to Bowyer in August 1732, which may have been corrected by Swift (see *Corr.*, iv, 483–4); but Pope succeeded in getting it included in the *Miscellanies*.

First printed in London for T. Warner, 1730. See facsimile of title-page, p. 151 (L).

Miscellanies. The Third Volume, 1732, pp. 173–205 (M), with some corrections in Swift's hand in his own copy. (S.)

Works, Dublin, 1735, Vol. IV, pp. 286–309 (35), from which the present text is taken, and collated with the earlier editions. Even then Faulkner did not dare to print the footnotes of the London editions, referring to Lord Allen and Richard Tighe.

Page	Line	PRESENT TEXT	VARIANTS
153	3–4	H.t. His Excellency, *John*, Lord *Carteret*	his Ex——y, the Lord C——, &c. D. his Excellency the Lord C——T, &c. L; the Lord Lieutenant of Ireland, the Lord Carteret, M
	23	*Blood*, D	*Blood*, &c. L, M
	b.	whence D	thence L, M
154	7	and just D	just L, M.
	10	although	tho' D, L, M
	13	Disposition D, L, M	Dispositions 35
	17	Youth, D, L, M	Youth; 35
155	1	unsupportable D	insupportable L, M

2B

Page	Line	Present Text	Variants
155	4	with all D, L	besides all M
	5	adding D, L	having M
	13	*affected*	affected D, L, M.
	19–20	and to the	and the D, L, M
	22	*orthodox*	orthodox D, L, M
		Patriots, (at the Head of whom I name with Honour *Pistorides*.)	Patriots; for M *Pistorides** (*Fn.* *The Rt. Hon. R—D T—*gh*, Esq.; whose Grandfather was a Baker. L
156	1	*Violante** (*Fn.* *A famous Italian *Rope-Dancer*.)	*Violante* D, L; *Violante** (*Fn. A famous Rope-Dancer*) M
	4	by her D	but by her L, M
	9	*Hartly Hutcheson*	*H— H—* D; *H—ly H—tch–n,* L, M
	24	and therefore	and consequently D, L, M
157	10	one Hundred	a hundred D, L, M
	14	its Owner	the Owner D, L, M
	22	*Traulus*	*Traulus** (*Fn. L—d V—t A—n,* who spoke against the Libel in the Privy Council, and likewise in the House of Lords.) L, M
158	2	*flay and dissect*	flay and dissect D, L, M
	5	*Three-Pence*	three Pence D, L, M
	8	mistaken L, M	mistaking D, 35
	15–22	I apprehend etc.	*omitted in* M
	4 *f.b.*	much	much more M
159	1	bestowed on him L, M	bestowed him D
	12	*Politicks* D, L	*Principles* M
	24	but whether	whether D, L, M.
	27	*Wenches*	Mistresses D, L, M
	8 *f.b.*	who D, M	and who L
160	2	heartily D, L, M	heartilly 35
	10	Supposition D, L, M	Suppositions 35
	18	What then must	What must, then D
	9 *f.b.*	those useless D	these useless L, M
	5 *f.b.*	until	till L, M
161	7	further D	farther L, M
	21	*take to their Books*	take to their Book D; Books L, M
162	6	morally D	mortally L, M
163	11	of almost	almost of L, M
	3 *f.b.*	of no large Dimensions of Body or Mind	of no large Dimensions of Body or Mind D, L, M
164	4 *f.b.*	drank D	drunk L, M
165	1	except that of *Party*	but *Party* D, L, M
	8	Friend* (*Fn.* *The Author)	Friend D, L, M
	13	*Gentleman* D, S	Gentlemen L, M
	10 *f.b.*	one Hundred	Hundred D; a hundred L, M
166	8	Lodging, a great Number of Pupils, and	Lodging, and D, L, M
167	17	*net* Profit	*neat* Profit D, L, M
	9 *f.b.*	particularly that of	particularly of D, L, M

Page	Line	PRESENT TEXT	VARIANTS
168	2	*Tory*, whatever M	Tory. Whatever D, L, 35
	13	Excellency *John, . . . Ireland*	E— the L—— L—— D, L; Excellency the Lord Lieutenant M
	2 *f.b.*	this dangerous	that dangerous D, L, M
169	4 *f.b.*	*Anti-Revolutioners,* *White-rosalists*	White-rosalists D, L, M
	2 *f.b.*	*seems to lie*	plainly lyes D; plainly lies L, M

14. AN ANSWER TO THE CRAFTSMAN

This Answer, together with a reprint of the original *Craftsman*, which prompted Swift to write, was first printed by Faulkner as a separately paged Appendix to Vol. IX of his edition of Swift's collected *Works* in 1758. The same was included in the London 4to edition in 1764, in Vol. VII, pt. i, pp. 103–108. For text of *Craftsman*, see Appendix C.

The present text is taken from Faulkner, and variants from the 1764 edition follow:

Page	Line	PRESENT TEXT	VARIANTS
173	18–20	which costeth . . . polish them	which it costeth us . . . polish 64
	6 *f.b.*	for the Letters	for letters 64
174	4	have had	have 64
	12	*D'Anvers*	D'ANVER 64
	16	Manufacture	manufactures 64
175	10	Affection to	affection for 64
176	3	the Owners	our owners 64
	18	imported 64	exported 58
	25	get drunk 64	be drunk 58
177	2	export to	export for 64
	7	still continue	continue 64
	24	by a	by 64
178	4	Bonnyclabber *Fn. Thick, sour milk 64	Bonnyclabber 58
		mingled . . . as they formerly did	milk mingled . . . as it formerly was 64
	6	Luxury, . . . began	when, luxury . . . beginning 64
	5 *f.b.*	the Merchants	merchants 64

15. ON THE BILL FOR THE CLERGY'S RESIDING ON THEIR LIVINGS

First printed in *Miscellaneous Pieces in Prose and Verse*. By J. Swift. C. Dilly, 1789.

But the original autograph manuscript is in the possession of Mr. William R. Lefanu, and he has kindly given me permission to print from it here.

It is evidently a corrected fair copy, in which a number of changes have been made in spelling, punctuation and capitalization. A few words have been written in by another hand, and it seems likely that the minor corrections may all be the work of a later editor. As Swift often asked his friends to perform this amount of correction for him, I have printed from the corrected text, but note below the original readings of the manuscript:

Page	Line	PRESENT TEXT	MANUSCRIPT READINGS
181	6	of friends, industry S	friends *inserted above the line*
	7	means and merits S	and merits *inserted above the line*
	12	loyal	loyall
		Hanover	Hannover
	13	implicit	implicite
	17	England; and	England; And
	20	Bishops meerly to promote Christianity among us, and S	Bishops as it were in particular meerly to advance Christianity among us.
		(*The rest of this sentence seems to have been inserted later by Swift in a smaller script.*)	
	23	Missionaries	Missionaryes
	25	farther	further
	5 *f.b.*	Churches are S	Churches were built
	3 *f.b.*	pretended authority S	pretended *added above the line*
	2 *f.b.*	several Abbies	severall Abbyes
182	3	forty	fourty (*and* passim)
	8	easily	easyly
	9	behaviour	behavior
	16	graze a few S	graze his
	23	fully cultivated S	well cultivated
		I mean for the general S	I speak for the generall
	27	dress; and	dress; And
	3 *f.b.*	an English	an honest English
183	2	or charitable endowments *inserted above the line* S	
	8	Kingdom divided among(st) them S	Kingdom between them.
	10	by others S	by those
	11	several	severall (*passim*)
	12	memories	memoryes
	14	only	onely
		debentures forfeited in 1641	debentures in fourty odd, who
	19–20	Colonies, by . . . called	Colonyes, (under . . . called)
	23	not: thus	no: thus
	26	are manifest S	were manifest
		The whole Lands of the see of Waterford were	The whole see of Waterford was
	7 *f.b.*	Counties	Countyes
	5 *f.b.*	favourites, was prevailed	Favorites, was prevayled
	4 *f.b.*	grant to some Sees S	grant both to some Bishops
	2 *f.b.*	did likewise endow many S	and endowing
184	5	the roots being,	the roots *inserted above the line*
	7	inconsiderable	unconsiderable
		colonies	colonyes

Page	Line	PRESENT TEXT	VARIANTS
184	20	demesne	demain
		land to let. *Then follows a line and a half of a new paragraph crossed out and endorsed* (comes in after)	
			But, as far as I am informed, the case is very different in all other parts of the Kingdom. S
	21	natural	naturall
	24	cultivate them	them *inserted above the line*
	25	levelled	destroyd
	28	for all which S	all *inserted above the line*
		appointed by Law, and S	*inserted above the line*
	9 f.b.	being too poor	being *inserted above the line*
	7 f.b.	churches, it	churches; It
	6 f.b.	join	joyn
	b.	in different parts; For, in the North	in some parts; particularly the North
185	2	prolific	profilick
	5	only	onely
		natural luxury S	natural *inserted above the line*
	8	travel	travell
	10	half their number tho' the revenue would be sufficient	half the number, and the revenue sufficient
	12	the times mend or that S	*inserted above the line*
	15–16	some Bishopricks S	many Bishopricks
		soil	land *corrected to* Soyl S
	18	foreign	forein
	24	income for a country Dean	revenue for a country Deanry
	26	two parishes, to the amount of that value	to the amount *inserted above the line by later hand*
186	10	for the Bishops S	for certainly the Bishops

The last leaf of the MS. had been previously used by Swift for the beginning of a letter, which he had discontinued. It is dated Dublin Dec^b 28th, 1731, and proves therefore that the pamphlet was finished some time after that date. The fragment of the letter is as follows:

Madam
  I have received for some time past many accounts of the Scituation your family is in at present

It seems possible that it may have been addressed to his sister, Mrs. Jane Fenton, to whom he was then paying an annuity of fifteen pounds per annum. See *Corr.* iv, 133.

16. CONSIDERATIONS UPON TWO BILLS . . . RELATING TO THE CLERGY OF IRELAND

First published in London, in March 1732, and advertised in the following notice (first brought to my attention by Professor Louis Landa) in the Dublin Journal of 21–25 March, 1732:

  The Clergy of this Nation, and all the young Gentlemen in our Universities, are wonderfully pleased with a Pamphlet lately transmitted from

Dublin (which we are informed was prohibited being printed there).
'Tis Entitled, Considerations on Two Bills lately sent down from the
R—— H—— the H—— of L—— to the H—— H—— of C——, relating
to the C——y of *****. 'Tis said some Copies are sent to Ireland.

I suggest that this must have been the pirated edition, evidently set up from
a ms. copy, containing many obvious errors, printed together with No. 17.
Considerations upon Two Bills, Sent down from the Rt. Hon. the House of
Lords to the Honourable House of Commons of Ireland, relating to the Clergy
of that Kingdom. By the Rev. Dr. Swift, D.S.P.D. To which is added, A
Proposal for an Act of Parliament, to pay off the Debt of the Nation, . . . by
A—— P——, Esq; Dublin, Printed; London, Reprinted for J. Roberts at the
Oxford Arms in Warwick-Lane. 1732. (Price Sixpence.) (R)

Advertised in *Fog's Weekly Journal* and *St. James Evening Post*, Mar. 25, 1732.

The first authorized London edition must have appeared several months
later, if it was that assigned to William Bowyer by Matthew Pilkington, who on
Augst 28 sent copies, in which the Dean had 'with his own hand made some
alterations in some of them.' (See Corr., iv, 484) and see facsimile of title-page,
p. 189 (M)

The text of this edition was reprinted by Faulkner in *Works*, 1738, Vol. VI,
pp. 137–156. (N.B. In all copies I have seen of this L4 is a cancel, and it is odd
to find that in the later edition of 1741, in which this sheet has been certainly
reset, that L4 is again a cancel. I do not know what change was made.) Faulkner's
text is clearly based on M and has no separate authority, though it is possible
that one or two changes have been made in the proofs by Swift. It has been
used here as a copy-text, because it is more convenient, since the many words
printed originally only with initials are there given in full. The variants in M are
given below. It would serve no purpose to list all the absurd misreadings of R.

Page	Line	PRESENT TEXT	VARIANTS IN M
	Title	Right Honourable	R—— H——
		House of Lords	H—— of L——
		Honourable	H——ble
		House of Commons	H—— of C——
		IRELAND	I*******D
191	6 *f.b.*	Bishops	B——s
	5 *f.b.*	Clergy	Cl——gy
		and passim	
193	5	too often	sometimes
194	4	100 *l.*	an 100 *l.*
	6 *f.b.*	Children,	Children, &c.
195	11	as good a M	a good
196	9	Neglect of Cure (*Errata*), M	Neglect of Care M
			Want of Care F

(*This is a significant correction, which proves that F printed from Moore, for the
compositor or reader faced by an obvious error corrected the wrong word, overlooking the
correction properly given in the 'Errata' list at the end of the text, but, indeed, given
with the wrong page reference.*)

Page	Line	PRESENT TEXT	VARIANTS IN M
	7 *f.b.*	the other	t' other
198	8	goes off	go off

Page	Line	PRESENT TEXT	VARIANTS
198	18	ten	two
199	17	living, which	living, that
200	7	have always	have
	19	their Rise	its Rise (*and in* F)
201	6 *f.b.*	such a *Prelate*	that *Prelate*
202	9	However, one	But one

17. A PROPOSAL FOR AN ACT OF PARLIAMENT TO PAY OFF THE DEBT OF THE NATION

First printed in Dublin in 1732; see facsimile of title-page, p. 206. *Works*, Faulkner, 1735, IV, 310–17.

The text is here printed from Faulkner, collated with the first Dublin edition (32), which was evidently also printed by him, on the evidence of the ornaments used on pp. 5 and 16, which occur also in *Some Reasons against the Bill for settling the Tyth of Hemp and Flax*, which he printed in 1734.

Page	Line	PRESENT TEXT	VARIANTS
209	12	36800 *l* 32	36800 35
	18	Information 32	Informations 35
211	7	Fines	Tythes 32
	9 *f.b.*	*true loyal*	loyal 32
212	3	on by the Bishops 32	on the Bishops 35

18. AN EXAMINATION OF CERTAIN ABUSES ETC.

First printed in Dublin in 1732; for facsimile of title-page see p. 215. Reprinted in London with the following title:

City Cries, Instrumental and Vocal: Or, An Examination of Certain Abuses, Corruptions, and Enormities In London and Dublin. By the Rev. Dr. Swift, D.S.P.D. Dublin. Printed; London, Re-printed for J. Roberts at the Oxford Arms in Warwick-Lane, 1732 (R). Advtd in *Grub Street Journal*, Mar. 16, 1732. *Works*, Faulkner, 1735, IV, 318–338.

The present text is printed from Faulkner, collated with 32 and R.

Page	Line	PRESENT TEXT	VARIANTS
217	H.t.	An EXAMINATION . . . Year 1732	AN EXAMINATION *of certain Abuses*, &c. 32 CITY CRIES: OR AN *Examination of certain Abuses, Corruptions*, &c. R
	13	*Dublin* 32	*Dublin*, 35
	15	those	these 32
	18	their profound	their most profound 32, R
	b.	touch the	touch at the 32, R
218	13	until	till 32 R

Page	Line	PRESENT TEXT	VARIANTS
218	15	those	these 32 R
	21	meant, for R	meant; for 32; meant? For 35
	28	until	till 32 R
	3-2 *f.b.*	*dead as a Herring*	*as dead as an Herring* R
219	2	*No fn. in* 35	from* *Howth*
			Fn. *The sea about eight Miles from *Dublin*, where they fish for Herrings. R
	18	Observation	Observations R
	19	and it is that	which is that R
	20	*Sweethearts	(*No fn. in* 32, R)
	4 *f.b.*	*Toupees	(*No fn. in* 32, R)
220	8	until	till 32, R
	17	the immense 32, R	an immense 35
	20	hath	have R
221	18	his own	their own R
	9 *f.b.*	Enmity	Malice 32 R
222	1	together into	together in R
	14	Parliament	P——t 32, 35
	2 *f.b.*	Cock, in the same posture	Cock. 32 R
223	1	fit	either fit 32, R
	10	Guests	Guest 32 R
	11	Not one . . . being	For not one . . . is 32, R
	12	*Punch*	Liquor R
		For, as they . . . they are	For the Birds, as they . . . are 32, R
	18	intended against the Government, by	against the present Government, intended by R
224	13	*true Protestant*	*Protestant* 32, R
	14	cannot	can't 32, R
	18	halloo	hallow 32; hollow R
	20	the Signs	those Signs 32, R
	22	common Understanding	most common Understanding 32 Understandings R
	27	these	those 32, R
225	16	the known	that known 32, R
	8-7 *f.b.*	*which . . . Detractors*	(*Italicized in* 35)
226	1	horrid, or indeed rather diabolical *Countenances*	horrid *Countenances* 32, R
	27	with much Offence	with great offence 32, R
	2 *f.b.*	*worst of Times*	(*Fn. added in* 35)
227	14	good Grounds	Grounds 32, R
	8 *f.b.*	until	after 32, R
	6 *f.b.*	the Cries	the fine Cries 32, R
228	7	this wicked	the wicked 32, R
	9	and is in	and in 32, R
	17	they have so long aimed at	after which they have so long aspired 32, R
	19	Whereby the	And the 32; and that the R
229	9	as to have the Honour of being	that he had the Honour to be 32, R

Page	Line	PRESENT TEXT	VARIANTS
229	17–18	*Alas . . . Bottom*	(*Italicized in* 35)
	22	since	often since 32, R
230	1	*Peyton (Fn. added in* 35)	P——*n* 32, R
	6 *f.b.*	so infamous a	this infamous 32, R
	4 *f.b.*	yet	but 32, R
231	11–13	*We hope . . .* TURNUPS	(*Italicized in* 35)
	2 *f.b.*	*worst of Times*	„ „
232	3	*Popery . . . Treason*	(*Italicized in* 35)
	6	*true Protestants*	(*Italicized in* 35)

19. THE HUMBLE PETITION OF THE FOOTMEN IN AND ABOUT THE CITY OF DUBLIN

Dated Dublin, 1732, but no edition found of that year.

Printed in London together with *A Serious and Useful Scheme etc.* (dated From my Garret in Moor-Fields, Aug. 10, 1733) for J. Roberts at the Oxford Arms in Warwick-Lane, 1733.

This volume was reprinted in Dublin by George Faulkner . . . G. Risk, G. Ewing and W. Smith, in 1733.

A second issue adds 'By the Rev. Dr. J.S.D.S.P.D.' on the title-page.

Reprinted again in 1734.

Works, Faulkner, 1735, IV, 371–374.

The present text is printed from this last (35) collated with the earlier edition (33). *A serious and Useful Scheme* was probably written by Matthew Pilkington, who may well have been responsible for providing Curll with copy for the 1733 volume.

Page	Line	PRESENT TEXT	VARIANTS
235	6 *f.b.*	of wearing our 33	of our 35

20. THE ADVANTAGES PROPOSED BY REPEALING THE SACRAMENTAL TEST

First printed in Dublin, Feb., 1732; see facsimile of title-page, p. 241.

Reprinted in London for J. Roberts at the Oxford Arms in Warwick Lane, 1732 (R). Advtd in *Grub Street Journal*, Mar. 9, 1732

Works, Faulkner, 1735, IV, 350–361.

The present text is taken from this 35 edition, collated with 32 and R.

Page	Line	PRESENT TEXT	VARIANTS
243	20	into Civil	into Religious or Civil 32, R
244	7–8	plead, that they	plead; they 32, R
	17	landed People	learned People 32, R
	20	or Confusion	or Tumults 32, R
	29	Part	Parts 32, R
	8 *f.b.*	spiritual who represent the *Church* are	spiritual are 32, R
	3 *f.b.*	*Independency, Muggletonianism, Brownism, Familism,* or	Independency, or 32, R

Page	Line	PRESENT TEXT	VARIANTS
245	7	*Presbytery* which I find stands the	*Presbytery*, which stands much the 32, R
	2 *f.b.*	It is obvious	It is easy 32, R
247	11–2	compromising among themselves, that	compromising that 32, R
	15	*Churchman* and *Dissenter*	*Churchmen and Dissenters* 32, R
	19	jealous 32, R	zealous 35
	22	Art;	Arts, R
	b.	shall be	is 32, R
248	15	*have it in Direction*	(*Italicized in* 35)
249	13	should be 32, R	shall be 35
	14	by Him	by one 32, R
	29	Print, exactly in the same Style and Manner with those of our modern *Presbyterian* Teachers: So	Print: So 32, R
250	1–2	Senators: Yet this was a Priviledge begun	Senators; which, however was an Institution begun 32, R
	4	our limited	this limited 32, R
	5	Method whereby	Method, by which 32, R
	13	Hardship for	Hardship upon 32, R
	14	exceeds	exceed 32, R
	18	these hard 32, R	those hard 35
	28	which some	as some 32, R
251	6	to accept an	for an 32, R
	15	not in the least doubt, that they will take	not doubt, their taking 32, R
	19	Disposition 32, R	Dispositions 35

21. QUERIES RELATING TO THE SACRAMENTAL TEST

First printed on a half-sheet of two pages, without imprint, with the following head title: QUERIES Wrote by Dr. *J. Swift*, in the Year 1732. (Very proper to be read at this Time by every Member of the Established Church.)

Reprinted in *The Dispute Adjusted* by Edmund Lord Bishop of London. Dublin 1733.

Works, Faulkner, 1735, IV, 362–370.

The present text is printed from 35, collated with the original half-sheet (32).

Page	Line	PRESENT TEXT	VARIANTS
256	20	thinks	think 32
	26	Apostolical	Apostolick 32
257	10 *f.b.*	to murder	or murder 32
	b.	the Monarchy	our Monarchy 32
258	10	lyes	lyeth 32
	17	loves	loveth 32
	27	lies	lieth 32
	3 *f.b.*	exceeds	exceedeth 32
	2 *f.b.*	remains	remaineth 32
259	28	stands	standeth 32
	6 *f.b.*	Enemy	Enemies 32

22. THE PRESBYTERIANS PLEA OF MERIT &c.

First printed in Dublin in 1733; see facsimile of title-page, facing p. 263 together with 'An Ode to Humphry French, Esq; etc.' (33)

Reprinted in London for G.F. and Sold by A. Dodd, near Temple Bar; and at the Pamphlet-Shops.

Another edition together with Nos. III and IV of *The Correspondent*.

Works, Faulkner, 1738, VI, 95–117.

The present text is printed from the collected edition of 38, collated with 33.

Page	Line	PRESENT TEXT	VARIANTS
264	21	were those . . . Libels	was that Libel
	23	us, until	us, that until
265	9	until	till
	15	until some Time before	till the very Time that
	23	that Prince	his Majesty
	7 f.b.	the General	their General
	6 f.b.	Members who	Members which
269	15	Part	a Part
270	12	in his	his
272	11	because they must else	because otherwise they must
275	21	Animosity	Animosities
276	4	even until	even till
	9	*Doctor (*Fn. added in* 38)	
	2 f.b.	allowing	granting
	b.	†Many (*Fn. added in* 38)	
278	b.	*Superiors appointed to defend it*	Commanders appointed to defend it

23. REASONS HUMBLY OFFERED TO THE PARLIAMENT OF IRELAND

First printed in POLITICAL TRACTS. VOL. II By the Author of GULLIVER'S TRAVELS. *LONDON*, Printed for C. Davis in Pater-Noster-Row. MDCCXXXVIII. (38)

Works, Dublin, 1746, VOL. VIII, pp. 81–99 (46)

The present text is taken from 38, collated with the later Dublin edition. There are no important variants, except in the title-page, and in the omission of a whole paragraph (see below, p. 288, ll. 13–21). In spite of the warning on the title that the arguments are put forward in the style of a Roman Catholic, this may have seemed too dangerous a paragraph to the editor of 1746, but it was at least restored in the next Dublin edition of 1752. It is possible that it was simply omitted by the carelessness of the compositor; for there are errors in other parts of this volume, which were also corrected in 1752. See Textual Notes in Vol. XIII of this edition.

Page	Line	PRESENT TEXT	VARIANTS
284	b.	Written in the Year 1733	Written in the Style of a *Roman* Catholick. London: Printed in the Year 1734. And

Page	Line	PRESENT TEXT	VARIANTS
			Dublin: Printed in the Year 1743.
284	*b.*	Part	a Part 46
285	18	Kingdom; until 46	Kingdom. 'Till 38
286	2	Kingdoms; whereas 52	Kingdoms. Whereas 38, 46
	10	Adherents: To 52	Adherents. To 38, 46
288	13–21	38 (*and in* 52)	*Omitted in* 46
289	3 *f.b.*	lessened: So	lessened. So 38, 46
290	22	the other Side:	t'other Side; 38, 46
	24	pass: 46	pass. 38

24. SOME FEW THOUGHTS CONCERNING THE REPEAL OF THE TEST

First printed by Deane Swift in *Works*, London, 1765, 4to. Vol. VIII, pt. i, p. 135 and reprinted in Dublin by Faulkner, *Works*, XII pp. 215–16.

There are no variants, and the present text is therefore simply reproduced here, with the footnote which was presumably added by the editor.

APPENDIXES

A. THE MEMORIAL OF THE POOR INHABITANTS OF IRELAND

The text is taken from a photostat of the small octavo pamphlet, which had been written by John Browne, and printed in Dublin anonymously and with no date in March, 1728, with the following title-page:

TO THE R——d Dr. J——n S——t, THE MEMORIAL Of the Poor *Inhabitants, Tradesmen,* and *Labourers* of the *Kingdom* of IRELAND.
Dublin: Printed by *Thomas Walsh* in *Skinner-Row*.

B. HINTS FOR *INTELLIGENCER PAPERS* AND *MAXIMS EXAMINED*

Among the Piozzi papers discovered by Professor James Clifford are the following drafts and fragments in Swift's own hand, now in the John Rylands Library (Eng. Mss. no. 659).

They were first brought to my attention by Professor Clifford, who is now editing them with Professor Irvin Ehrenpreis. They are reproduced here as far as I can decipher them, with the permission of the Librarian of the John Rylands Library. They are of importance in proving the authenticity of *Maxims Examined* and in providing examples of Swift's manner of setting down 'hints' to be used for Intelligencer papers. Each item is usually separated by a short pen-stroke, and they are struck out or crossed apparently after being dealt with, as shown on the illustration facing p. 131 above.

1. *Hints Education of Ladyes.* 2 leaves (9) within another leaf, folded and endorsed
on the outside   Hints
                 Educ^ti de Dames
                      pour une Intelligencer
and within some early drafts of a few lines in verse, headed 'Gay
   Maitre d'hotel'

2. (10) headed 'Intelligencer,' and containing a list of nine hints for topics.
3. (11 a and b) 2 leaves written on 3 pages headed 'Maxims Examind'. One leaf is torn at the bottom and pasted to the other one. These 'heads' were originally intended for the paper on *Maxims controlled in Ireland*, though one or two points seem to be used for the *Proposal that all Ladies should wear Irish Manufactures*.

C. THE CRAFTSMAN for Nov. 7, 1730

The present text is taken from a copy of the original paper. It was included in the first collected edition of the *Craftsman* with the wrong date, December 12, and from this text was reprinted by Faulkner at the end of Swift's *Works*, 1758, Vol. IX.

INDEX

Abernethy, John, *The Nature and Consequences of the Sacramental Test* &c., xliii
Absentees. *See* Ireland
Acheson, Sir Arthur, xvii, 166–8
Addison, Joseph, Secretary of State, 48
Africa, slave trade of, recommended for Ireland, 135
Agesilaus, riding a hobby horse, 161
Ajax, the madness of, 19
Allen, Joshua, 2nd Viscount, his attacks upon Swift, xxv, xxvi, 141, 145; 'miserable creature *Traulus*', xxvii, 157–9
America, Irish immigration to, 59–60, 136; Plantations in, xxi, 58, 176, 289; 'a very knowing American', 111
Anabaptist, 244, 245, 275
Anne, Queen of England, 47, 229; grant of First Fruits, 147; last ministry of, 226–7, 273; death of, 266, 286
Annists, 169
Anti-Glorious-Memorists, 169
Anti-revolutioners, 169
Arcadia, 176
Aristotle, 49, 155
Army, 'only School for Gentlemen,' 49
Astrea, 57
Atheism, 286
Attorney-General, not competent to decide on Irish recruits, 313

Bacon, Francis, Lord Chancellor, 39, 48
Bankers in Ireland, 56
Barebone, Dr., of London, a bankrupt, 135
Bath, 71
Bedlam, 158; government of, 131, 309
Bible, 256; *Gen.* xlix, 6, 7, quoted, 279; *Exod.* v, 17 quoted, 11; *Prov.*, quoted, 23; the Gospel, 291
Bolingbroke, Henry St. John, Viscount, ix, x, 47
Bolton, Theophilus, Archbishop of Cashel, xxxix
'Bonnyclabber,' 178
Boulter, Hugh, Archbishop of Armagh, letters to Duke of Newcastle quoted, xxx, xl, xlvi

Bowyer, William, printer in London, xxxviii
Boyle, the Hon. Henry, afterwards Lord Carleton, Secretary of State, 47
Boyle, Michael, Dean of Cloyne, afterwards Archbishop of Armagh, 294
Brentford, Kings of, 267
Bridewell, 236
Bridgeman, Sir Orlando, 47
Broglio, Count, 311
Browne, John, *The Memorial of the poor Inhabitants* etc., xii, xiii, 17, 20, 23; text: 303–5; notes: 348
Brownism, 244, 286
Burnet, Gilbert, Bishop of Salisbury, 77, 246, 268, 289

Caesar Augustus, playing with boys, 161
Cain, 295
Calvin, John, 264; Calvinists, 278
Caroline, Queen, wife of George II, xxxv
Carr, Charles, Bishop of Killaloe, xxxix
Carteret, John, 2nd Baron, afterwards Earl of Granville, Lord Lieutenant of Ireland, xiv, 305; patronage of Tories, xxviii, 153f., 162; relations with Swift, xxv, xxix; and silver coinage, 56
Catholics, Roman, unlikely to be authors of innovations, 290. *See* Ireland
Cavaliers, 267
Cavan, county of, renowned for thievery, 111
Cervantes, 32
Charles I, king of England, martyr, 153, 184, 257, 260, 285, 293; peace concessions, 265; rebellion against, 286, 288, 289; reign of, 39, 47, 264
Charles II, king of England, 47, 96, 268, 287, 293
Christ Church Cathedral, Dublin, chancellorship of, 165
Churchill, John. *See* Marlborough
Church of England, Established, xl; 184, 244, 258, 264, 274, 292; clergy of, 181f., 197, 276; episcopacy, 244, 256; hierarchy, 286

351

FAULTS ESCAPED

P. ix, l. 9   *for* June 15 *read* June 14
    fn. 2   1936   1937

P. xxv, for fn. 2 substitute the following:
    Professor Ehrenpreis kindly informs me that he has found that the date of
    the presentation to the Dean of the Freedom of the City was May 27, 1730,
    the day after the Archbishop had received his.

P. 51, l. 4   *for* Span-Fathing *read* Span-Farthing

P. 59, l. 3fb   *for* not *read* nor

P. 66, l. 5fb   *for* about raising *read* about the raising

P. 156, between l. 2 and line 3 insert the following:
    hath ever been *offered the Oaths to the Government*: On the con-

P. 160, l. 23   *for* Professors *read* Possessors

P. 338, textual note to p. 160, l. 23, insert:
    Possessors L, M   *Professors* 35